catching
schools

THE RESEARCH-INFORMED CLASSROOM SERIES

There is no doubt that having just one great teacher can make a difference in the life of a child. But having a series of great teachers can make a much bigger difference. The work of a single, outstanding teacher can be largely undone if subsequent teachers are less effective and engaging. And variation from one teacher to the next—in everything from terminology used to strategies emphasized—can cause students confusion as they transition from one year to the next.

This is why *Catching Schools* is so important. *Catching Schools* approaches improving literacy at the whole-school level. It is designed to help every teacher in the school become a better literacy educator and get everyone in the school on the same page in their literacy instruction. This increases the coherence and cohesion of instruction, not only making learning easier for students but improving the quality of life for teachers as well.

Whole-school reform is one of the most complex topics in education. We can't trust a topic like this to just anyone. In Barbara Taylor we have a wonderwoman up to the task. Barbara has logged thousands of hours in hundreds of schools and classrooms. She has taken on day-to-day questions about what works in literacy instruction and long-term questions about how to turn around schools. She has the nitty gritty details about making schools better places for literacy learners, and she has the big picture research data and syntheses to show that what she recommends works. I'd trust her with my own children's schools and you should trust her with yours.

I am so proud to have *Catching Schools* in the *Research-Informed Classroom* series. The series aims to bring rigorous classroom-based research to bear on persistent challenges of classroom practice. Surely helping struggling schools become more effective in their literacy instruction is a persistent and formidable challenge, and Barbara Taylor meets it commandingly with her own research and research of trusted colleagues as well as insights from top-notch teachers and years of experience in schools across the nation. My aspiration for the *Research-Informed Classroom* series is to make research accessible, appealing, and actionable. In *Catching Schools* we learn about the actions we can take tomorrow, next week, next month, and every year to catch schools and turn them into the literacy learning environments all students deserve.

—*Nell K. Duke*

MICHIGAN STATE UNIVERSITY

catching
schools

AN ACTION GUIDE TO SCHOOLWIDE READING IMPROVEMENT

Barbara M. Taylor

HEINEMANN
Portsmouth, NH

Heinemann
361 Hanover Street
Portsmouth, NH 03801–3912
www.heinemann.com

Offices and agents throughout the world

Library of Congress Cataloging-in-Publication Data
Taylor, Barbara M.
    Catching schools : an action guide to schoolwide reading improvement / Barbara M. Taylor.
        p. cm. —(Research-informed classroom series)
    Includes bibliographical references and index.
    ISBN-13: 978-0-325-02658-9
    ISBN-10: 0-325-02658-0
    1. Reading (Elementary)—United States. 2. Educational change—United States. 3. Effective teaching—United States. I. Title.
    LB1573.T348 2011
    372.73—dc22   2010046525

Editors: Wendy Murray and Margaret LaRaia
Production editor: Patricia Adams
Video editor: Sherry Day
Video producer: Bob Schuster, Real Productions
Cover design: Lisa Fowler
Typesetter: Gina Poirier Design
Manufacturing: Valerie Cooper

Printed in the United States of America on acid-free paper
15   14   13   12   11   ML   1   2   3   4   5

This book is dedicated to the many elementary
teachers in schools across Minnesota and the U.S.
who contributed to this book through their
participation in school-wide reading improvement
as they used the School Change in Reading
framework. Thank you for providing motivating
instruction that meets your students' needs,
challenges them all, and is instrumental
to their success in reading.

Contents

LOOKING
INSIDE
CLASSROOMS

28, 32, 35, 41, 46, 49

**LOOKING
INSIDE
CLASSROOMS**

3 Teaching Practices That Work for Readers 52

4 Time to Collaborate
Launching a Schoolwide Plan 77

5 The People Factor
Launching the Meetings and Collaboration 94

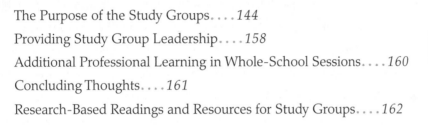

Teacher and Administrator Resources on the DVD

Chapter I

Chapters 2, 3, and 4

No additional resources for these chapters.

Chapter 5

Chapter 6

Chapter 7

Chapter 8

Chapter 9

On the DVD

See-It-in-Action Video Clips

Downloadable Classroom Reproducibles

More than 100 pages of full-size forms and teaching resources.

Foreword

The title of Barbara Taylor's new book says it all. *Catching Schools: An Action Guide to Schoolwide Reading Improvement*. The metaphor of catching schools is powerful because each of its possible meanings captures a part of the genius of Barbara's work with schools and teachers. One can "catch" a school before it falls too far—just as we catch a toddler before she loses her balance and tumbles to the ground. Thus, Barbara talks about the importance of focusing our attention, as a profession, on those schools whose students are most at risk of failing to learn to read well. We need to catch those schools before they tumble toward, or beyond, mediocrity. One can also "catch" a school in its ascendancy, just after it has begun the improvement process, to provide just that little nudge here and there, just that perfect planning form or reflection tool at just the right time—not too early and not too late—to help accelerate the faculty's progress on their self-determined improvement trajectory.

I had the enormous privilege of working as Professor Taylor's collaborator in what I like to call the "middle phase" of her work on school-based reading reform—the CIERA School Change work that stretched from 1998–2004. I consider her earlier work with EIR (Early Intervention in Reading) to be the early phase and her work on Reading Excellence and Reading First in Minnesota to be the final (really the most recent) phase of the development of the approach she unfolds in this book. So I saw a lot of the principles she discusses in this book in action—in the schools we worked with in that project. More importantly, I witnessed the approach and the practices she recommends in a range of "beating the odds" and "aspiring" schools. The "beating the odds" schools were performing well beyond the level that would be predicted by their demographics; the "aspiring" schools were working to achieve that status.

The signature of this book, what sets it apart from other books that address the same challenge of guiding school reading reform, is its balance. And it is balanced in many ways—between research and practice, between different kinds of assessment, between code and meaning instruction, and between top-down and bottom-up approaches to professional development.

Research and practice. Because Professor Taylor has spent her career with one foot firmly planted in the research traditions of the academy and the other just as firmly planted inside classrooms in our public schools, she settles for reform activities and classroom pedagogy that serves two masters: (a) rigorous standards of empirical research (other things being equal, she directs us toward practices that come with the weight of empirical evidence), and (b) equally rigorous standards of practical wisdom (other things being equal, she directs us toward practices that acknowledge the goals, constraints, and opportunities that operate inside schools and classrooms). That is a very high bar to meet, but the good news is that those of us who follow her guidance will not be led astray.

It is important to remember that research, operationalized as gathering evidence about the efficacy of one's practice, is also critical in Barbara's approach. In fact, she is insistent that schools gather hard data from their own formative and summative assessments about student progress throughout the year; she is equally insistent that they meet as grade level and cross-grade level teams to interpret those data as a way of guiding future instruction. Again, a tight link between research and practice—but in this instance coming from inside the school.

Balance in assessment. Professor Taylor also gets assessment right, in terms of two kinds of balance—one between formative and summative assessment for gauging student progress and the other between assessing learning and assessing teaching. She encourages us to develop our own *school-wide system of formative assessments* that can be used to (a) evaluate progress over time and (b) to shape future instruction in the short run and to use some sort of external, standardized summative assessments to determine whether the progress that students demonstrate on our formative assessments transfer to more distant contexts of performance. She encourages teachers, and by implication schools, to evaluate their own teaching by completing self-evaluation surveys, sharing videos with peers, or inviting others into their classrooms to conduct highly analytic observations. This last balancing act—between assessing learning and assessing instruction—is critical for reform because we cannot expect learning to change unless it is preceded by changes in teaching. And we won't know that until and unless we evaluate teaching and then reflect on what we see.

Balance between code and meaning. Barbara has long been an advocate of ensuring that students possess the enabling skills (word identification, decoding and phonemic awareness, vocabulary and fluency) that contribute to comprehension, but she rightly points out that those skills are never ends unto themselves but only a means to the greater end of comprehension. And she makes it clear that when it comes to priorities, comprehension is first amongst equals. My favorite feature of her recommendations about instruction is that she demands that teachers model and guide students in USING decoding, vocabulary, AND comprehension strategies "on the fly" during real time reading. She knows that you have to get ALL strategies off workbook pages and into the flow of everyday reading (and there is no question whatsoever about her commitment that EVERY child spend a sizeable fraction of EVERY reading period doing everyday independent reading. Otherwise kids will draw a "workbook activity box" around those strategies and put them away when they are reading. For Professor Taylor, the value of any skill or strategy is indexed by its capacity to help readers solve the problems they encounter along the way in authentic reading activities.

Balance between top-down and bottom-up approaches to professional development. No one has worried more about how to balance teacher agency versus demonstrated teacher needs as the primary basis for determining a school's professional development agenda. This is the classic tension between grass roots (the bottom-up model) and externally imposed (the top-down model) approaches to setting the agenda. If you examine Barbara's approach, it has a little bit of both. The agenda is really set by a confluence of forces: (a) any and all district level standards or mandates that are in place, (b) the evidence emerging from both formative and summative assessments used in the school, and (c) the collaborative negotiations that go on inside a faculty as they determine specific professional development activities for the year. But when push comes to shove, Barbara ultimately sides with the bottom-up model because she knows that when the agenda is entirely determined by external mandates or decision-makers, teachers will engage in "mock compliance," going through the motions while waiting for the current regime to run its course. She knows that when teachers have a major (not the only but a major) voice in setting the agenda, buy-in and compliance are much more likely. It breeds the right kind of accountability—one based on a keen sense of professional responsibility.

But when all is said and done, the most important feature of this book is its practicality. It may be grounded in research—about reading development, reading pedagogy, and professional development (and I, for one, am glad it is so grounded), but it is ultimately a "how to" manual to help teachers and administrators build strong and vital programs of schoolwide reform. You'll find suggestions for each and every facet of reading program change, from assessing needs, to setting goals, to establishing priorities, to developing assessment systems, to settling on school-wide instructional principles, to setting the professional development agenda, to using data to evaluate progress, to recalibrating in light of new evidence. About the only thing she doesn't tell us how to do is how to organize a celebration of student and school progress. She leaves that to us. I guess she figures we'll figure that one out for ourselves. School leaders who are committed to student learning through teacher learning and improved curriculum and pedagogy will find everything they need in this book. I wish you well in "catching schools" in your corner of the educational world.

P. David Pearson
Berkeley, CA

Acknowledgments

This book is the result of ten years of collaboration with many elementary teachers and colleagues across the United States. I want to thank them all for their invaluable contributions to this book.

Inspired by the research on effective schools, teachers, and school reform, I began, with colleagues, to develop the School Change in Reading (SCR) framework in the late 1990s. My goal was to help elementary teachers within schools help all of their students succeed in reading through research-based, motivating instruction that meets all students' needs and challenges them all. With colleagues, I have refined the SCR process over the years by working with and learning from many teachers and their students. Without the opportunity to visit teachers in their classrooms, I would not have been able to modify and improve the collaborative professional learning practices described in this book. Thus, I want to thank the several thousand teachers I have visited and learned from over the past ten years through my work on effective reading instruction and schoolwide reading improvement. I especially want to thank the exemplary teachers who have contributed so much to this book by sharing their thoughts and lessons related to effective reading instruction.

I owe a special thanks and a debt of gratitude to my colleagues, P. David Pearson, a professor at the University of California, Berkeley, and Debra Peterson, a faculty member in the Minnesota Center for Reading Research at the University of Minnesota. David began the SCR work with me under the umbrella of CIERA (Center for the Improvement of Early Reading Achievement). Debra worked tirelessly with me to refine the framework, primarily through our work in Minnesota REA and Reading First schools.

I also want to thank the many people at Heinemann who have made this book possible. In particular, I want to thank Patty Adams, my production editor, who has consistently done a top-notch job on a complex project to get this book and companion DVD ready for publication. Whenever I called with questions or concerns she responded cheerfully and promptly. Many others at Heinemann have also contributed to this book and I thank them for their efforts.

It is my sincere hope that elementary teachers and administrators within will find this book useful as they engage in ongoing, collaborative school-wide reading reform and professional learning in their efforts to teach all students to be confident, motivated, successful readers. I want to say thank you to all teachers reading this book for the important work you do for our children!

Barbara M. Taylor
University of Minnesota

A Good Beginning to School Reform? Schoolwide Reading Improvement

Considering any kind of schoolwide change can be like getting ready to create a beautiful garden. Imagine looking at the backyard where you want to put the garden. How do you start? How do you envision it will look when you're done? How will you nurture it and keep it growing and changing? These are the kind of questions you might be asking yourself about schoolwide reading reform as well. This book will show you the way.

A considerable body of research indicates that one sound route to improving student achievement and teacher effectiveness overall is by improving reading instruction. When students achieve as readers, many other facets of effective teaching and learning come into high relief. The children's reading advances, they are thinking, happier, more engaged, and on task, and you will find there will be greater collaboration among staff. School reform needs a starting point, and reading is a great one. The processes used for reading improvement are ones around which other reforms can be carved.

Let's begin by considering some key questions this book will help you answer:

▶ How do we teach children today to become successful readers, people who read with good comprehension throughout their lives?

▶ How do we combine the research of the past decades with our own expertise to help us as individuals—and as a school staff—develop a clear vision of effective reading instruction?

The good news is, we know a lot about teaching reading and the critical role teacher expertise plays in student learning. This knowledge is the engine that powers this book. I share the practices for teaching reading that have been proven to work along with a model for a schoolwide change process that is embedded in practice. It's a model deeply rooted in the belief that when teachers see what works and are given a way to work alongside one another to hone their teaching abilities, student learning improves. I show you how you can put the practices into action in your own reform effort.

Whether you are a teacher, staff developer, college professor, or administrator, the accounts of school reform and the professional development model in this book will help you bring change to your school. Wonderful things are possible when teachers and administrators commit to ongoing conversations about and examinations of the school culture (both spoken and unspoken), the reading curriculum, reading assessments, and, most importantly, reading instruction. See Figure 1-1

Some Questions to Start the Journey

Throughout this book, I encourage you to maintain a questioning stance. Pause and reflect on how the ideas sit with you and how they relate to the school within which you teach. Jot down notes, underline, express doubt, and talk with colleagues. Use a list like the one that follows in Figure 1–2 to draft your own school's version of starter questions discussed at staff meetings to launch your collaborative professional learning journey. Many of your questions and responses will need to be revisited as you continue on your journey. Reform takes reflection and, like much in life, it's done best at a slow but steady pace. In time, as a result of this experience, teachers more purposefully and effectively instruct in ways that meet students' varied needs, reading scores increase, and students become more successful, motivated learners in the classroom.

Why This Reading Improvement Model Works: Research Highlights

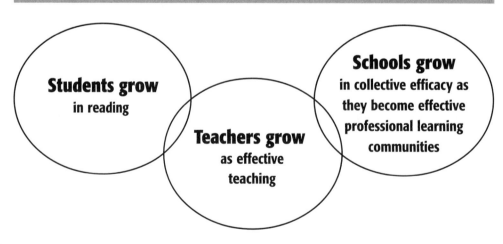

Figure 1-1 Outcomes of This Model

See pages 16–18 at the end of this chapter for summaries of the supporting data.

Questions to Discuss as a Staff	Notes/Next Steps
▶ What do we currently do well as a school?	
▶ What are our current strengths?	
▶ In general, what are our weaknesses as a staff?	
▶ What do we consider effective, engaging reading instruction for students?	
▶ What are we not on the same page about?	
▶ What is our schoolwide approach to reading? Do we have one?	
▶ What are the hallmarks of a successful lesson?	
▶ How do we measure if students have learned from it?	
▶ In addition to the state and district tests, what assessments do we have in place?	
▶ What are teachers using to make instructional decisions? Are we looking at data effectively in order to help bring about optimum achievement?	
▶ What reading materials and/or literature anthologies or curriculum do we have in place and what do we think of them? What kinds of texts are we missing?	
▶ How are we meeting the needs of our English language learners and students who need more support as readers?	
▶ What do we need to do to be the best teachers we can be?	

Figure 1-2 *Sample Starter Questions to Launch Your Professional Learning Journey*

Catching Schools © 2011 by Barbara M. Taylor (Heinemann: Portsmouth, NH).

Listening to the Language of Change: Quotes from Participants

I want to share with you some comments from the participants in the School Change in Reading (SCR) process that is the focus of this book. So often school improvement is voiceless, faceless—goals and statements that are hard to get excited about. I want you to hear the participants' voices, letting their language wash over you as a way to pick up on the recurring qualities of successful professional development and reform. In later chapters I'll go into these elements in more detail. As you read these quotes, think about:

▶ collaboration

▶ staff relating to each other in new ways and with common goals

▶ high expectations for students' academic abilities

▶ high expectations for students to become ever more independent as learners as they proceed through the grades

▶ the benefit of a reform effort operating with a clear structure of "why and how" as well as "who, what, and where," as opposed to rigid mandates for change, to make the process less stressful for participants

▶ the benefits of professional learning communities focused on a specific content—reading—rather than floundering in the changing winds of overly general improvement initiatives

▶ a developing sense of ownership and collective efficacy

These educators work in four elementary schools that are engaged in a multiyear journey to improve their reading program and students' reading scores as part of the SCR process. The firsthand experiences of principals, literacy coordinators, and teachers reveal the elements that make professional learning successful and lasting. Most of all, these stories convey the teachers' and administrators' enthusiasm for the process. Without engagement and enthusiasm, school improvement is impossible. (These teachers and schools will be revisited in subsequent chapters.)

Lincoln Elementary

The context

Lincoln Elementary is a K–5 urban school in a large midwestern city. For many years Lincoln was a small, neighborhood school, but a few years ago it merged with a nearby school as part of district reorganization. Eighty percent of the students at Lincoln receive a subsidized lunch, 10 percent are special education students, and 25 percent are English language learners (ELLs). Lincoln is a culturally diverse school: almost half of the students are black; a little more than half, in fairly equal numbers, are white, Asian, and Hispanic; and a few are Native American. In the past, the school was on the state's adequate yearly progress (AYP) watch list, but the school made AYP in reading for the past five years, the first three of which the SCR process was in place. During those three years, students in grade 3 went from the thirty-sixth to forty-fifth percentile on average on the spring score in comprehension on a standardized test. Grade 2 students went from a mean spring score in comprehension at the forty-sixth percentile in the first year to the sixty-first percentile in the third year.

The principal

Janet Jones sees her role as "the instructional leader and manager of daily operations with the ultimate responsibility of making sure we provide the best educational programs possible to ensure student success." To accomplish this success, she visits classrooms, reviews data, talks to teachers, and encourages them to talk to her. She has her most highly skilled teachers work with the students who are at the lower end in terms of ability.

> *On participation in the SCR* process, she says,
>
> I now understand what good reading instruction is and how to make it happen. Also, the project changed the way staff thinks about instruction; it changed relationships in a good way; and it gave everyone confidence, pride, and satisfaction in their work. We make sure we are having professional conversations about instruction. Teachers are now more discriminating about what and how they teach reading. They are teaching differently because they are more confident about their instructional choices.

Second-grade teacher

Matthew Thompson is an exceptional second-grade teacher. He accompanied his students from first to second grade during the third year of the school's SCR process. His students entered second grade reading seventy-four words correct per minute (wcpm) on average and ended the year reading 108 wcpm on average. On a standardized reading test, his students improved on average from the fifty-fourth percentile in vocabulary in the fall to the seventy-third percentile in the spring.

> *On helping students achieve grade-level expectations,* he says,
>
> All students need to be at their instructional level. Missing pieces identified by assessments need to be filled in, whether it is decoding strategies or reading with expression. Students need to learn how to think about a story and to answer questions on their own. Most need fluency building. They all need to write regularly and thoughtfully about what they have read.

> *On cultivating students' independence,* he comments,
>
> I want my students to be motivated to learn on their own, to not need me telling them what to do every moment.

Throughout the year, he carefully scaffolds how to work with a partner and in a small group, how to ask for and give help, and how to engage in student-led discussions. In Chapters 2 and 3, you will learn more about Matthew's approach to getting second graders, many of whom are ELLs, involved in student-led discussions related to high-quality literature.

> *On how reform leads to openness to change,* Matthew says,
>
> We learned a lot and once you know better ways of doing things, you want to keep doing them. Initial support from our external partner was very helpful, but now in the third year most of the staff development is internal. We work extraordinarily

well together. We are sharing with one another, discussing what we've read, and talking about what we're doing. I've never heard so much discussion about how we're teaching and what we're noticing about the children's learning as I have these past three years. I'm really proud of our staff.

Special education teacher

Kathy Little has high expectations for her at-risk first-grade readers.

Reflecting on the components of her instruction, Kathy says,

Collaborating with other teachers, creating lessons and using research and assessments to drive my instruction, and reflecting on what's working and what isn't are three critical pieces.

On how her teaching has changed, Kathy reflects,

My lessons are more intentional. I am especially focusing on vocabulary and comprehension. I'm using writing as a way for students to respond. I'm also being more purposeful in relating to students' lives. I'm seeing more excitement in my students than before, and this makes me more excited.

In Chapter 2, you'll learn more about Kathy's reading instruction for struggling readers.

On the benefits of collegiality, Kathy says,

I attribute success to study groups, good peer relations, and collaboration across grade levels. Having a focus during study groups is really improving my teaching; everyone shares experiences with the same strategies and reflects on changes that need to be made. Our monthly student progress meetings, where we share reading data on our students, help us focus on what we're teaching and what modifications are needed to get our students to the next level.

Westside Elementary

The context

Westside Elementary is a K–6 urban school in which 95 percent of students receive subsidized lunch and 95 percent are students of color. The largest demographic is Spanish speaking, the second is Somali. During the SCR process, Westside became a school for newcomers to the United States, and the percent of ELLs at the school increased from 66 to 87 percent. On a standardized test, over the three years that data were collected, grade 3 students increased from a mean spring comprehension score in the first year at the eighteenth percentile to a mean score at the thirty-third percentile in the third year. They also went from a mean spring vocabulary score at the sixteenth percentile in the first year to a mean spring vocabulary score in the third year at the twenty-fourth percentile. The school still has a long way to go but is making steady progress.

The principal

With six years at Westside under her belt, Carla Herrera continues to rally her staff to get to know each individual child and his or her academic and social needs. The school's approach to differentiated instruction is impressive.

On leadership style, Carla says,

I oversee all of the professional development planning, observe teachers, and coach them in the classroom. I believe in connecting individually with each teacher around the data of their students. To improve instruction in their schools, principals need to get into classrooms and recognize what their teachers are doing and be a support to teachers. Principals need to know good instruction themselves and know how to coach teachers when needed. I am in classrooms every day and I join team meetings, so I know what is going on in the classrooms.

On the school's reading program, she comments,

We run a readers workshop model of instruction, with a minilesson followed by an independent work period that includes time for small-group instruction and/or partner work. The workshop closes with a sharing at the end. We have allotted 120 minutes of reading in grades K–3 and 90 minutes in grades 4–6 each day. Our students are grouped based on their needs. We assess them with a variety of measures. We provide interventions, such as Early Intervention in Reading for grades K–3, and in our 4–6 grades we have an intervention model that was created by our intermediate reading coach, a former Reading Recovery teacher. We have an adopted basal series, but we rely heavily on our extensive leveled books and also use the library collection to fill the book bags children take home for independent reading.

On the biggest challenge, Carla shares,

. . . is continuing to differentiate to meet the needs of all learners and to manage the behaviors and serious emotional needs of some of our children while running a workshop model of instruction.

On the role of the literacy leadership team, Carla says,

The literacy leadership team is made up of a teacher from each grade, K–6, and co-facilitated by the school's two literacy coaches, one working with K–3 and one 4–6. The leadership team members look at the data on students and on teaching practices to come up with overarching goals for literacy instruction at Westside. They are the venue for communicating with grade-level teams around building-wide expectations and implementation of our readers workshop model.

On study groups, Carla shares,

Teachers [for grades] K–6 met in study groups around the theme of reading comprehension this year, often sharing and discussing videos of their teaching. What felt awkward and cumbersome at the beginning is now becoming routine.

On how a reflective stance leads to change, Carla says,

Because of our involvement in schoolwide reading improvement, we're more reflective and intentional about our practice and more intentional about our research-based instruction. We have learned to open our doors and be more comfortable with peer observation and feedback.

Literacy coordinator

Estella Butler knows she has a crucial position in a school engaged in substantive efforts to improve its reading program.

Estella says,

Working directly with teachers, I set up study groups and whole-group meetings focused on literacy, and I make sure that we are studying research-based strategies. I organize materials and handouts, and I help teachers videotape their lessons to share in study groups. I engage in classroom observations that include pre- and post-conversations with teachers. I meet with a member of our external support team to plan ways to assist teachers as they are implementing what they are learning. I collect assessment data, meet with teachers to look at their data, and help them figure out what instructional modifications to try next.

On professional learning and changes to reading instruction, Estella shares,

Many teachers are willing to try what they are learning in study groups in their classrooms; if it doesn't seem to be working, most of them will adjust to meet the needs of their students, and that is a good thing. Also, teachers are beginning to drop some of their old habits and practices and turning to research-based techniques and data to drive their instruction. Before, our professional learning was all about reading and talking and now it's about action.

Teachers really understand that higher-level questioning is important and this is going really well. Teachers are seeing the importance of modeling and using accountable talk. Also, vocabulary learning is being stressed and that's new. A lot of the teaching was whole-group in the beginning and now I'm seeing so much small-group teaching, maybe almost too much at times. I think a lot of things have changed for the better with instruction due to the study groups and whole-group meetings.

On coaching, Estella reflects,

What I've learned about coaching from our external partners has really helped me. In the beginning I was in the classroom doing a lot of teaching and modeling myself, and I wasn't really sure how to get teachers to do more of the teaching when I was there. I've learned how to put the ownership on the teachers. I have a pre-conference, go in to observe, and then have a post-conference. I ask questions to get teachers to come up with their own ideas and changes. Now we are teaching teachers how to engage in peer coaching using the same coaching model.

Teacher of ELLs

Angelina Ipson says her reading instruction has improved and her students are doing well.

She notes,

My English learners are able to apply more reading strategies than in previous years. Our scores are higher and that's good. In fact, most of our kids have shown improvement. My students are asking each other questions more, they are telling why more and proving why, not just saying, "I liked this book." Their written responses are much more meaty, too.

On reading/writing connections, Angelina says,

This year I am connecting written responses with students' reading more often, and this is making their reading more meaningful to them. The kids can really make some connections to their reading on their own now. I have also made a greater effort to help the kids see how reading and writing, speaking and listening are all connected.

On communication and professional learning, Angelina comments,

Communication across the school is strong because we meet in cross-grade-level study groups and talk about what works and what we are doing. The professional development is rigorous and much is expected. I like the fact that we read about best practices and apply them to our daily work. I think the application piece will make us better teachers and a better school.

On leadership, Angelina shares,

Our principal, Carla Herrera, is very supportive, reasonable, and tuned in to the reality of our day-to-day situations. Also, she sets a tone for collaboration. She works best by bouncing ideas off a group. She is willing to sit down and talk with people about problems they are having and how to resolve them.

On the literacy coordinator, Angelina says,

Estella observes in our classrooms and we talk about what we could do better. She pushes us to move forward. If we didn't have her leadership we would probably get lazy! She also helps us share our successes. After she has been in to watch me teach, I find that a lot of her comments simply affirm what I'm doing. She also makes suggestions and encourages us to go out to watch what others are doing in the school. Estella's coaching has been most helpful in that it has caused us to reflect more closely on what we are doing and to dig deeper. She has helped us think and make our conversations about our teaching more academic and metacognitive.

Fourth-grade teacher

Benice Daniels's students went from the thirtieth percentile on average in both comprehension and vocabulary to the thirty-ninth percentile in both areas by spring in the third year of the schoolwide reading improvement process.

On her biggest challenge in teaching reading, Benice says,

It is the varied levels of the students. Some kids are so behind the other kids and the biggest challenge is to instruct them in the right way so they can catch up. Keeping children motivated and not frustrated or afraid is another challenge.

On improvements she's made, Benice adds,

I have increased my ability to teach fluency and vocabulary effectively. Now I am focusing on comprehension-strategies instruction based on what I am learning in one of my study groups. I plan to keep expanding my repertoire in this area. I need a lot of practice and good examples when I am trying new things because it is so unfamiliar to me.

On schoolwide change, Benice comments,

Everything in our professional development model has a purpose and is useful, including feedback. Looking at the progress students have made from fall to spring has motivated teachers. There are individual students who made great gains. Also, the assessments drive our instruction because we see where our students' needs are and have a study group in that area, for example in comprehension, to provide more effective instruction.

Edgewood Elementary

The context

Edgewood Elementary is a suburban school that has changed significantly in the past ten years. Historically, it was a school with little diversity, but now 35 percent of the students are from diverse backgrounds, 35 percent of the students receive a subsidized lunch, and there are very affluent students in the school as well. Edgewood made adequate yearly progress (AYP) for the three years it was involved in the SCR process, as well as the year that followed. The mean spring comprehension score on a standardized test for grade 3 students increased from the fifty-fourth to fifty-sixth percentile from the first year to the third year and the mean spring vocabulary score increased from the fiftieth to sixtieth percentile over this three-year period.

The principals

Mike O'Connell, the principal for two years of the reform effort, attributes his success to an emphasis on collective leadership and a can-do attitude:

> Through collaboration and a strong sense of collegiality we are really able to do some wonderful things for kids and look at change as a process over time.

During the third year of the grant, Tricia Calhoun took over as principal. To her credit, she did not try to move the school in a new direction based on her personal vision but worked hard to build on the successes of the prior two years. Her approach to leadership was similar to Mike's. She says,

> I am an educational and instructional leader. It's my responsibility to keep us focused on our collective vision and school goals. I try to support teachers individually and collectively with their professional development and instructional practices. I'm a liaison with parents, the community, and the district. I support teachers with student management and discipline. She visits classrooms frequently.

On the role of parents, Tricia says,

> I think that we have a group of very engaged parents and they are very satisfied with our school's community. Also, I think they are generally very happy with how we support them as educators of their children. However, the Edgewood staff feels it can do a better job with our parents—that some aren't as engaged as they could be. We have a task force to increase parent involvement and partnership in their child's education. As a school, we want to assist families in the education of their children.

Tricia explains the leadership team's roles,

> Our leadership team consists of the literacy coordinator, four classroom teachers, a special education teacher, a basic skills teacher, and me. But leadership really is a collaborative effort among all the teachers. The leadership team is responsible for identifying areas of need and the types of professional development that will support change. Individual classroom teachers and teams make decisions about literacy instruction such as determining what learning targets to teach at what point in time, the formative assessments they give, and the daily instructional decisions that need to be made relating to their students' needs.

On the school's reading program, Tricia comments,

Our reading curriculum consists of our learning targets, our assessments, and our resources. Teachers use our core basal program, but they are driven by students' progress toward learning targets, not the basal. We know that students need varied instruction, and we're using our assessments as much to inform our instruction as to measure results.

We are training all teachers who hadn't previously been trained in the EIR small-group intervention program because we saw how effective that was for students who received it. A related initiative in our school is identifying and implementing an effective system of interventions for all of our at-risk readers as well as challenging supplemental instruction to support all students.

We are more aware of students' engagement. Teachers are always thinking about motivation now in their instruction and the role that it plays in how students learn to read. Teachers are releasing responsibility to the students over time. They are doing less teacher talk and allowing the children to be more actively engaged in questioning and in monitoring their reading.

On what made the biggest difference in professional learning, Tricia says,

I think the sustained study of topics makes a real difference. Teachers' opportunities to reflect on and share their practices with others seem to have a real impact on students' learning. I also think that teachers' ongoing use of current data from teacher observations has really helped them change their teaching, and classroom visits by external partners have helped us look at our practices through another lens.

Literacy coordinator

About her job responsibilities, Anna Berglund explains,

I visit classrooms to help move instructional practices forward for individual teachers by modeling and by coaching with guided reflective questioning and constructive feedback. Hopefully, this reflection and support leads to changes in instruction, which in turn leads to increased student learning.

On important changes in the past few years, Anna reflects,

One thing that's changed is that we have specific names to describe what we are doing. We are also much more aware of why we are doing what we are doing, and we are explicit about this with our students so they understand what they are doing and why. We are much more aware of what's happening at other grade levels and how instruction is building from one grade level to the next throughout the school. We are also paying more attention to individual student data and the need to differentiate instruction to help individual students.

On professional learning, Anna comments,

The School Change in Reading process has given us a structure to work within that leads to productive, reflective discussions about teaching and learning. Also, talking about the school reading program gives us a schoolwide perspective of what we are doing to help our students. It breaks down the feelings of isolation, and it gives staff ideas and strategies to make it more effective. Learning together builds common language and common vision and goals.

Things that were important this year for us were study groups that focused on comprehension strategy instruction, higher-level questioning, and getting kids to talk to one another about books they were reading. Schoolwide, we have seen all students' fluency scores increase. But more important, we have seen students deepen their comprehension and their ability to engage in dialogue with other people. Overall we've seen our kids thinking at higher levels.

First-grade teacher

Becky Saunders does an amazing job teaching her first graders how to engage in student-led discussions. In the third year of the SCR process, her students went from the fifty-sixth percentile on average on a prereading test in the fall of grade 1 to the seventy-second percentile in decoding and comprehension by the end of the year.

On recent changes in her instruction, Becky adds,

I have been working hard at implementing student-led discussion groups in which students ask and respond to challenging questions. Students are writing their own high-level questions. They also learn how to coach each other for a high-level response.

I am also more focused on comprehension strategies. This, along with student discussions, leads to more student engagement. The research we've read on student engagement points out that students learn more as they are more engaged in their learning. Also, access to quality books is a key component.

On what contributed to these changes, Becky says,

It's come from what we've been learning in our study groups and also what we've learned through workshops conducted by our external partners. I'm a member of the higher-level questioning study group. I find that's a daily application in my room. I'm also in an EIR intervention study group, which is something we are using daily. I really value study groups because of the opportunity to learn from readings and from one another. As we talk, we are able to reflect together on what we are doing and if it's best for students.

On receiving support from the literacy coordinator, Becky adds,

I've appreciated the opportunity to sit down with the literacy coordinator to talk about things I'm doing or thinking of doing. I like to bounce ideas off her one-on-one. Also, the feedback on what she sees students [are] able to do when she comes to my room or what else I might think about doing is helpful. It has caused me to think about my instruction in different ways and make modifications.

On students' reading achievement, Becky says,

I see students meeting higher standards and targets. So I am able to raise the bar and know that students will still be able to succeed. We all take great joy in seeing the children accelerate in a way we haven't seen before.

Madina Elementary

The context

Madina Elementary is a small school in a rural farming community in which most of the students are white and a small percentage are Native American. Fifty-eight percent of the students receive a subsidized lunch, and 15 percent have been identified as having special learning needs. The responses from the principal, literacy coordinator, and teachers at Madina to interview questions were very similar to those from administrators and teachers at Lincoln, Westside, and Edgewood. Madina made AYP in reading during the five years it received support in the SCR process from an external partner and for the two years after this support ended. Over the three years data were collected, the mean spring comprehension score for grade 3 students on a standardized test went from the fifty-fourth to sixty-third percentile.

The principal

At the end of the SCR process, principal Judy Hunter said,

> It has been a rewarding experience. Our literacy coordinator has provided outstanding support and leadership for the staff. The leadership team, made up of one representative from each grade level, has been the direct connection to the staff. They are also the ones who have been most active in creating our sustainability plan. Study groups have been invaluable as our forum for reflecting and processing, helping us go from the research and student data to implementation in the classroom. Feedback data from teacher observations during the reading block have been another way for us to look at our progress and for teachers to individually reflect on their teaching.

The literacy coordinator

Jane Larson, the literacy coordinator, reflected,

> The School Change in Reading process is based on research on effective schools and what works. Through this change process, we have collaborated on reading instruction. Talking with others has led to professional growth for all teachers in our school. It is important to talk with colleagues about instruction and assessments to reflect on your own teaching and make changes.

Kindergarten teacher

Melissa Norris, an exemplary kindergarten teacher, reflected *on changes in her instruction since the SCR process began,*

> I have more of a focus, like the reciprocal teaching piece I have added that includes predicting, clarifying, questioning, and summarizing. I have really noticed a difference in student engagement since I started the reciprocal teaching work. Also, my students are excited about reading books and discussing them with their peers.

Third-grade teacher

Maggie Voss, an excellent third-grade teacher, reported,

> People who have visited my classroom mention over and over again how excited the students are about reading. The children are really into informational text. Part of this is because the students know how to use strategies and they have better comprehension. Also, I get so much positive feedback about reading from the students at the school. They love to discuss their books and monitor their own comprehension. They have more ownership of their own learning.

The Take Away: Similarities Among Schools

These four schools have similar stories. The principals, literacy coaches, and teachers believe that the reform effort had a significant impact on their school's sense of collective efficacy, on the quality of classroom instruction and teachers' sense of self-efficacy, and on students' reading achievement and motivation to learn.

Principals saw themselves as instructional leaders:

▶ They understood what good reading instruction entailed and looked like in the classroom.

▶ They visited classrooms in order to build rapport, provide support, coach, and communicate to teachers that they were serious about ensuring there was excellent reading instruction at their school.

▶ They had a collaborative style. They listened to their teachers, who in turn felt they could come to their principals for help.

▶ They were engaged in the reform process and were members of their literacy leadership teams. But they did not try to take charge; rather they fostered collaborative leadership.

Leadership team members took an active role in leadership. They, not the principal or literacy coordinator, were seen by teachers as the group in charge of the literacy improvement efforts at their schools.

The *literacy coordinator* was regarded as an instructional leader and excellent teacher:

▶ She was seen as the manager of the reform process who, as a member of the leadership team, worked with the other members to keep all aspects of the improvement effort moving forward.

▶ She helped teachers collect student data when needed and, more important, set up and participated in meetings in which teachers looked at this data together to make instructional modifications to better meet students' needs.

▶ She was valued as an exemplary reading teacher who modeled effective practices in classrooms.

▶ She was respected by her colleagues and was accepted, even appreciated, as a peer coach who had learned how to ask questions and provide suggestions to get teachers to reflect on their reading instruction and generate their own next steps to make their instruction even more effective (Peterson et al. 2009).

Teachers felt they had made significant improvements in their reading instruction and demonstrated enthusiasm for the changes they had made:

▶ They expressed greater satisfaction with and confidence in their ability to provide balanced instruction that was differentiated to meet varied student needs.

▶ They said they were now teaching comprehension strategies, engaging students in high-level talk and writing about text, and teaching students how to take part in student-led discussions.

▶ They expressed their great satisfaction in seeing students' reading scores increase, especially in the area of comprehension; in seeing greater engagement in and enthusiasm for learning in their students; and in seeing students develop greater independence as learners.

All the educators showcased in this chapter felt that participation in the SCR improvement process had been successful because it increased collaboration and cohesiveness throughout the school. It led to more reflection on and professional conversations about reading instruction through study groups, whole-group meetings, student data retreats, reflections on observation data, and coaching conversations.

What's Ahead in This Resource

In the chapters that follow, you will learn about the processes these schools put in place and the different types of learning opportunities that teachers and administrators engaged in. Ultimately, it gives you a blueprint to help you plan your own schoolwide professional development plan.

Chapters 2 and 3 focus on the content and practices of effective reading instruction and showcases successful teachers such as Matthew Thompson, Kathy Little, Angelina Van Ipson, Benice Daniels, and Becky Saunders. Use these chapters as a springboard to develop teachers' knowledge of literacy; use them to galvanize professional inquiry and conversations about effective reading instruction, effective classroom discussions, and so on.

Chapter 4 presents the research on school-based reading improvement and an overview of the theory and research behind the SCR model. Increasingly, school leaders are asking, *can you show me the data that shows that this framework works?* They don't want to waste precious time or resources—and most of all, they want to serve their students. The SCR model has strong research support on its efficacy (Peterson et al., 2009, Taylor and Pearson, 2004, Taylor et al., 2000, Taylor et al. 2003, Taylor et al. 2005, Taylor and Peterson, 2007, Taylor and Peterson, 2008, Taylor et al., 2007). These studies and others are summarized at the end of this chapter.

Chapter 5 describes the meetings and processes you need to foster organizational change in your school. Chapter 6 provides suggestions for how to use data on students, classrooms, and the school to help foster change. Chapter 7 focuses on the specifics of teachers' professional development so you have a vision for the teacher-centeredness of this reform. Chapter 8 details the coaching techniques that a literacy coach or teacher peers can use to support one another as they try out new instructional techniques. Chapter 9 offers a kind of case study of teachers and administrators in Westside Elementary, so you can spot the factors of their success and anticipate common roadblocks and take actions that keep a can-do spirit in your school community. For external support on how to engage in processes covered in this book, go to www.earlyinterventioninreading.com.

Questions for Reflection and Discussion

1. Which comments made by these teachers, principals, or literacy coordinators stuck with you? Why?

2. In what ways is your school similar to the four schools featured in this chapter? In what ways is it different?

3. In what ways is leadership in your school similar to the leadership described in this chapter? In what ways is it different?

4. In what ways is professional learning at your school similar to the professional learning described in this chapter? In what ways is it different?

5. Based on what you learned thus far from the schools described in this chapter, what questions do you have and what changes might you like to work toward in your school?

Supporting Your Practice: Research Studies to Share

As a teacher, you may be looking for research to support best classroom practices. With your needs in mind, we offer the following studies to provide the very evidence you need, ready to share with others: principals, professional developers, parents, and school boards.

The School Change in Reading (SCR) reform model has been used in many states across the country, particularly in Minnesota (see Chapter 4). This model has been extensively researched, and relevant studies are briefly summarized here.

Characteristics of Effective Teachers and Schools

Taylor, B. M. 2002. Highly Accomplished Primary Grade Teachers in Effective Schools. In *Teaching Reading: Effective Schools/Accomplished Teachers*, edited by B. M Taylor and P. D. Pearson, 279–88. Mahwah, NJ: Erlbaum.

> Four exemplary primary-grade teachers in schools that were beating the odds had high expectations for student learning and behaviors; taught and coached in instructional level groups; enhanced literacy through authentic, engaging learning activities; and fostered independent learners.

Taylor, B., P. D. Pearson, K. Clark, and S. Walpole. 2000. "Effective Schools and Accomplished Teachers: Lessons About Primary Grade Reading Instruction in Low-Income Schools." *The Elementary School Journal* 101: 121–65.

> Effective schools had strong links to parents, systematic assessment of pupil progress, strong communication and collaboration, and a collaborative model for the delivery of reading instruction, including early reading interventions. Effective teachers, compared to others, spent increased amounts of time in small-group reading instruction, gave students more time to engage in independent reading, had high levels of pupil on-task behavior, and strong home–school communications. Effective teachers, as compared to others, and teachers in more effective schools, as compared to other schools, supplemented explicit phonics instruction with coaching in word-recognition strategies and employed a greater number of higher-level questions in discussion of texts. Effective teachers also asked students to do more writing in response to reading than other teachers.

Taylor, B. M., M. Pressley, and P. D. Pearson. 2002. Research-Supported Characteristics of Teachers and Schools That Promote Reading Achievement. In *Teaching Reading: Effective Schools, Accomplished Teachers*, edited by B. M. Taylor and P. D. Pearson, 361–74. Mahwah, NJ: Erlbaum.

This review found that effective teachers had excellent classroom management, provided balanced reading instruction, used small-group instruction more than other teachers, and stressed higher-order thinking. High-poverty schools with high achievement focused on improved student learning, had strong school leadership, had strong teacher collaboration, engaged in consistent use of data on student performance, focused on professional development and innovation, and had strong links to parents.

Schools Using the SCR Framework to Become Highly Effective

Taylor, B. M., P. D. Pearson, D. S. Peterson, and M. C. Rodriguez. 2003. "Reading Growth in High-Poverty Classrooms: The Influence of Teacher Practices That Encourage Cognitive Engagement in Literacy Learning." *The Elementary School Journal* 104: 3–28.

> In schools involved in schoolwide reading improvement, the teachers in grades 2 through 5 who saw the most growth in their students' reading during the school year asked more high-level questions about text, taught less phonics, did more coaching and involving students in active reading practice, and had more students on task, as compared to other teachers.

Taylor, B. M., D. P. Pearson, D. S. Peterson, and M. C. Rodriguez. 2005. "The CIERA School Change Framework: An Evidenced-Based Approach to Professional Development and School Reading Improvement." *Reading Research Quarterly* 40(1): 40–69.

> In a study of thirteen schools across the United States using the SCR framework over a two-year period, schools more successful in implementing the essential components of the reform (including staff participation in frequent study-group meetings to learn about and reflect on research-based practices, as well as sustained staff efforts to provide effective, research-based instruction in classrooms) saw substantially greater growth in their students' reading than schools less successful in implementing the reform.

Taylor, B. M., and D. S. Peterson. 2007. *Year 2 Report of the Minnesota Reading First (Cohort 2) School Change Project.* Minneapolis, University of Minnesota, Minnesota Center for Reading Research.

> In a study of twenty-four Minnesota Reading First schools, second and third graders saw greater growth in reading comprehension, vocabulary, fluency, and decoding (grade 2) if they were in classrooms where teachers engaged in more high-level questioning relative to other teachers. They also saw greater growth in reading comprehension and vocabulary if they were in classrooms where teachers engaged in higher levels of comprehension strategies instruction as compared to other teachers. Second graders saw less growth in vocabulary, fluency, and decoding if they were in classrooms where teachers engaged in more phonics instruction than other teachers. First graders saw greater growth in reading comprehension and decoding if they were in classrooms where teachers engaged in more high-level and low-level questioning.

Taylor, B. M., and D. S. Peterson. 2008. *Year 3 Report of the Minnesota Reading First (Cohort 2) School Change Project.* Minneapolis, University of Minnesota, Minnesota Center for Reading Research.

In a study of twenty-three Minnesota Reading First schools, students in grade 3 had significant growth in comprehension (+3.1 normal curve equivalent points, NCEs) and vocabulary (+5.6 NCEs) on a standardized reading test from fall to spring. Students in grade 2 had significant growth in decoding (+4.4 NCEs) and comprehension (+1.3 NCEs). First graders had significant growth in decoding (+4.6 NCEs) and comprehension (+2.5 NCEs). Second and third graders saw greater growth in reading comprehension, vocabulary, and decoding (grade 2) if they were in classrooms where teachers engaged in more high-level questioning than other teachers. Students saw greater growth in reading comprehension, vocabulary, fluency, and decoding (grade 2) if they were in classrooms where teachers engaged in more comprehension strategies instruction.

Taylor, B. T., D. S. Peterson, M. Marx, and M. Chein. 2007. Scaling up a Reading Reform Effort in 23 High-Poverty Schools. In *Effective Instruction for Struggling Readers, K–6,* edited by B. M. Taylor and J. Ysseldyke, 216–34. New York: Teachers College Press.

In a study of 23 Reading Excellence Act schools in Minnesota, students in grades 2 and 3 had greater growth in reading comprehension and vocabulary in classrooms in which teachers engaged them in more high-level questioning and less phonics instruction relative to other teachers. Schools that did a better job of implementing the SCR framework saw greater growth in their students' reading comprehension scores than other schools.

Specific Elements of the SCR Framework

Peterson, D. S., B. M. Taylor, R. Burnham, and R. Schock. 2009. "Reflective Coaching Conversations: A Missing Piece." *The Reading Teacher* 62(6): 500–09.

Teachers in Minnesota Reading First schools made important research-based changes to their reading instruction and students made accelerated progress in their reading comprehension scores. Teachers' instructional changes were stimulated through collaborative conversations about practice that included video sharing, data sharing, and coaching conversations with the building literacy coach. Through coaching conversations, teachers focused on elements of effective instruction and set goals for future reading lessons.

Taylor, B. M., and P. D. Pearson. 2005. Using Study Groups and Reading Assessment Data to Improve Reading Instruction Within a School. In *Current Issues in Reading Comprehension and Assessment,* edited by S. Paris and S. Stahl, 237–55. Mahwah, NJ: Erlbaum.

This chapter describes the efforts of teachers at one high-poverty, diverse school that used the SCR framework with great success. The teachers, teacher leaders, and principal at Howard Elementary worked very well together as a collaborative, learning community, and they saw excellent growth in their students' reading scores.

For related studies, see Chapter 4, as well as B. M. Taylor, T. E. Raphael, and K. H. Au (2010). Reading and School Reform. In *Handbook of Reading Research, Volume 4,* edited by M. Kamil, P. D. Pearson, P. Afflerbach, and E. Moje. New York: Routledge.

Teaching Reading Well

• •

Essential Content

One of the most prevalent comments teachers make to me is, "You can't believe the range of readers in my classroom." Across the nation, from Washington to Florida, many teachers seem unsure of how to address the dramatically different levels of proficiency in their classroom. While it's beyond the scope of this book to go into the demographic and economic factors that underpin current literacy challenges, the reform model in this book addresses the complexity of meeting all students' needs by keeping teachers' sights trained on two truths:

1. There are core practices that work for all readers.

2. In order to help all students achieve, all teachers within a school have to know and put into practice many of the same fundamental aspects of effective reading instruction.

This last point is almost too obvious to state, and yet in my own research, I've found that one of the biggest obstacles to reform is that there isn't a clear, shared vision of effective reading instruction that anchors the school.

In this chapter, I offer an *overview* of research-based practices that help all children in the elementary grades succeed in reading to their fullest potential. The What the Research Says sections in this chapter summarize the research on each topic, and question prompts in the Talk About It sections offer you a starting place for conversations with colleagues. The goal is to develop a collective vision of how to develop independent, proficient, motivated readers in every grade of the school. What factors are the same across grades? What is key to grades K–3 reading instruction that is less crucial in grades 4 and up?

To start, it's helpful to focus on two basic facets of teaching: the *content* and *pedagogy*. Having teachers reflect on these two facets helps them tease out the what from the how of their daily teaching, which in turn helps them see that improving their practice is often a matter of improving their decision making before, during, and after teaching. That is, as they deliver their reading instruction, they must continuously make good instructional choices to meet individual students' needs and to provide intellectual challenge to them all, based on these reflections in conjunction with ongoing assessment data.

First, let's look at the *content* of sound reading instruction—the components of effective reading instruction supported by scientifically based reading research that are related to the abilities that students must develop to become competent readers. These components include instruction in phonemic awareness, phonics, fluency, vocabulary, and comprehension. Instruction in the first three components, which are related to decoding, is important when students are learning how to read, especially in kindergarten and grade 1; instruction in the last two components, vocabulary and comprehension, is important in every grade. (Remember, though, that there is a lot more to sound reading instruction than providing lessons in decoding, fluency, vocabulary, and comprehension.)

Phonemic Awareness, Phonics, and Decoding Instruction

Most developing readers benefit from systematic, explicit instruction in phonemic awareness and phonics. Most kindergarteners and many students in early first grade benefit from small-group, focused instruction in phonemic awareness that deals, in particular, with learning how to hear the individual phonemes, or sounds, in words (*phonemic segmentation*) and how to blend phonemes together to pronounce words (*phonemic blending*). Having students see and/or manipulate letters while working on segmentation and blending is also beneficial. Focusing on a few important aspects of phonemic awareness (e.g., segmentation and blending) is more effective than focusing on many aspects, and phonemic awareness instruction is most effective when presented in short lessons spread out during the first year or two of school.

What the Research Says: Phonemic Awareness Instruction

To develop phonemic awareness, teachers engage students in activities in which they identify the sounds in words or blend sounds together. In the following chart, you can see the recommendations from prominent researchers; while researchers have their unique findings, just about all agreed that children benefit from deliberate, explicit instruction that focuses on segmentation and blending. Research has found:

▶ Most students in kindergarten and some in grade 1 benefit from systematic, explicit phonemic awareness instruction.

▶ Instruction that focuses on segmentation and blending is the most effective.

▶ Phonemic awareness instruction coupled with opportunities for students to manipulate letters is effective.

▶ Phonemic awareness instruction of 5 to 18 hours spread out over time has been found to be most effective as opposed to longer amounts of total time spent on it.

	Explicit Phonemic Awareness Instruction	Focus on Blending and Segmentation	Phonemic Awareness Combined with Letter Manipulation	Total Time: 5–18 hours total spent on phonemic awareness
Adams (1990) (review)	X			
Fuchs and Fuchs (2005)	X		X	
National Reading Panel (NRP 2000) (review)	X	X	X	X
Schneider et al. (2000)			X	
Snow, Burns, and Griffin (1998) (review)	X			
Stahl (2001) (review)	X			

talk About it

* Do you teach too much, not enough, or just about the right amount of phonemic awareness in kindergarten and early first grade?

* Is this instruction specifically focused on phonemic awareness or do you cover it incidentally as you review letter names and sounds?

* Do you focus in particular on helping students hear and blend the sounds in words?

Some Effective Instructional Approaches

Expose children to rhyming texts. Intentionally draw the children's attention to *rhyming words.* As you read books that have rhyming words, ask children to specifically identify the words that rhyme on each page. Ask children to make up their own rhyming words.

Read a variety of alphabet books to children. Specifically point out *words that begin with the same sound.* Ask children to point out objects within the illustrations that have the same beginning sound. There are lots of wonderful alphabet books available.

Use read-alouds to demonstrate segmenting sounds. While reading a book to children, stop and model how to *segment the sounds* in a two- or three-phoneme word. For example, when reading the book *Go, Dog, Go!* by P. D. Eastman you could ask the children, "What sound do you hear at the beginning of the word *go*? What sound do you hear at the end of *go*?" Some of the children may respond with the letter name. Redirect them to the sound they hear. It is important that they are able to identify the sounds in words in addition to naming the letters that make these sounds. A three-phoneme word from the same story would be segmented in the following way: "What sound do you hear at the beginning of *red*? What sound do you hear next in *red*? What is the last sound you hear in the word *red*?"

Use read-alouds to model blending sounds. While reading a book to children stop and model how to *blend the sounds* in a two- or three-phoneme word. For example, when reading the book *Do Like Kyla* by Angela Johnson, tell the children, "I'm going to give you three sounds and you see if you can tell me the word. /B/ /e/ /d/. Let's say the sounds a little faster. What is the word? *Bed*."

Incorporate guided writing. With this method, you model writing on chart paper while inviting students to practice writing along with you, using individual whiteboards, chalkboards, or clipboards. In other words, have *every* child participate in writing every letter in every word of the sentence rather than having them come up to you to "share the pen" which takes time and the disadvantage of one child at a time writing. The thinking aloud you do is focused on building phonemic awareness. For example, after reading *Rosie's Walk* by Pat Hutchins, have the class generate a short sentence about the story like "The fox chased the hen." After the students write *the*, ask them, "What word comes next in our sentence? What is the first sound in the word *fox*? What letter makes the /f/ sound? What is the next sound you hear in *fox*? What letter makes that sound? What is the last sound we hear in *fox*? What letter makes that sound?" Use the same approach with the word *hen*.

Have children work with sound boxes. Children identify, represent, and blend the individual sounds of words effectively when using sound boxes. For example, after reading the book *The Mitten* by Alvin Tresselt, give the children each a sheet that is numbered 1 to 3. After each number there should be three boxes. Tell children, "We are going to be writing some words from our story. Put your finger on the number one. The first word is *hop*. Remember how the cricket said she would just hop over and see if she could squeeze in, too? In the first box after the number one we will write the first sound in the word *hop*. What letter makes the /h/ sound? Write an *h* in the first box. What sound comes next in the word *hop*? What letter makes that sound? Now write the letter *o* in the second box. What is the last sound we hear in the word *hop*? What letter makes that sound? Write the letter *p* in the third box. Now put your pencil down and use your finger to point to each box as we say the sounds. /h/ /o/ /p/. Let's say it a little faster. Good, the word is *hop*." Continue on with the words *red* and *rip*. You can also do sound box activities with four boxes per word for four-phoneme words like *cold* and *snap*.

Resources on Phonemic Awareness

McCormick, C. E., R. N. Throneburg, and J. M. Smitley. 2002. *A Sound Start: Phonemic Awareness Lessons for Reading Success.* New York: Guilford.

Rog, L. J. 2001. *Early Literacy Instruction in Kindergarten.* Newark, DE: International Reading Association.

Taylor, B. M. (in press). *Catching Readers: Grade K.* Portsmouth, NH: Heinemann.

Instruction in Phonics and Word Recognition Strategies

Children, especially in kindergarten and first grade, also benefit from systematic, explicit phonics instruction. A variety of approaches are effective, including learning letter-sound correspondences, letter-by-letter decoding, and decoding by onset and rime. A combination of approaches may be most effective (Lovett et al. 2000), and most teachers report that they use several of them (Baumann, Hoffman, Duffy-Hester, and Ro 2000). Also, teachers need to help children use word recognition strategies and apply their phonics knowledge accurately and fluently in their daily reading and writing activities (National Reading Panel 2000a). Importantly, children need the opportunity to read books in which newly learned phonic elements occur. Teachers see more growth in their students' reading during kindergarten, first grade, and second grade when they coach students as they try to decode words while reading, as opposed to telling children unknown words (Taylor, Pearson, Clark, and Walpole 2000; Taylor and Peterson 2006b, 2006c).

What the Research Says: Phonics and Word-Recognition Strategies

In phonics instruction, teachers guide students to attend to symbol/sound correspondences, letter-by-letter decoding, decoding by onset and rime or analogy, or decoding multisyllabic words. There is no "one best sequence" for introducing phonics elements systematically. However, the authors of *Direct Instruction Reading* (Carnine, Silbert, Kame'enui, and Tarver 2004) recommend the following:

- most common consonants (*b, c, d, f, g, h, k, l, m, n, p, r, s, t*) and short vowels (*a, i, o*)
- less common consonants (*j, q, z, y, x, v, w*) and short vowels (*u, e*)
- CVC words starting with continuous sounds (*m, s, a*)
- CVC words starting with stop sounds (*b, d, t*)
- blends, consonant digraphs, vowel pairs, and long vowels

In word recognition instruction, teachers help students use one or more strategies to figure out words while reading, often by prompting children during whole group, small group or one-on-one conferring.

The following chart summarizes some of the research conducted about phonics. Research has found:

- Most students, especially in grades K and 1, benefit from systematic, explicit phonics instruction.
- A variety of approaches to systematic phonics instruction are effective.
- Phonics instruction in small groups, as opposed to whole class, is effective.
- In addition to systematic phonics instruction, students benefit from opportunities to apply phonics to reading, especially with support from a teacher.
- Differentiated phonics instruction is beneficial, based on students' needs. In grades 2 through 5, effective teachers provide focused phonics instruction as needed by students. Average and above average readers are less likely to benefit from systematic, explicit phonics lessons than below average readers.

	Systematic, Explicit Instruction	Variety of Approaches	Small Group	Application to Reading of Texts	K–1 Focus	Differentiated
Adams (1990) (review)	X			X		
Baumann et al. (2000)	X	X				
Camilli, Vargas, and Yurecko (2003)	X			X		
Christensen and Bowey (2005)	X	X				
Ehri (1991) (review)	X					
Juel and Minden-Cupp (2000)	X	X			X	X
Lovett et al. (2000)	X	X				
Mathes et al. (2005)	X	X				
NRP (2000) (review)	X		X	X	X	X
Snow et al. (1998) (review)	X			X		
Stahl (2001) (review)	X	X		X		
Taylor et al. (2000)			X	X		
Taylor et al. (2003)	X		X	X	X	X

❞❞ talk about it

＊ Is your phonics instruction systematic and explicit? Do you have a scope and sequence you follow for the phonics elements you introduce and review?

＊ Do you differentiate the amount and type of phonics instruction you provide based on students' reading abilities and needs?

＊ Do you spend as much or more time helping students apply their phonics knowledge to texts they are reading as you spend providing explicit phonics lessons?

Some Effective Instructional Approaches

Engage in sound boxes. Teach letter–sound correspondences to children through writing. In the sound boxes activity, children write one sound in each box to focus on hearing the sounds in words, which helps them develop their phonemic awareness, and to associate the appropriate letter with that sound. As they gain skill with this activity, exaggerate the sounds less and let them do it on their own as needed. It is helpful if they actually say the words as they are writing them in the sound boxes. You may also want to ask them how many sounds they hear in a word, which will tell them how many boxes they will be using.

After writing all the sounds in the words, it is important that children touch the words with their finger as they reread them. This helps them make the transition from hearing the sounds in words and writing the letters for these sounds to reading the words.

The words that are best for sound boxes depend on the children's level of development and what you are stressing in terms of phonics at a particular point in time. For the most part, you should select words with two to four phonemes that have phonetically regular long and sort vowel sound represented by the CV, CVC, CVCC, or CVCE pattern (e.g., hen and time from *Rosie's Walk*). Once children begin to hear the phonemes in words, you may want to add initial consonant blends (e.g., pl, br) or digraphs (e.g., she, ch, th).

 Engage in guided sentence writing. Naturally, this collaborative activity is powerful for building phonics knowledge as well as phonemic awareness. The teacher models and coaches students as they write a sentence together about a story or an event they have shared as a class. It can be done as a whole class, in small groups, or as individual conferring. For example, a kindergarten class might write, "He went to the store," after hearing the story *Just Grandpa and Me* by Mercer Mayer. Students might write the sentence on whiteboards as the teacher wrote on the board. The teacher would coach students by saying such things as, "What do you hear first in *he* and what letter is this? What do you hear next in *he*?"

ADDED BENEFITS TO USING SOUND BOXES AND GUIDED SENTENCE WRITING ACTIVITIES

The sound box and guided sentence writing activities also help children grasp the concept of *letter-by-letter sequential decoding.* When students write, they *apply* sequential decoding as they segment and blend the sounds in the words; teachers coach them as needed helping them identify missing letters, and more generally, helping children hear and write as many sounds in words as possible.

Use a short vowel chart. On this chart, short vowels are represented by five pictures and labels that start with the short vowel sounds. For example, a chart might include the words *apple, elephant, insect, octopus,* and *umbrella.* If a child can't tell what vowel is at the beginning of the word *up,* ask, "Is it the sound you hear at the beginning of *apple*? Is it the sound you hear at the beginning of *elephant*? *Insect*? *Octopus*? *Umbrella*?" By giving children a chart to refer to, the teacher is providing them with a tool for figuring out words on their own. A short vowel chart can be useful in decoding and in writing.

Model letter-by-letter decoding. Beginning readers need the teacher to model how to go about segmenting and blending sounds to decode unfamiliar words (Taylor 2010a; Taylor, Short, Frye, and Shearer 1992). In early first grade, a teacher might follow a reading of *Rosie's Walk* with a demonstration of how to segment and blend the sounds in *hen, past,* and *got.* Teachers can also demonstrate segmenting and blending using the words that occur in morning messages or guided writing.

Engage in the Making Words activity (Cunningham 2009). This is a highly effective way for students to grasp the concept of letter-by-letter decoding. In the Making Words activity students are taught to spell words with letter–sound patterns using sets of letters on small cardboard squares. Children spell and say a word the teacher has given them, and then, per teacher direction, substitute letters within the word with other letters to form new words. For example, after reading *The Chick and the Duckling* by Mirra Ginsburg, the teacher might have students use the letters *c, d, g, k, l, n, i, u* to spell *lid*, then *kid, kick, lick, luck, duck,* and *duckling*. Then the students would sort words that went together in some way. Children often want to sort words that start the same way, which is fine. However, we do want to steer them toward sorting words that share a common phonogram: *lid, kid; lick, kick; luck, duck*. The teacher would then explain to students how looking for a rhyming part in a word might help them decode the word while reading.

ADDED BENEFITS OF MAKING WORDS ACTIVITY

The word sorting within the Making Words activity boosts students' ability to *decode by onset and rime*. I encourage teachers not to overlook this component, and have children sort the words they have made. Take the time to teach children how to sort words they have made that share a common phonogram, which will help them start to recognize common phonograms. It is also important to model and talk about how recognizing a phonogram and adding the first letter is a good strategy to use to figure out an unfamiliar word.

What the Research Says: Coaching Students to Apply Phonics Knowledge During Reading

In addition to learning about phonics, children need to be able to apply their phonics knowledge to actual reading of high-quality literature. Generally speaking, this application comes down to children using their understanding of phonics to recognize words. There are a number of ways to coach students during reading to attend to word recognition (Taylor 2010a, b, c). In one study, the observations of four of the most accomplished teachers in the most effective schools (Taylor et al. 2000) were analyzed for similarities in practice pertaining to coaching in word recognition across the four teachers. Five categories of practice emerged and are summarized here.

1. **The teacher guides a metacognitive dialogue on strategies.** Before reading and with the students, the teacher reviews the strategies for figuring out a word.

   TEACHER: *The point is to be able to read on your own this summer. What if you come to a big long word? Yes, sound it out. What else can you do? Yes, you can twist it a little (e.g., try a different vowel sound in <u>terrible</u>). Also you can ask yourself if it makes sense. And if you try these things, then what do you do? Yes, skip it, or what else? Yes, you can ask someone.*

2. **The teacher guides a metacognitive review of strategies used.** After reading, the teacher prompts students to recall what they just did to figure out particular words.

   TEACHER: *How did you figure out <u>squirt</u>, Tom?*

   TOM: *I sounded it out.*

TEACHER: *You could also look at the picture.*

TOM: *Also make sure it makes sense.*

3. **The teacher positively reinforces students' use of strategies.** The teacher commends a student either during reading or after reading for figuring out a word or at least trying to do so.

> **TEACHER:** *I noticed that Mara got stuck and skipped it and read around it and then came back to it. That's good thinking.*

4. **The teacher provides general prompts to students to figure out words.** The teacher prompts a child to figure out a word without suggesting a specific strategy.

> **TEACHER:** *What could give you a clue on that word?*

5. **The teacher prompts students and suggests a specific strategy.** The teacher prompts a child to figure out a word by suggesting a specific strategy to try (e.g., sound it out, look for a phonogram, think of what would make sense that starts with___, etc.).

> **TEACHER** [HELPING A GROUP READING ALOUD]: *Whoa, back up there. Frame the work with i–n. What is the first sound? What is the second sound? What's the word?*

During Reading: Prompts to Use

Becoming an expert at knowing when to prompt children—and when to wait while they puzzle through a word or a passage—takes time. The more you do it, the more skilled you will be. The overarching goal is to help children to use a *variety* of strategies as they are engaged in reading during small-group instruction or one-on-one reading time. Typical prompts include phrases such as:

- What do you do when you come to a word you don't know?
- Let's sound it out and see if the word looks right and makes sense.
- Does that word that you sounded out look right and make sense? (*tease* for *teach*)?
- What do the letters *ea* say?
- How do you know it can't be *dripped*? (for *dressed*)
- Do you see a chunk you recognize? (in *nothing*)

Decoding Strategies to Teach for Longer Words

Chunk a challenging longer word. Students in second grade and above need to learn a general chunking strategy for decoding multisyllabic words (Taylor 2010b, c; Taylor, Harris, Pearson, and Garcia 1995). Students can first break the word into chunks (approximate syllables) with one vowel or vowel team per chunk. For example, the word *cardinals* can be chunked as either *car-din-als* or *card-in-als* and the word *temperature* as either *tem-per-a-ture* or *temp-er-a-ture*. Emphasize the importance of being flexible as they sound out the chunks, especially with the vowel sounds. If one sound doesn't work, try another. After students have sounded out the chunks, they say the word more quickly. This strategy will get students close to the right word. Like any comprehension strategy, this needs to be taught in tandem with others, such as using the context of the passage to help them infer word meaning and activating their background knowledge.

▶ **Develop knowledge of morphology.** Young readers not only must learn to quickly and accurately associate letters with sounds and to recognize word families or phonograms—groups of letters that share a consistent form and pronunciation (e.g., *-ate, -ed, -oat*)—but also learn to recognize the units that change the meanings of the words to which they are added (e.g., *pre-, un-, dis-, -ful, -able*). Students need to be taught and given ample opportunities to use their knowledge of morphology (roots, prefixes, suffixes) to recognize words.

Resources on Phonics and Word Recognition Instruction

Bear, D. R., M. Invernizzi, S. Templeton, and F. Johnston. 2007. *Words Their Way: Word Study for Phonics, Vocabulary, and Spelling Instruction.* 4th ed. Upper Saddle River, NJ: Pearson/Merrill Prentice Hall.

Beck, I. 2006. *Making Sense of Phonics: The Hows and Whys.* New York: Guilford.

Carnine, D. W., J. Silbert, E. J. Kame'enui, and S.G. Tarver. 2004. *Direct Instruction Reading.* 4th ed. Upper Saddle River, NJ: Pearson.

Cunningham, P. 2009. *Phonics They Use: Words for Reading and Writing.* 5th ed. Boston: Pearson.

Gaskins, I. W., L. C. Ehri, C. Cress, C. O'Hara, and K. Donnelly. 1996. "Procedures for Word Learning: Making Discoveries About Words." *The Reading Teacher* 50: 312–27.

McGill-Franzen, A. 2005. *Kindergarten Literacy.* New York: Scholastic.

Taylor B. M. 2010a. *Catching Readers: Grade 1.* Portsmouth, NH: Heinemann.

——— 2010b. *Catching Readers: Grade 2.* Portsmouth, NH: Heinemann.

Taylor, B., R. Short, B. Frye, and B. Shearer. 1992. "Classroom Teachers Prevent Reading Failure Among Low-Achieving First-Grade Students." *The Reading Teacher* 45: 592–97.

LOOKING INSIDE CLASSROOMS

What does all this good teaching look like in real classrooms? In the vignettes that follow, teachers Seth Brown and Choua Vang lead lessons rich with phonemic awareness, phonics, and word-recognition strategies. Notice their pacing, the way they explicitly state the purpose of the lesson, and the way they differentiate instruction.

DIFFERENTIATING PHONICS INSTRUCTION

Seth Brown, a kindergarten teacher at Edgewood Elementary, begins his reading block with a 20-minute lesson during which he reads aloud the picture book *Owen's Blanket* by Kevin Henkes to his class of twenty-two children.

Next, Seth instructs his students to summarize the beginning, middle, and end of the story with pictures and words. When they're finished they know that they are to read from their book boxes while Seth meets with small groups for differentiated phonics lessons followed by the reading of leveled books.

Seth spends 15 minutes with group 1. These students know the consonant sounds and are learning how to blend beginning sounds, short vowel sounds, and ending sounds into words. Seth teaches students the sound for the letter *a* by introducing the Andy Apple picture card. He engages the students in phonemic awareness by having them blend the sounds *h-a-t*, *s-a-t*, *r-a-t*, and *c-a-n* into words as he writes them on a whiteboard. Students, with help from Seth, each write *h-a-t* and *s-a-t* in sound boxes, and they write *mat* on their own at the bottom of their papers. As the students get up to go to their tables to read independently from their book boxes, Seth exclaims, "You did such a good job! High fives for all!"

Seth then spends 20 minutes with group 2. These students do not yet know all of their consonant sounds. Seth introduces the sound for the letter *h* to the group with the Hattie Horse picture card. "Do like you are checking your breath, /h/," Seth says as he models making the sound. He writes on a whiteboard as he has his students blend /h/ with /at/ to make *hat*; /h/ with /it/ to make *hit*; /h/ with /ot/ to make *hot*. Seth reads the leveled reader with his students and then they read it on their own. Seth coaches individual students as they decode words in their story.

Seth spends the next 15 minutes with group 3, which is made up of students who are already reading. Seth first reads through the leveled reader with his students but lets them lead. The second time through he has them read on their own as he coaches individuals. "Good readers use their strategies to figure out words, so I want you to practice reading on your own and use your decoding strategies like good readers do." A student reads *trick* in the sentence, "They are going to the track." Seth coaches, "Does that make sense? Try switching the vowel sound, try /a/." The student says *track*, and Seth asks, "Does that make more sense? Good job."

TEACHING PHONICS EXPLICITLY WITHIN STORYBOOK READING

Choua Vang teaches kindergarten in an urban setting at Westside Elementary. Since many of her students still don't know the letter names and sounds, she begins a whole-group reading lesson with an efficient 3-minute review. She explains the purpose: "You need to know your letter names and sounds so you can read new words."

Before she reads their new book, *Things I Like* by Anthony Browne, Choua takes a few minutes to introduce two basic sight words they'll encounter in the story, *what* and *I*. She also has students share with a partner things they like, as a way of engaging children with the story's theme and giving them greater buy-in. She keeps the pace quick—this interactive exchange of ideas takes just a few minutes. Choua then spends 10 minutes reading the story to the students, modeling how to sound out and blend words like /d/ /i/ /g/ *dig* and /r/ /u/ /n/ *run* as she reads.

After finishing the story, she works on phonemic awareness by having students tell her the words from the story as she gives the sounds, /l/ /i/ /k/ *like* and /d/ /i/ /g/ *dig*. She has twelve students go to their tables to reread the story with a partner and then write a sentence and draw a picture of something they like. Choua works for 15 minutes at a table with the other six students, who need more help to reread their story and write their sentence. She speaks to a few of her students in Hmong as she is coaching them on their writing.

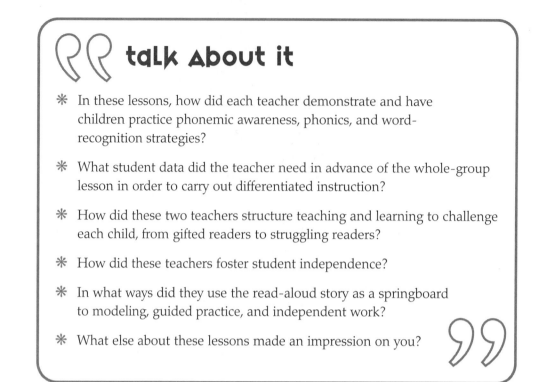

talk About it

✳ In these lessons, how did each teacher demonstrate and have children practice phonemic awareness, phonics, and word-recognition strategies?

✳ What student data did the teacher need in advance of the whole-group lesson in order to carry out differentiated instruction?

✳ How did these two teachers structure teaching and learning to challenge each child, from gifted readers to struggling readers?

✳ How did these teachers foster student independence?

✳ In what ways did they use the read-aloud story as a springboard to modeling, guided practice, and independent work?

✳ What else about these lessons made an impression on you?

Fluency Instruction

Oral reading procedures in which students receive guidance or support in developing fluency have a significant impact on students' reading. Effective fluency procedures include *repeated reading* of the same text while receiving feedback from a teacher or other coach and *assisted reading* of varied texts with support from a teacher or other skilled reader or after listening to a skilled reader. Kuhn and colleagues (2006) found that fluency-oriented reading instruction (FORI), a fluency development approach which focuses on scaffolded, repeated reading of grade-level texts, and wide reading were both effective. Stahl (2004) found that fluency practice was most important in first and second grade, with other aspects of reading gaining importance in third grade and above.

What the Research Says: Fluency Instruction

Oral reading procedures to develop decoding fluency, in which students receive guidance or support, have a significant impact on students' reading. Key findings from fluency researchers are:

▶ Oral reading procedures to develop fluent reading, including repeated reading and assisted reading, are effective.

▶ Wide reading is effective.

▶ Focus on fluency in grades 1 and 2 is most useful.

	Repeated Reading	Assisted Reading	Wide Reading	Focus in Grades 1 and 2
Kuhn et al. (2006)	X		X	
Kuhn and Stahl (2003) (review)	X	X		
NRP (2000) (review)	X	X		
Stahl (2004) (review)				X

talk about it

* What is the difference between repeated reading and assisted reading? Do you use both techniques?

* Do all students get sufficient opportunities to engage in independent, wide reading of texts to develop their fluency?

* Do you differentiate fluency practice, beyond wide reading for all, based on students' needs?

Some Effective Instructional Approaches

▷ **Repeated reading.** In repeated reading (Samuels 1997), children read a passage multiple times to increase accuracy and fluency. In the original techniques, a student reads a 50- to 300-word passage multiple times until he can read it 50 words per minute (wpm) faster than when he started (e.g. 50 words per minute faster).

▷ **Paired repeated reading.** In paired repeated reading, students select a short passage from their reading group book to read three times to a partner. At the end of the reading, they evaluate their own and their partner's reading (Koskinen and Blum 1986).

▷ **Assisted reading.** In assisted reading, a student reads with support from a skilled reader or reads a passage after listening to a skilled reader read the passage on a tape (Shany and Biemiller 1995; Stahl and Kuhn 2002). In the latter case, it is important, however, that students are monitored to ensure that they are actually reading, not just following along, as they listen to a tape. With both assisted and repeated reading, the text should be at the student's instructional level, the level at which the student can read a passage with 92 to 95 percent accuracy (Stahl and Kuhn 2002).

▷ **Cross-age partner reading.** In cross-age partner reading (Taylor 2010c; Taylor, Hanson, Justice-Swanson, and Watts 1997), an older elementary student reads to a younger elementary student and vice versa. The older student learns how to coach the younger students during reading. The older student also reads a picture book multiple times for three days before reading it to the younger student and prepares comprehension and vocabulary questions to ask the younger student.

- **Readers theater.** In readers theater, students practice reading the lines of characters. Then they share their story with an audience (Martinez, Roser, and Strecker 1998–99).

- **Fluency-oriented reading instruction.** In FORI (Stahl and Kuhn 2002), students engage in a number of activities to build fluency including the following: reading many texts at an independent level (at 95% accuracy or higher); reading a text repeatedly with support from a teacher or aide until they can read it fluently; reading with a partner and on their own to increase the amount of time spent reading at school; and increasing the amount of time spent reading at home. In the second grade, students read for a 15-minute, free-reading period at the beginning of the school year and for 30 minutes by the end of the school year. They also kept out-of-school logs in which they were to read for 15 minutes at least four days a week.

- **Reading practice through reading for pleasure.** Students read books from different genres for 20 to 30 minutes a day. After reading, ask students to complete their reading log. Encourage students to read different books from a favorite author, share favorite books in a book sharing club, and write about favorite books on cards for a book file that other students can look through for book suggestions.

Resources on Fluency

Johns, J. L., and R. L. Berglund. 2005. *Fluency Strategies and Assessments*. Dubuque, IA: Kendall-Hunt.

Rasinski, T. V. 2000. "Speed Does Matter in Reading." *The Reading Teacher* 54(2): 146–51.

———. 2003. *The Fluent Reader: Oral Reading Strategies for Building Word Recognition, Fluency, and Comprehension*. New York: Scholastic.

Samuels, S. J., and A. Farstrup, eds. 2006. *What Research Has to Say About Fluency Instruction*. 3rd ed. Newark, DE: International Reading Association.

Stahl, S. A., and M. R. Kuhn. 2002. "Making It Sound Like Language: Developing Fluency." *The Reading Teacher* 55(6): 582–84.

Taylor B. M. 2010a. *Catching Readers: Grade 1*. Portsmouth, NH: Heinemann.

——— 2010b. *Catching Readers: Grade 2*. Portsmouth, NH: Heinemann.

——— 2010c. *Catching Readers: Grade 3*. Portsmouth, NH: Heinemann.

LOOKING INSIDE CLASSROOMS

BUILDING FLUENCY WITH PARTNER WORK

Kathy Little is a special education teacher at Lincoln Elementary. Kathy Little knows that it is important to help her students develop into fluent readers and clearly focuses on building fluency. She demonstrates many elements of effective pedagogy in her lesson.

Kathy's second graders come to her for a 45-minute reading class using the processes in the Early Intervention in Reading (EIR) model (Taylor 2010b) and are greeted with Kathy's morning message: "Good morning, fantastic readers! Today we'll reread to work on our fluency. We'll use the strategy of monitoring to help us better understand what we read. Have a great day!" Before the lesson begins, Kathy reviews her homework chart and checks off students' work.

Kathy says, "Today we are going to reread our story from yesterday, *Animals Should Definitely Not Wear Clothing* by Judi Barrett. What will you do if you get stuck? Turn to the person next to you and tell them what you will do." Students share their ideas: "Skip the word and come back to it." "Sound it out." "Look for chunks." "Ask for help." Kathy replies, "Good ideas. Remember that good readers ask themselves questions if something doesn't make sense."

Kathy continues, "I'm going to partner you up to reread the story, and we'll work on our fluency. What does fluency sound like?" Students answer: "Read fast." "No mistakes." "Smooth reading." Kathy adds, "Remember voice level and good expression, too." One student reads to the group to model fluency. "Good expression, Jamal," Kathy responds. Another student reads as the group listens. Kathy points to the fluency poster. She reminds students not to drop their endings.

Kathy then listens to students read and coaches when they get stuck on words. One student is trying to sound out *sneakers* but says *snackers* instead. Kathy asks, "Does that make sense? Can you be flexible with your vowel sound? What other sound can *ea* make? Sound it out. Say it faster. One more time."

Kathy and her students spend 10 minutes making words. They build *mist, mast, steam, steak, sake, take,* and *mistake,* the "mystery word" from their story.

Next, Kathy and the students discuss *Animals Should Definitely Not Wear Clothing.* They talk about parts of their story that were confusing and the fix-up strategies they could use to clarify the text's meaning. One student says she chunked the word *manage* to sound it out. Kathy also discusses vocabulary that students may find difficult. "Who knows what the word *disastrous* means? Can you give me an example of something that would be disastrous?" Kathy also asks students what their favorite parts of the story are and why.

❝❞ talk about it

* What kinds of fluency instruction does Kathy Little employ in this lesson?

* How else might the children have practiced fluency in ways that were connected to authentic literature? [*Individual reading of just-right books for pleasure, small-group reading of plays (readers theater), reading nonfiction to write a report.*]

Vocabulary Instruction

Vocabulary instruction leads to gains in reading comprehension, which is not a surprising finding given the strong relationship between vocabulary knowledge and the ability to comprehend what is read (Nagy and Scott 2000). Using a variety of instructional approaches is beneficial. Effective techniques include direct instruction in specific words, prereading instruction in words in the text, learning words in rich contexts, learning to use strategies to determine word meanings, and learning words incidentally through wide reading. Words studied should generally be those the learner will find useful in many contexts. Repeated exposure to words in authentic contexts is helpful, as is active engagement in learning words.

What the Research Says: Vocabulary Instruction

Building vocabulary is an extremely important factor in students' reading development. A robust vocabulary often overlaps with strong background knowledge—because learning word meanings is often learning important concepts, whether directly tied to the curriculum or not. There is a strong research base supporting students learning vocabulary in a variety of settings so they get the multiple exposure to words that is necessary for sustaining vocabulary acquisition. Teacher demonstrating, peer collaborating, talking, writing—all this instruction and practice with words in authentic contexts, and with high-quality texts, is critical to reading development. Some key general findings from research are:

▌ Vocabulary instruction leads to gains in reading comprehension.

▌ A variety of approaches are effective.

▌ Use of multiple approaches is effective, including direct instruction, words in context, wide reading.

▌ Words studied should be those readers will find useful in many contexts.

▌ Repeated exposures to new vocabulary in meaningful contexts is effective.

	Variety of Effective Approaches	Use of Multiple Approaches	Focus on Useful Words	Repeated Exposure to Words in Meaningful Contexts
Baumann and Kame'enui (2004)	X			
Beck, McKeown, and Kucan (2002)			X	X
Biemiller and Boote (2006)				X
Blachowicz and Fisher (2000) (review)	X			
Graves (2007)	X			
Nagy and Scott (2000) (review)				
NRP (2000) (review)	X	X	X	X

❝❝ talk About it

* Do you use a variety of approaches to teach vocabulary, or is your vocabulary instruction almost always the same?

* Do you focus on words that students will find useful in numerous contexts in the future?

* Do you teach a fair number of the word meanings you want to cover as students come across these words in their reading?

* Do you give students opportunities to see and use vocabulary in meaningful contexts as opposed to in isolation or in drill activities? ❞❞

Some Effective Instructional Approaches

▶ **Teach word at point of need.** Discuss the meanings of unfamiliar words at point of contact in the text (Beck et al. 2002).

▶ **Connect the known to the new.** Explicitly relate new words to students' prior learning and their lives. Relevance is a huge factor in vocabulary acquisition. For example, if a new word in grade 2 or 3 from a George and Martha story (*George and Martha, Tons of Fun,* by Ed Marshall) is *concentrate*, after discussing the meaning of the word in the context of the story, ask students to tell about a time they had to concentrate.

▶ **Extend word learning to independent reading.** On sticky notes or in a vocabulary journal, have students write down interesting, unknown, or newly learned words that come from the books they are reading. Students can share words and possible meanings either with the teacher in whole- or small-group lessons or by turning vocabulary journal in to teacher, or with a volunteer, educational assistant, or older classroom helper.

▶ **Use graphic organizers.** Have students complete a concept map or web of "juicy" words identified by their teacher from books they are reading. Talking about words in relation to one another helps children connect the dots of word meanings, cements their knowledge of word parts, and helps them "order" new vocabulary in a bigger universe of curriculum concepts and language. For example, a graphic could display words relating to camouflage or it could highlight "juicy" adjectives or new vocabulary that signals personality and character's mood in books.

Resources on Vocabulary

Baumann, J. F., and E. J. Kame'enui, eds. 2004. *Vocabulary Instruction: Research to Practice.* New York: Guilford.

Beck, I. L., and M. G. McKeown. 2002. "Text Talk: Capturing the Benefit of Read-Aloud Experience for Young Children." *Reading Teacher* 55(1): 10–20.

Beck, I., M. McKeown, and L. Kucan. 2002. *Bringing Words to Life: Robust Vocabulary Instruction.* New York: Guilford.

Blachowicz, C., and P. Fisher. 2002. *Teaching Vocabulary in All Classrooms*. 2nd ed. Upper Saddle River, NJ: Pearson/Merrill Prentice Hall.

Graves, M. F. 2007. "Conceptual and Empirical Bases for Providing Struggling Readers with Multifaceted and Long-term Vocabulary Instruction." In *Effective Instruction for Struggling Readers K–6,* ed. B. M. Taylor and J. E. Ysseldyke, 55–83. New York: Teachers College Press.

LOOKING INSIDE CLASSROOMS

Sandy Grayson and Joan Meyer, both teachers at Madina Elementary, have been part of a schoolwide study group focusing on vocabulary instruction. They have worked hard to translate research on effective vocabulary instruction into practice. Their students demonstrate good vocabulary growth on a standardized reading test given at the beginning and end of the year.

EMBEDDING WORD LEARNING WITHIN A READ-ALOUD

Sandy Grayson begins a lesson by reading a picture book about bears with her kindergarteners. "We are going to learn new words from our story. Good readers learn as many words as possible so they can understand the story. After we learn new words, you can use them when you speak and write. Does this book seem similar to one we already know?" A student shouts out, "*Goldilocks and the Three Bears!*" Sandy replies, "Thumbs up if you agree with Sam."

As she reads, Sandy gets her students involved: "Whose house do you think it is? Pair-share with a neighbor." "Show me the face the wolf has. Give me a nod if you think the wolf is nice." "How are you like the bears in the story and how are you different? Pair-share with your partner."

After reading the story, Sandy spends 6 minutes on challenging words in the story, beginning with *launched*. She reads the page from the text on which the word is used. She shows the word on a card. She asks the students if they could launch fireworks. They all say the word *launched*. Sandy continues, "The next word is *gleeful*." The students say the word, and Sandy gives them the meaning and relates the word to the story. "Show me a gleeful look on your faces. Thumbs down if a party at school would make you gleeful. How about if you were going to the dentist? What if you had to stay home from school because of a big snowstorm?" Sandy moves on to the third word. "Our last word is *astonished*." She reads a portion from the text, gives a meaning, and uses the word in a sentence. "Touch your nose if you would be astonished if the grass is green. How about if your dog said hello?" Students say the word *astonished*. Sandy ends with praise: "You did a super job learning our new vocabulary words today." Sandy calls a small group to the reading table and the other students take out their book browsing boxes and begin to read.

INTRODUCING VOCABULARY BEFORE READING, RETURNING TO VOCABULARY AFTER READING

Joan Meyer is an excellent second-grade teacher at Madina Elementary. Focusing on word learning from the get-go, she gives a group of her students sticky notes before they begin to read their basal story independently. "Write down interesting words and questions you would like to discuss next time we meet," she tells them. She then begins to work with a second small group on the book about visiting the Grand Canyon. They find the Grand Canyon on the map. "You are going to read independently. I want you to find out why the Grand Canyon became a place people visited. But first, look for the words *ancient ruins* on page three. What do you know about ancient ruins?" A student answers, "It means it's from a long time ago." Joan responds, "That's true, but I want you to learn more about ancient ruins as you read."

After reading they discuss the concept of ancient ruins and then Joan turns to the word *eroded*. "What does it mean? Look on page five. Share with your partner how the canyon was formed and use *eroded* in your conversation." Joan writes *culture* on the whiteboard. "Look on page six. Let's reread the sentence with *culture* in it. What does the word mean?" A student says that it is about people's lives. Joan continues, "Let's look in the glossary for more information." At the end of the lesson, Joan tells students that at their seats they are to write three interesting facts from their story. "This will help us when we have a discussion on our story the next time we meet."

Comprehension Strategies Instruction

Skilled readers call upon strategic thinking processes to support and sustain their comprehension. Instruction in strategies students use as they read has been found to improve their comprehension. In a meta-analysis, Gajria, Jitendra, Sood, and Sacks (2007) found that explicit instruction in comprehension strategies applied to expository text improved the reading comprehension of learning-disabled students in the elementary, middle, and high school grades.

Explicit lessons in the following strategies are most effective: summarizing, monitoring comprehension, using graphic and semantic organizers, using story structure, answering questions, and asking questions. Perhaps most important is teaching students how to use multiple strategies in naturalistic contexts, such as in whole-class or small-group interactions (National Reading Panel, 2000).

What the Research Says: Comprehension Strategies Instruction

A major goal of comprehension instruction is to help students use a set of procedures when reading independently that will yield deep comprehension of a text. The key here is that the teaching scaffolds students toward independence. Research has shown that explicit lessons in the following strategies are most effective:

▶ summarizing

▶ comprehension monitoring

▶ use of graphic and semantic organizers

▶ use of story structure

▶ higher-level question answering about text

▶ question generation before, during, and after reading

▶ use of multiple strategies in the context of reading texts

	Strategies Instruction Improves Reading Comprehension	Teach Students to Use Multiple Strategies	Strategies Instruction Is Difficult But Possible
Duffy et al. (1987)	X		X
Foorman et al. (2006)	X		
Gersten et al. (2001)	X		
Guthrie, Wigfield, and VonSecker (2000)	X	X	
Guthrie et al. (2004)	X	X	
NRP (2000) (review)	X		
Pressley (2006)	X	X	X
Symons et al. (2001)	X	X	
Taylor et al. (2007)	X		X

talk about it

* Do you focus on teaching comprehension strategies that have a sound research base?

* How are you currently teaching comprehension? Do you have students practice these strategies with fiction more than with expository texts? Or is it the other way around?

* Do you have a scope and sequence of comprehension strategies taught across the grade levels in your school?

* Do you teach students to use multiple strategies as they read and to talk about when they find particular strategies to be useful?

Some Effective Instructional Approaches

▶ **Summarize a story.** You may want to use a story map (graphic organizer), which follows a story grammar to help students include information on the important parts of a story. First, model for students how you would summarize a story. Also, you may wish to show students how one summary is better than another. Next, construct a story summary with students. Then, have students do a summary with a partner and on their own (Taylor 2010c). Baumann and Bergeron (1993) found that first-grade students who used a similar procedure over six 40-minute sessions had better comprehension of new stories than control students.

  ▶ *Why summarize the gist of a story?* Summarizing the gist of a story is an important thing to do when a parent, teacher, or friend asks you to tell them about what you read. None of these people wants to hear you tell them everything about the story. They just want the most important points in about three sentences.

- *Start with the beginning.* Give an important sentence or two from the beginning of the story. What happened at the beginning? This would include something about the main characters (Who?), the setting (Where and When?), and an initiating event or problem (What is the problem?) following a story map or story structure.

- *Move to the middle.* Give an important sentence or two from the middle of the story. What happened in the middle? This would include more events related to the problem (following a story map or story structure).

- *Move to the end.* Give two important sentences from the end of the story. What happened at the end? This would include something about how the problem was solved (What was the solution?). Students should also give an important sentence on a theme of the story (e.g., What is the author saying to you about _____?).

- **Engage in comprehension monitoring.** Have students specifically engage in comprehension monitoring once a week over a four- to six-week period. Ask them to tell you when and why they need to engage in comprehension monitoring. Share strategies you may have used successfully with your students to help them engage in comprehension monitoring. Have students talk about times they noticed they engaged in comprehension monitoring at week 1 and at week 6 (or at the end of your sequence of lessons on comprehension monitoring) to be able to assess students' growth. At the beginning of each study group, keep a journal reflecting on your skill in helping students grow in their ability to engage in comprehension monitoring. Have you modeled enough? Have you been releasing responsibility to the students? Are you giving each of your students a chance to practice instead of participating in a turn-taking experience related to engaging in comprehension monitoring?

- **Summarize informational text.** Students summarize informational text once a week over a six- to ten-week period. Ask them to tell you when and why they will need to be able to summarize informational text. Share strategies you may have used successfully with your students to help them summarize informational text. Have students write or tell a story summary at week 1 and at week 6 (or at the end of your sequence of lessons on summarizing informational text) to be able to assess students' growth. At the beginning of each study group, keep a journal reflecting on your skill in helping students' grow in their ability to summarize informational text. Have you modeled enough? Have you been releasing responsibility to the students? Are you giving each of your students a chance to practice instead of participating in a turn-taking experience related to summarizing informational text?

- **Use reciprocal teaching.** Reciprocal teaching (Palincsar and Brown 1984, 1986) is one of a number of integrated instructional routines that develop students' abilities to use multiple comprehension strategies. It has been found to be effective in increasing the reading comprehension of lower-achieving and higher-achieving readers (Rosenshine and Meister 1994). It has primarily been researched with students in grade 4 and above. Students are taught to employ four strategies: asking and answering an important question about the text; summarizing the important ideas in a sentence or two; clarifying anything that is confusing; making a prediction about upcoming text. At first the teacher assumes responsibility for leading students, in groups of about four, through the strategy cycle as they read short passages of text. As students gain control over the strategies, they assume increasing responsibility for leading one another through the cycle. With time, they lead themselves through the strategy cycle while reading independently. (Taylor 2010c; in press Taylor b.)

▶ **Employ multiple strategies instruction.** A logical step after teaching students how to use reciprocal teaching is to help them become more independent in terms of using different strategies at different points in time. Instruction that helps students to become more strategic, self-regulated learners and active readers has been called *transactional strategies instruction* (TSI) (Bergman 1992; Brown, El-Dinary, Pressley, and Coy-Ogan 1995). Through TSI students learn why, when, and how to engage in multiple strategies: getting the gist, predicting, visualizing meanings, summarizing information, thinking aloud, and problem solving related to comprehension monitoring. As students read, they identify (jot down) places in the text where they choose and use a particular strategy. They talk in a group about what strategy they used at a particular point in time and why. (Taylor, in press b.)

Resources on Comprehension Strategies

Block, C., and M. Pressley, eds. 2002. *Comprehension Strategies: Research-Based Practices.* New York: Guilford.

Duke, N. K., and V. S. Bennett-Armistead. 2003. *Reading and Writing Informational Text in the Primary Grades: Research-Based Practices.* New York: Scholastic.

Englert, C. S., T. V. Mariage, C. M. Okolo, C. A. Courtad, R. K. Shankland, K. D. Moxley, A. Billman, and N. Jones. 2007. "Accelerating Expository Literacy in Middle Grades: The ACCEL Project." In *Effective Instruction for Struggling Readers K–6*, ed. B. M. Taylor and J. E. Ysseldyke, 138–69. New York: Teachers College Press.

Kelley, M. J., and N. Clausen-Grace. 2007. *Comprehension Shouldn't Be Silent.* Newark, DE: International Reading Association.

Kletsien, S. B., and M. J. Dreher. 2005. *Informational Text in K–3 Classrooms: Helping Children Read and Write.* Newark, DE: International Reading Association.

Klingner, J. K., S. Vaughn, M. E. Arguelles, M. T. Hughes, and S. A. Leftwich. 2004. "Collaborative Strategic Reading: Real World Lessons from Classroom Teachers." *Remedial and Special Education* 25: 291–302.

Oczkus, L. D. 2003. *Reciprocal Teaching at Work: Strategies for Improving Reading Comprehension.* Newark, DE: International Reading Association.

Raphael, T. E., K. Highfield, and K. H. Au. 2006. *QAR Now.* New York: Scholastic.

Swan, E. 2003. *Concept-Oriented Reading Instruction: Engaging Classrooms, Lifelong Learners.* New York: Guilford.

Taylor B. M. (in press b). *Catching Readers: Grades 4/5.* Portsmouth, NH: Heinemann.
———. (in press b). *Catching Readers: Grade 3.* Portsmouth, NH: Heinemann.

Comprehension strategies are difficult to teach well, perhaps in part because teachers have to model them by talking aloud about something they do subconsciously as skilled readers. As a result, strategy instruction can become over-ritualized (Hacker and Tenant 2002), that is, the strategies are applied in ways that are unnatural to children's reading or overshadow the appreciation of the text's meaning.

However, with ongoing professional development, teachers can become skilled in providing effective comprehension strategies instruction that enhances students' reading abilities. This was true for Melissa Norris and Benice Daniels, who learned how to provide effective comprehension strategies instruction in their cross-grade-level study groups.

WORKING WITH KINDERGARTENERS ON SUMMARIZING A STORY

Melissa Norris and her kindergarteners are about to read a story about toads who are fighting over bugs in a pond. When a storm blows in, two of the toads get stuck in the mud. A third toad saves them, and the three toads are happy to share the bugs in the pond at the end of the story. Melissa says, "We are going to read a fable, which is a story with a lesson in it. Let's read to see if we can figure out what the lesson is in the story. As we read, we will ask questions in order to understand what we are reading. We will also summarize the story when we get done. We will talk about what happened in the beginning, the middle, and the end of the story. Why is it important to summarize a story?" Students respond: "So we know it better." "It helps us to understand." Melissa asks, "When else can you ask questions or summarize a story?" Students reply: "At home." "At school." As Melissa reads, students ask what a quarrel is. She answers, "They are mad at each other; a quarrel is a fight." When she reads *The water is mine,* a student asks what that means. Melissa replies, "It means it belongs to me. You guys are doing something good. You are asking questions when you don't understand. That is a good strategy."

After the students have read the story, Melissa asks them to tell her what happened at the beginning, what happened in the middle, and what happened in the end, thus reinforcing their sense of story structure. Then she asks, "What is the author's message?" Students answer: "It is good to share." "It is good to all get along." They discuss this, and Melissa tells them, "You did a good job summarizing!" (If your students can't come up with the author's message in a story, you can tell them. The exposure to an author's message is a first step in getting them to be able to talk about it.)

Melissa asks, "How did the toads change from the beginning to the end of the story?" Students say the toads went from mad to happy. Melissa has the students, at their tables, write words and draw pictures that capture the beginning, middle, and end of the story.

HELPING FOURTH GRADERS UNDERSTAND NONFICTION

Benice Daniels, a fourth-grade teacher at Westside Elementary, works with her students on comprehension strategies as they read an article on natural resources in their basal. "I want to review the comprehension strategies we have learned to help you continue to get better at using them," she says, pointing to strategy charts she has displayed in front of the room. "Why do we do comprehension monitoring?" Students respond: "To help us better understand." "To help us take a test." Benice asks, "What things do you do to clarify?" Students answer: "I go back and reread." "I read on, then go back, or ask someone."

Benice asks, "Did anyone *visualize* today as we read the first two pages of our story? Did anyone make a *purposeful prediction*?" Students offer examples. Benice reviews the strategies of *generating questions* to ask others during a discussion and *summarizing main ideas and important supporting details.* She reads the last page of the article, talking aloud as she summarizes it.

She ends the lesson by saying, "As you read pages 216 through 218 today, I want you to use sticky notes to mark where you use strategies. Use a yellow one to mark where you used clarifying, visualizing, or making purposeful predictions; just write down a word or two to help you remember what you did. Use a pink one to write down good questions to ask others and to summarize. I'll work with some of you at the front table, and some of you will work at your seats. Then we'll all get together to share what we did."

❝❝ talk about it

* What are some features of effective comprehension strategies instruction?

* What did you learn from these lessons that you can bring to your own reading instruction?

* What are some challenges you've faced in demonstrating comprehension strategies or guiding students as they use these strategies?

* How can you work with grade-level colleagues to shape your comprehension instruction so that it's embedded with reading, writing, and discussion?

Fostering Comprehension Through High-Level Talk and Writing About Texts

Teaching students how to engage in high-level talk and writing about text is an important aspect of comprehension instruction that has been found to improve students' reading skills. Teachers see more reading growth in their students when they ask challenging questions—those that students must pause and think about before answering, that ask students to interpret a story at a high level and focus on theme, and that get students to make connections between a text and their own experiences or with events in the world about them (Taylor et al. 2003; Taylor and Pearson, 2004). In one study, students who generated higher-level questions had higher standardized comprehension scores, after accounting for prior knowledge, than students who generated lower-level questions (Taboada and Guthrie 2006).

Unfortunately, too, teachers ask low-level questions much more frequently than high-level questions (Taylor and Peterson 2006a, 2006b; Taylor et al. 2003). However, teachers can also make important changes in the frequency with which they engage all students in high-level talk and writing about text (Taylor et al. 2005, 2007). Matthew Thompson and Maggie Voss have increased their focus on higher-level questioning in recent years as part of their school-based reading improvement effort.

What the Research Says: High-Level Talk and Writing About Texts

When students participate in high-level discussions about texts, their reading comprehension is enhanced. High-level writing about texts is also extremely beneficial to developing thinking, motivated, and proficient readers. High-level talk and writing about reading engages students in higher-level thinking about a text's ideas and can include both aesthetic and efferent responses. Talk and writing also fosters a metacognitive stance in readers. Students become more and more aware of what they do—and need to do more of—to comprehend and enjoy texts. It's a challenging, gradual process to help children attain a high level of text interpretation. Effective instruction helps students discuss and write analytically in ways that go beyond a yes or no answer about the text. Their responses need to show they can summarize, synthesize, evaluate, and apply. The following researchers have done considerable work proving the connection between talk, writing, and reading comprehension:

▶ High-level talk and writing about text leads to gains in reading comprehension.

▶ Teaching students how to engage in high-level talk and writing about text is difficult, but with ongoing professional development teachers can learn to be successful.

	Engage in High-Level Thinking About Text to Improve Comprehension	Teaching High-Level Thinking Is Difficult, But Possible
Guthrie et al. (2000)	X	
Guthrie et al. (2004)	X	
Juel and Minden-Cupp (2000)	X	
Knapp (1995)	X	
Pressley et al. (2007)	X	
Saunders and Goldenberg (1999)	X	
Taylor and Pearson (2004)	X	
Taylor et al. (2003)	X	X
Taylor et al. (2005)	X	X
Taylor et al. (2007)	X	
Taylor and Peterson (2006a)	X	X
Taylor and Peterson (2006b)	X	X
Van den Branden (2000)	X	

talk about it

* Do you spend at least as much time on questions that promote high-level thinking about texts as you do on low-level questions that do not require students to stop and think before they answer?

* Do you coach students to elaborate on or clarify their answers to high-level thinking questions?

* Do you encourage students to take an active role (with you not asking all the questions) as they engage in discussions about texts?

Some Effective Instructional Approaches

▶ **Put a premium on high-level thinking during discussions.** Lead a discussion instead of a recitation (e.g., rapid fire Q&A). Teach students how to agree and politely disagree as well as how to add to someone's idea. Also teach them about not talking too much, being a good listener, and making sure that everyone gets a change to talk. Try to stay out of the conversation as much as possible (or at least try not to do as much of the talking as the students), and instead look at yourself as a coach who is helping the students express and/or clarify their ideas. Give the students enough wait-time, and let them know you really are interested in their ideas rather than them simply telling you what you are looking for in the way of answers. (Taylor in press b.)

▶ **Cultivate student-led discussions.** Implement student-led discussion groups over a six- to ten-week period or longer. Teach students how to agree and politely disagree as well as how to add to someone's idea. Also teach them about not dominating discussions, being a good listener, and making sure that everyone gets a chance to talk. Teach students how to take turns being the discussion leader and how to bring "juicy" questions to their book club meetings. (Taylor in press b.)

Examples of Interpretive Questions Based on the Text

1. What do you think is an important event that happened in the story? Why do you think it is important?

2. What did you like or not like about (name a character)? Why? What in the story helped you think this way?

3. Why do you think (character in the story) did _____? If you were the main character, would you have done the same things the main character did? Why or why not? What might you have done differently?

4. How did (character in the story) change? Why do you think this happened?

5. What was one of the author's messages (themes) in the story? What did you learn from reading this story?

6. What caused X to happen? Why do you think this?

7. What were main ideas (important ideas the author wanted you to know) that you learned from this text (nonfiction)?

Examples of Higher-Level Questions Relating to Children's Lives

1. How are you like (character in the story)? How are you different?

2. Which character would you like to be like? Why?

3. Can you compare anything in this story to (name another story or something else you have done in your classroom that could be compared)? Why do you think these are similar (alike) or different?

4. What is your opinion about X? Why do you think this?

5. Nonfiction-type questions could relate to your state (e.g., Could you find these animals, events in your state? Why or why not? Where might they happen if they could be in your state?).

Resources on Comprehension: High-Level Talk and Writing About Text

Anderson, N. A. 2007. *What Should I Read Aloud?* Newark, DE: International Reading Association.

Beck, I. L., and M. G. McKeown. 2002. "Text Talk: Capturing the Benefit of Read-Aloud Experience for Young Children." *Reading Teacher* 55(1): 10–20.

Beck, I. L., M. G. McKeown, R. L. Hamilton, and L. Kucan. 1997. *Questioning the Author*. Newark, DE: International Reading Association.

Cunningham, P. M., and D. R. Smith. 2008. *Beyond Retelling: Toward Higher Level Thinking and Big Ideas*. Newark, DE: International Reading Association.

Day, J. P., D. L. Spiegel, J. McLellan, and V. B. Brown. 2002. *Moving Forward with Literature Circles*. New York: Scholastic.

Galda, L., B. Cullinan, and L. Sipe. 2009. *Literature on the Child*. 7th ed. Elmont, CA: Thomson/Wadsworth.

Goldenberg, C. 1992/1993. "Instructional Conversations: Promoting Comprehension Through Discussion." *The Reading Teacher* 46: 316–26.

Heffernan, L. 2004. *Critical Literacy and Writer's Workshop*. Newark, DE: International Reading Association.

Kelley, M. J., and N. Clausen-Grace. 2007. *Comprehension Shouldn't Be Silent*. Newark, DE: International Reading Association.

McMahon, S. I. 1997. "Book Clubs: Contexts for Students to Learn to Lead Their Own Discussions." In *The Book Club Connection,* ed. S. I. McMahon and T. E. Raphael, 89–108. New York: Teachers College Press.

Olness, R. 2007. *Using Literature to Enhance Content Area Instruction: A Guide for K–5 Teachers*. Newark, DE: International Reading Association.

Raphael, T. E, L. S. Pardo, and K. Highfield. 2002. *Book Club: A Literature-Based Curriculum*. 2nd ed. Lawrence, MA: Small Planet.

Raphael, T. R., S. McMahon. 1994. "Book Club: An Alternative Framework for Reading Instruction." *Reading Teacher* 48(2): 102–16.

Wood, K. D., N. L. Roser, and M. Martinez. 2001. "Collaborative Literacy: Lesson Learned from Literature." *Reading Teacher* 55(2): 102–11.

Taylor, B. M. (in press b.) *Catching Readers: Grades 4/5.* Portsmouth, NH: Heinemann.

LOOKING INSIDE CLASSROOMS

DEEPENING UNDERSTANDING WITH STUDENT-LED DISCUSSIONS

One of Matthew Thompson's strengths is his ability to get his second graders at Lincoln Elementary engaged in student-led discussions. He begins by teaching his high-ability students how to engage in small-group discussions full of high-level questions about chapter books they are reading. (These students then demonstrate and coach the rest of the class. However, as we see later, Matthew spends a great deal of time coaching them before they do so.) They are discussing the chapter book *Justin and the Best Biscuits in the World* by Mildred Pitts Walter, about a boy and his grandfather, who is the boy's best friend. The story is also about black cowboys who helped to settle the West.

First, Matthew goes over the roles students have in their discussions. "What is your job in the group? How do you know if you are doing a good job?" One student answers, "Jump in respectfully." Matthew asks him to elaborate: "What does that sound like?" Another student answers, "If you hear a space you can jump in." Matthew asks the student acting as facilitator what to do if two people talk at once and what other roles he has. The student replies, "I would let one talk and then the other. Also, I need to make sure everyone gets to answer. Oh, that reminds me, Lorinda, you need to sit by me as your support person since it is hard for you to talk."

The facilitator selects one of the questions the group has come up with to discuss about the chapter they are reading. Matthew watches from the sidelines. As the students discuss the main character's feelings about men's work and women's work, they politely disagree with one another and look in their books for evidence to support their opinions: "I think Justin is embarrassed to tell his grandpa he doesn't know how to clean fish, which is a man's work." "I disagree. I think he is afraid his grandfather will laugh at him." "I disagree with both of you. I think he doesn't want to disappoint his favorite person." The facilitator, with prompting from Matthew, asks Lorinda, a shy girl, if she has anything to add. She agrees with the ideas of the last student and repeats them. At the end of the discussion, Matthew gets his students to focus on a theme of the chapter, that men can do "women's work" and women can do "men's work." He also has them evaluate how they did in the discussion. Abe says, "I think I only did so-so. I did not give many answers." Matthew asks the facilitator to respond. The facilitator says to Abe, "I think you did a good job, and you looked back in the book." Matthew adds that when someone disagreed with Abe, Abe said he'd have to go back to the book and think about his answer which was a good, but hard, thing to do. The facilitator gives Lorinda a compliment about participating, and she says thank you with a smile on her face.

Matthew next checks in with students who are working in other groups of four. One group is working on *Will and Orv* by Walter A. Schulz. Matthew has given them the choice of reading on their own or with a partner. He listens to each of the four read; coaches each one in word-recognition strategies; jots down notes on students' abilities related to word recognition, fluency, vocabulary, and comprehension; and individually asks students questions about their story. The group members can answer the study questions in their book on their own or with a partner, but everyone is responsible for writing down answers that they then share. Matthew teaches his students how to give one another compliments when they hear good ideas.

USING GRAPHIC ORGANIZERS TO SUPPORT STUDENTS' RESEARCH PROJECTS

Maggie Voss, a fourth-grade teacher at Madina Elementary, has asked her students to research desert animals. "Yesterday, you and your partner chose a topic and came up with three or four questions you wanted to answer. Your purpose is to learn about your topic. Look for answers to your questions, but also go beyond that and find other information. Don't limit yourselves; look for other fascinating facts." Maggie shows the students a graphic organizer on which they can write down topics and main ideas in the circles and use the lines coming from each circle to add important and interesting details related to these topics. "We'll share our reports later in the week. I know you'll enjoy this! Plus, once we know how to do research projects, we can do them as independent or partner activities for the rest of the year!"

talk about it

* What elements of effective instruction in high-level talk and writing about text were present in Matthew Thompson's or Maggie Voss's lesson?

* What are some stumbling blocks you've faced when trying to raise the level of thinking during discussions? What can you take from these lesson vignettes and apply to your classroom?

Balanced Reading Instruction

Direct Teaching and Opportunities for Student Application

Beginning reading instruction is most effective when children are provided with systematic skills instruction in phonemic awareness and phonics along with authentic experiences with literature emphasizing the construction of meaning. A balanced approach to reading instruction involves direct teaching of reading skills and strategies as well as providing students with opportunities to apply these skills and strategies to texts through reading, writing, and discussing.

What the Research Says: Balanced, Differentiated Content Instruction

A balanced approach to reading instruction involves direct teaching of word-recognition and comprehension skills and strategies as well as providing students with opportunities to apply skills and strategies to engaging texts through reading, writing, and discussing. Also, effective teachers make good choices in the use of instructional materials based on students' abilities, as determined by assessment data, and teaching purposes, which will vary at times for different students (Pressley et al. 2007). For example, some second graders may need explicit phonics lessons in the sounds for letter combinations, but others who are already reading chapter books fluently may not.

▶ Effective teachers provide a balance in teaching skills and strategies and in helping students apply reading skills and strategies to reading, speaking, and writing about texts in authentic contexts.

▶ Effective teachers regularly make conscious content choices to differentiate instruction to meet students' needs.

	Balance Teaching Skills and Strategies with Students Using Skills and Strategies in Authentic Literacy Activities	Provide Differentiated Instruction to Meet Individual Needs
Connor, Morrison, and Katch (2004)		X
Juel and Minden-Cupp (2000)		X
National Reading Panel (2000) (review)	X	X
Pressley (2006)	X	
Pressley et al. (2001)		X
Pressley et al. (2007)		X

talk About it

✳ Do you make conscious decisions about providing explicit skill or strategy instruction and giving students opportunities to apply strategies to texts they are reading?

✳ Do you select materials or lessons in teacher manuals based on students' varying needs?

Resources About Balanced, Differentiated Instruction

Lapp, D., D. Fisher, and T. D. Wolsey. 2009. *Literacy Growth for Every Child: Differentiated Small-Group Instruction, K–6.* New York: Guilford.

Pressley, M. 2006. *Reading Instruction That Works: The Case for Balanced Teaching.* 3rd ed. New York: Guilford.

Southall, M. 2009. *Differentiated Small-Group Reading Lessons.* New York: Scholastic.

Taberski, S. 2000. *On Solid Ground: Strategies for Teaching Reading K–3.* Portsmouth, NH: Heinemann.

Walpole, S., and M. C. McKenna. 2009. *How to Plan Differentiated Reading Instruction: Resources for Grades K–3.* New York: Guilford.

Choosing Instructional Content to Meet Individual Students' Needs

Students in any given classroom are at different levels of competence related to phonemic awareness, phonics knowledge, decoding abilities, fluency, vocabulary, and comprehension. Effective teachers choose their instructional materials based on students' abilities, as determined by assessment data, and their teaching purposes, which will vary at times for different students (Pressley et al. 2001; Pressley et al. 2007). Juel and Minden-Cupp (2000) found that low-ability first-grade readers benefited from substantial exposure to explicit phonics lessons and high-ability students benefited from vocabulary, text discussions, and reading a variety of texts. As low-ability readers began to be able to read independently, they benefited from the same activities that benefited the better readers. Connor, Morrison, and Katch (2004) found that students who had difficulty with decoding benefited from teacher-directed explicit decoding instruction but that high-ability students benefited from child-managed activities such as reading aloud and sustained, silent reading.

LOOKING INSIDE CLASSROOMS

Seth Brown, one of the teachers mentioned earlier in this chapter, provides an excellent example of a teacher making good content choices to meet the varying needs of his students. Instead of teaching phonics to his kindergarteners in a whole group, he differentiates his phonics instruction by teaching students in small groups based on their needs. In his lesson, he focuses on the sound for the letter *h* with his lowest students and the sound for the letter *a* with his average students, and he coaches his high-ability students in word-recognition strategies as they read leveled readers.

Like Seth, most kindergarten and first-grade teachers are able to differentiate their phonics instruction by teaching phonics using leveled readers within guided reading groups. Comprehensive commercial reading programs, like a series of basal readers, include many suggestions for teaching phonemic awareness, phonics, fluency, vocabulary, and comprehension—more, in fact, than a teacher could ever use. Thus, when teachers use a basal reader for their large- and/or small-group instruction, they need to make deliberate decisions, tied to instructional goals and students' varying reading abilities, about which activities to use. The high-ability readers in Matthew Thompson's second-grade classroom who were reading and discussing a chapter book, for example, would not need to complete isolated phonics activities covered in their grade 2 basal reader program.

Kathy Little, in the earlier section on fluency, provides another good example of balanced instruction in her 45-minute lesson with special education students. She stresses fluency, but she also coaches students in word-recognition strategies as they reread their story. She reinforces phonics learning by having her students make words. She also engages students in a discussion of their story, focusing on vocabulary and the strategy of comprehension monitoring.

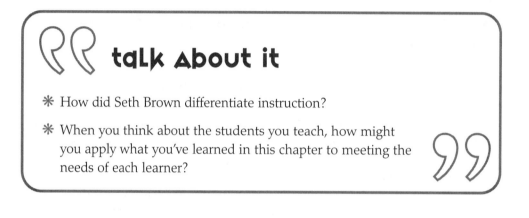

talk about it

* How did Seth Brown differentiate instruction?

* When you think about the students you teach, how might you apply what you've learned in this chapter to meeting the needs of each learner?

Swift-Paced, Balanced Instruction for ELLs

Angelina Ipson is an English language learner (ELL) teacher at Westside Elementary. The following are the rapid-paced, balanced reading lessons she uses for her six second-grade ELLs.

1. *Conducts word sorts.* The students spend the first 5 minutes doing a word sort with words from the *-ill* and *-ell* word families. Students sort the words on cards by word family and then read all of them at the end.

2. *Previews a leveled reader for vocabulary and content.* For the next 3 minutes, Angelina introduces a new leveled reader. Her students quickly look at the pictures in the book about trees. Angelina turns the pages and talks briefly about some of the vocabulary words. She asks, "What do you think we are going to learn about in this book?" Two students share ideas. Angelina reads the first page of the book to the group and asks, "What things are made of wood?" Students share ideas.

3. *Invites students to read on their own.* Then Angelina has students read on their own for 7 minutes as she coaches individual students as they read.

4. *Coaches one-on-one.* The group has a 5-minute discussion about the book and the vocabulary that may be unfamiliar is highlighted. Angelina asks questions such as: "What is lumber? What could you use lumber to make?" One student answers, "Shelves." Another says, "A table." Angelina asks, "What did you learn?" Students offer ideas.

5. *Asks students to write about their reading.* Angelina explains the last 10 minutes of the lesson. "Now I want you to write about what this world would be like without trees." Students share ideas with a partner for 5 minutes and then write for 5 minutes as Angelina coaches individuals.

Additional Aspects of Balanced Instruction

To provide balanced instruction, teachers must also consider the amount of time students spend in whole- and small-group instruction as well as in cooperative learning and independent activities. Grouping practices and independent learning activities will be discussed in Chapter 4.

Deepen Your Literacy Content Knowledge

This chapter provided an overview of the content of reading instruction—the knowledge, skills, processes, and strategies you need to teach students so they become successful readers. Use this information as a jumping-off point for further professional study. See Appendix 7–9 on the DVD for a list of recommended professional books on effective reading instruction. To recap, here are some basics: Teachers in the primary grades need to teach students the names and sounds of letters (*knowledge*) and how to decode words while reading (*strategies*). Teachers need to help students in the primary grades read fluently (*skill*). Teachers at all grades need to develop students' vocabulary (*knowledge*) as well as help them use vocabulary *strategies*, such as using context clues or looking up the meaning of words in the dictionary. Teachers at all grades need to engage students in high-level thinking (e.g., inferencing, interpreting, making connections, evaluating; these are all *reading processes*) about what they have read through the questions they ask students to respond to verbally or in writing. Teachers, especially in the intermediate grades, need to teach students to use *comprehension strategies* (e.g., summarizing, monitoring comprehension, self-questioning) in a conscious way to help them better understand and remember what they are reading.

Of course, there is a lot more to reading instruction than covering content (knowledge, strategies, etc.) in reading lessons. Teachers have to make many decisions about how to teach reading lessons, the *pedagogy* of teaching reading. Is a skill or strategy best taught in a whole-group setting or to a small, guided reading group? How much time needs to be spent on various parts of a lesson? How are the purposes of lessons made clear to students? How are lessons differentiated as needed to best meet students' needs? How do students get actively involved in lessons? How do students get the opportunity to practice and become independent in the skills, processes, and strategies they have been taught? How do teachers keep all of their students motivated and challenged as readers and as learners? How do teachers gather pupil performance data to inform their instruction and to assess students' reading abilities? How do teachers collaborate when more than one teacher provides reading instruction to a group of students? How do teachers provide interventions to struggling readers?

Teaching reading is complex. Here, we've covered the "what" of effective instruction. In the next chapter, we look at the "how"—the pedagogy of teaching reading.

3

Teaching Practices That Work for Readers

Teaching effectively so that all children are reading to their fullest potential is challenging. Sometimes we forget what a tall order it is. During a 90- to 120-minute reading block, teachers need to orchestrate many different components of their lessons and students' learning activities. Often, other classroom or resource teachers collaborate instructionally during parts of this block (Valli, Croninger, and Walters 2007), so the classroom teacher needs to coordinate instruction with them as well.

Every day, teachers need to move seamlessly between whole-group and small-group instruction; consider and make clear to students the purposes and timing of their lessons; provide students with challenging, motivating activities as they are working with the teacher, on their own, or with other students (Pressley et al. 2003); and provide culturally responsive instruction (Au 2006). Teachers also need to foster students' active involvement in their learning activities (Guthrie, Wigfield, and VonSecker 2000) and maintain a balance between leading students' learning, questioning, and other activities during large- and small-group lessons and providing support through judicious coaching and effective feedback as students actively participate in literacy learning activities (Connor, Morrison, and Katch 2004; Pressley et al. 2003; Taylor et al. 2003). All of this takes plenty of planning, and the recognition that becoming an effective teacher takes time. In this chapter, I provide an overview of practices that underpin good teaching and encourage you to read them with an eye to reflecting on how these practices match up to your own teaching.

Seeing is believing! In Video 1 on the DVD, we see Matthew Thompson, whom we met in Chapters 1 and 2, and again in this chapter, teaching his second graders, who are in a diverse, high-poverty school, to engage in discussions about literature. As you read this chapter, think about the things Matthew is doing to provide motivating, effective instruction to his students.

see it iN ActioN

Effective Reading Instruction

Matthew Thompson is teaching his second-grade students how to engage in book club discussions. Many important elements of effective instruction are present in his lesson. He provides a great deal of careful scaffolding and deliberately releases responsibility to his students as they are able to do more on their own. His group of above-average readers, whom he calls the green group, are reading *Charlotte's Web* by E. B. White. They are also serving as coaches for the rest of the students in the class who are just learning about book clubs. We see Matthew introduce *The Legend of the Indian Paintbrush* by Tomie dePaola, to his average and below-average readers, the blue group. Students are to read the story twice on their own, one time to work on decoding and a second time to work on fluency and comprehension. Michael moves around and coaches students in word recognition and comprehension individually as they read their new story. As we see, he individualizes this one-on-one support, focusing on decoding and comprehension with one student and on comprehension only with a stronger reader.

After 20 minutes, Matthew checks in on the green group that is reading *Charlotte's Web* and writing questions for their book club discussion the following day. On the next day, we see the green group having an authentic discussion about the latest chapters they have read in *Charlotte's Web*. Two leaders from the blue group are watching and learning about how to lead a book club discussion on their book, *The Legend of the Indian Paintbrush*, and with Matthew's support they are also giving feedback to the green group on their participation in their discussion. On the third day, the students reading *The Legend of the Indian Paintbrush* have a book club discussion with support from Matthew. Observers from the green group give feedback on the group's discussion.

Whole-Class and Small-Group Instruction: The Right Balance Is Key

Grouping practices are a key piece to look at as a part of your professional development work, because there is a strong correlation between classrooms that have sufficient small-group instruction and students' reading progress. Teachers who maintain a good balance of whole- and small-group instruction (Chorzempa and Graham 2006) can deliver expert reading instruction. I can't overemphasize that the *balance* is key. Research that Deb Peterson and I conducted showed that teachers who provide mostly whole-group or mostly small-group instruction see less reading growth in their students during the year than teachers who use a combination of whole- and small-group instruction (Taylor and Peterson 2006a, 2006b, and 2006c). Too much whole-group instruction can bore students, but too much small-group instruction leaves students on their own for too long.

While there are no magic numbers for the amount of whole- and small-group instruction that students need, in a study of effective schools and teachers in grades 1 through 3 (Taylor et al. 2000), I found that the students of teachers in the most effective schools spent 25 minutes a day in whole-group instruction and 60 minutes a day in small-group learning activities, including guided reading groups. The students of teachers in the least effective schools spent 30 minutes a day in whole-group instruction and 38 minutes a day in small-group instruction. When we looked at teachers irrespective of the school they were in we also found that the students in classrooms of the most accomplished teachers spent more time in small- than whole-group instruction, whereas students in classrooms of the least accomplished teachers spent more time in whole- than small-group instruction. (See Tables 3–1 and 3–2.)

Time Spent by Students in Reading Instruction by School Effectiveness Level

	Minutes spent in whole group	Minutes spent in small group	Minutes of independent reading	Minutes writing in response to reading	Minutes in other independent activities	Total minutes in Reading
Most effective schools	25	60	28	14	7	134
Moderately effective schools	37	26	27	15	7	112
Least effective schools	30	38	19	9	17	113

Table 3–1. Time Spent by Students in Reading Instruction by School Effectiveness Level

Time Spent by Students in Whole- and Small-Group Instruction by Level of Teacher Accomplishment

	Minutes spent in whole group	Minutes spent in small group
Most accomplished teachers	25	48
Moderately accomplished teachers	29	39
Least accomplished teachers	48	25

Table 3–2. Time Spent by Students in Whole- and Small-Group

Similarly, Bogner, Raphael, and Pressley (2002) found that motivational first-grade teachers provided a good balance between whole-class and small-group instruction, whereas unmotivational first-grade teachers provided mostly whole-group instruction. Furthermore, Chorzempa and Graham (2006) found that low-ability readers received unchallenging instruction in their small groups compared with their peers, such as being read to by the teacher and doing worksheets. Below-average readers in grades 1 through 3 also spent less time reading silently, answering high-level comprehension questions, reading expository texts, and selecting their own texts compared with peers in higher-ability groups.

Teachers need to consider when whole-group or small-group instruction will best meet instructional objectives. For example, it may be most efficient to introduce and model a comprehension strategy such as summarizing a story in a whole-group lesson, but it may be more effective to have students practice summarizing a story in small guided reading groups, using texts at students' instructional reading level, as the teacher provides more or less support based on students' needs.

What the Research Says: Grouping Practices

▶ Effective teachers provide a balance of whole- and small-group reading instruction.

▶ Teachers provide small-group or one-on-one interventions to accelerate struggling readers' reading development.

	Balance whole- and small-group instruction	Provide small-group or one-on-one interventions
Bogner, Raphael, and Pressley (2002)	X	
Camilli, Vargas, and Yurecko (2003)		X
Foorman and Torgesen (2001)		X
Graves, Gersten, and Hayes (2004)		X
Gunn et al. (2005)		X
Hiebert and Taylor (1998) (review)		X
Mathes et al. (2005)		X
Taylor and Peterson (2006a)	X	
Taylor and Peterson (2006b)	X	
Taylor and Peterson (2006c)	X	
Vaughn et al. (2006)		X
Wasik and Slavin (1993) (review)		X

Some Effective Instructional Approaches

▶ Start with a whole-group lesson, using a text from core material, such as a basal reader. Provide explicit instruction (tell, model, review) on a comprehension concept (e.g., understanding the difference between a fact and an opinion, understanding what a main idea is), skill or process (making inferences while reading, identifying main ideas, understanding the theme of a story), or strategy (consciously practicing comprehension monitoring or summarizing after reading) related to the text. Coach students as they practice comprehension concept, skill/process, or strategy while reading part of the text. Discuss vocabulary at point of contact in the story, and engage in high-level talk about the text during or after reading. (Taylor 2010a, b, c; in press b.)

While finishing the story have students (independently, with a partner, or in a small group) actively engage in and continue to practice comprehension concept, skill/process, or strategy as well as engage in high-level talk and/or writing about text.

Following a whole-group lesson in guided reading, small groups continue to work on the same comprehension concept, skill/process, or strategy with leveled texts at students' instructional reading level.

▶ Teach phonics, for those who need it, in small, guided reading groups instead of in a whole-group lesson. This way, you can focus on what students need to learn about symbol–sound correspondences and decoding strategies, based on their reading level. You can coach them in using word-recognition strategies as they read level texts. Also, students who no longer need explicit phonics lessons can spend their time on learning activities that are more useful to them.

▶ You, or a resource teacher, should provide a second shot of high-quality intervention instruction each day that is intensive, explicit, comprehensive, and supportive to students who are struggling with reading. Students who are behind their peers need a motivating, challenging guided reading small-group lesson and a motivating, challenging intervention lesson each day to accelerate their literacy learning and reading abilities.

Resources on Grouping Practices and Support for Struggling Readers

Fuchs, D., L. Fuchs, and S. Vaughn, eds. 2008. *Response to Intervention: A Framework for Reading Educators*. Newark, DE: International Reading Association.

Gaskins, I. W. 2004. *Success with Struggling Readers: The Benchmark School Approach*. New York: Guilford.

Lapp, D., D. Fisher, and T. D. Wolsey. 2009. *Literacy Growth for Every Child: Differentiated Small-Group Instruction, K–6*. New York: Guilford.

Manning, M., G. Morrison, and D. Camp. 2009. *Creating the Best Literacy Block Ever*. New York: Scholastic.

McCormick, R. L., and J. R. Paratore, eds. 2005. *After Early Intervention, Then What?: Teaching Struggling Readers in Grades 3 and Beyond*. Upper Saddle River, NJ: Pearson.

McCormick, S. 2007. *Instructing Students Who Have Literacy Problems*. 5th ed. Upper Saddle River, NJ: Pearson.

Morrow, L. M. 2003. *Organizing and Managing the Language Arts Block: A Professional Development Guide*. New York: Guilford.

Pressley, M. 2006. *Reading Instruction That Works: The Case for Balanced Teaching*. 3rd ed. New York: Guilford.

Southall, M. 2009. *Differentiated Small-Group Reading Lessons*. New York: Scholastic.

Taberski, S. 2000. *On Solid Ground: Strategies for Teaching Reading K–3*. Portsmouth, NH: Heinemann.

Taylor, B. (2010a). *Catching Readers: Grade 1.* Portsmouth, NH: Heinemann.

———. (2010b). *Catching Readers: Grade 2.* Portsmouth, NH: Heinemann.

———. (2010c). *Catching Readers: Grade 3.* Portsmouth, NH: Heinemann.

———. (in press a). *Catching Readers: Grade K.* Portsmouth, NH: Heinemann.

———. (in press b). *Catching Readers: Grades 4/5.* Portsmouth, NH: Heinemann.

Tyner, B. 2009. *Small-Group Reading Instruction: A Differentiated Teaching Model for Beginning and Struggling Readers.* Newark, DE: International Reading Association.

Tyner, B., and S. E. Green. 2005. *Small-Group Reading Instruction: A Differentiated Teaching Model for Intermediate Grade Reader, Grades 3–8.* Newark, DE: International Reading Association.

Vaughn, S., J. Wanzek, and J. M. Fletcher. 2007. "Multiple Tiers of Intervention: A Framework for Prevention and Identification of Students with Reading/Learning Disabilities." In *Effective Instruction for Struggling Readers K–6,* ed. B. M. Taylor and J. E. Ysseldyke, 173–95. New York: Teachers College Press.

Walpole, S., and M. C. McKenna. 2009. *How to Plan Differentiated Reading Instruction: Resources for Grades K–3.* New York: Guilford.

LOOKING INSIDE CLASSROOMS

Many of the teachers introduced in earlier chapters begin their reading blocks with a whole-group lesson in which they provide explicit instruction in a reading skill or strategy. They then provide follow-up instruction in this skill or strategy in small guided reading groups.

However, differentiating skill or strategy instruction in guided reading groups can be challenging. In grade-level meetings or study groups, teachers should discuss effective ways to do this.

Joan Meyer, a second-grade teacher at Madina Elementary, begins a lesson in January with a whole-group lesson on the crucial process of making inferences while reading. She asks questions as she reads a basal story about a goldfish. "Does the text actually say that Goldie is a fish?" Students shake their heads no. "What clues did we use to figure this out?" Students mention the words *tank* and *wiggling* from the story. Joan says, "We were making an inference. Some of the information came from our prior knowledge, from ideas we already had in our heads. Making inferences is important because they help us better understand what we are reading." At the end of the brief minilesson, Joan tells students they will talk more about making inferences during their guided reading lessons. In these small groups she provides more or less support based on students' needs.

Sally Hecht, a third-grade teacher at Edgewood Elementary, provides an example of embedding small-group instruction within a whole-group lesson. She begins her reciprocal teaching lesson with the whole class, using the first few sections of the students' science textbook to model the strategies of predicting, clarifying, questioning, and summarizing. Then she has students, in groups of four, use the strategies collaboratively while reading other sections of their science book. As the groups work, Sally moves from one to another, providing feedback and coaching based on different groups' needs.

talk about it

* What did you pick up about grouping practices in Joan Meyer's and Sally Hecht's lesson?

* What are your own current grouping practices? Are there things you'd like to change so that the balance and flow between whole group, small group, and individual learning is more explicit?

* Do you clearly tell students the purpose of each lesson? Do you explicitly make connections between some of the small-group and individual work and the whole-class lesson, so students can benefit from the clear trajectory of what they're learning and practicing?

* What daily oral and written activities might you use to reinforce students' learning in the various grouping structures of the day? (For example, partner work, pair-share, reflection logs, and so on.)

Small-Group Intervention Lessons for Struggling Readers

Virtually every classroom has at least a few children who need extra support in order to catch up to grade-level expectations. When possible, it is beneficial if this *additional* intervention instruction is delivered by the classroom teacher or a resource teacher who comes into the classroom. This way, struggling readers can participate in the regular literacy instruction and aren't stigmatized by leaving the classroom for support. The small-group intervention lessons need to stay small—seven students, maximum. Some children can also work one-on-one with the teacher, or resource teachers, as time allows. Small-group interventions and one-on-one tutoring increase the reading achievement of struggling beginning readers, ELLs, and special education students. Foorman and Torgesen (2001) found that struggling readers need additional small-group or one-on-one instruction that is more intensive, explicit, comprehensive, and supportive than the small-group instruction typically provided in guided reading groups in general.

Many of the schools with whom I've worked said that starting with teacher professional development for reaching struggling readers with intervention lessons was a great way to take on schoolwide reform "one step at a time." (See Chapter 6 for more about the Early Intervention in Reading (EIR) framework, as well as *Catching Readers: Day-By-Day Small-Group Reading Interventions* series, K–5 [Taylor 2010a, 2010b, 2010c, in press a, in press b], which explains the EIR framework and coordinates with the reform model in this book.)

Nora Johnson, a first-grade teacher at Lincoln Elementary, begins her explicit, intensive 20-minute Early Intervention in Reading (EIR) lesson with a group of struggling readers by stating its purpose: "One purpose today is to work on our fluency. Another is to review strategies for when we come to words we don't know, and a third purpose is to practice responding to higher-level questions so we better understand the story that we are reading. Rereading helps us build our fluency. What is reading with good fluency like?" Students answer: "Reading with good expression." "Reading like you are talking." Nora replies, "Yes, that's right. Let me model for you." Nora reads the first part of *Herman the Helper* fluently and then the students try. "That is very good. Be sure to keep it up!"

Nora continues: "Now we are going to help each other read this story, *Herman the Helper*, which we read yesterday. When you read with a partner you will help by giving them a strategy to try when they get stuck. Good readers use strategies, so what are some strategies we can use?" Students reply: "Sound it out." "Give the first sound." "Look at the picture." "Look for a chunk."

As students read with partners, Nora takes a running record on one student for the first one hundred words of *Herman the Helper* and she coaches the student on the next one hundred words. The student reads *helped* as *help-ed*. Nora asks, "Does that sound right?" The student corrects himself. Next Nora helps the student with *hurried*. "That is a hard one. Give me the first three sounds and I'll help you with the rest." Finally Nora asks, "Why do you think Herman liked to help?" The student replies, "He has more arms to help."

Nora then does a quick activity to reinforce the short vowel sounds these students worked on the day before. Students have the letter cards for *a, e, d, m, s,* and *h*. With Nora's guidance they make the following words: *me, he, she, shed* ("I put the rake in the shed"), *had* ("Tell me the sounds you hear in *had*"), *sad, mad, mash,* and *mashed*. "Where did we come across *mashed* in our story?" Students answer. Then they reread the words they have made.

Before the students return to their seats, Nora focuses on comprehension. She asks them to talk briefly about how they thought Herman felt when he helped others and how they feel themselves when they are helpful.

Instructional Purpose and Pacing to Meet Individual Needs

Effective teachers are well prepared with well-planned lessons (Wharton-McDonald, Pressley, and Hampston 1998). They continually reflect on the purpose of their lessons in relation to their students (Guthrie et al. 2004; Pressley et al. 2001) and on the pacing of different aspects of a lesson, keeping this pacing as efficient as possible (Pressley et al. 2001). Michael Pressley and his coauthors found that effective teachers carefully match learning tasks to students' ability levels, accelerating the demands of tasks as students' abilities improve. Their lessons are fast-paced, and students are engaged in many varied learning activities involving authentic reading and writing.

However, purpose and pacing tied to students' varying needs are areas that many teachers tell me they find challenging. I tell teachers that as they are planning, they need to continually ask themselves, "Why does this group need this learning activity; how will it move them forward? How long do I need to spend on this activity with this group of students, given that I want every minute to be worthwhile?" For example, many beginning first-grade readers will definitely benefit from reading decodable texts multiple times to build their fluency, but other students who come to first grade already reading books on an end-of-first-grade level will probably not benefit from multiple readings of decodable texts. This will not move the latter group forward. Some children in kindergarten will benefit from a 5-minute review of letter names and sounds, but a 10-minute review may be longer than is beneficial, especially considering all the important things, like vocabulary, oral language, and comprehension development related to texts, that can and should be covered in literacy lessons in kindergarten. Children who already know their letter names and sounds will not benefit from a review of this at all; the activity will not move them forward.

What the Research Says: Purpose and Pacing

▶ Effective teachers are well prepared with well-planned lessons.

▶ Effective teachers are clear about the purposes of their instruction and reflect on them as related to the students they are teaching.

▶ Effective teachers reflect on the pacing of their lessons and are efficient in their teaching.

	Well-planned lessons	Clear purpose	Good pacing
Guthrie et al. (2004)		X	
Pressley et al. (2001)	X	X	X
Wharton-McDonald et al. (1998)	X		

Some Effective Instructional Approaches

▶ Planning ahead always pays off. If you are using a teaching manual you want to read the selection before you teach so you have time to decide on what learning activities you will engage in with your students. You may decide to come up with some of your own learning activities, questions, and vocabulary, instead of those suggested in the manual, if these will be more motivating to your students, better meet their needs, and help you achieve your teaching objectives and district learning standards. If you are not using a teaching manual, you will also need to decide on learning activities, questions, and vocabulary ahead of time tied to the texts you are using to have the most successful lessons possible.

▶ State lesson purposes at the start of every whole-group lesson, small-group lesson, and independent learning activity so that you and the students are clear about what you are teaching and what they are learning and why this is important.

▶ Be as efficient as possible, and spend no more time on a learning activity than is needed. Think of, or ask colleagues about, ways to be more efficient in your teaching.

For example, instead of taking 5 minutes to have one kindergarten student at a time come up to your chart to circle a place they find the letter p (or the letter a in words with the short a sound), have students write or copy one or two words containing the letter p (or words with the short a sound) on their own whiteboards and circle or touch the letter p (or a) in these words. This may take 5 minutes as well, but all students will have been actively engaged in the activity, so the lesson has been more effective as well as efficient.

Or, instead of having one student at a time answer the same question, have students turn to a partner to answer the question. You can listen to a few pairs to see if they are coming up with good answers. This will take less time, and again, all students will get a chance to be actively involved in answering the question.

LOOKING INSIDE CLASSROOMS

Benice Daniels, in her comprehension strategies lesson in Chapter 2, covers the content on natural resources from the basal reader with all of her fourth graders, and she reviews the strategies they have learned to enhance their comprehension. However, she has different purposes for follow-up activities, based on students' abilities. Some students are ready for independent practice using strategies at their seats, but other students, whom she knows will need more support to be successful, work with her in the front of the room, using strategies as they read about natural resources.

Nora Johnson, in the lesson described earlier in this chapter, explicitly states lesson purposes for her first graders at the start of their intervention lesson: "One purpose today is to work on our fluency. Another is to review strategies for when we come to words we don't know, and a third is to practice responding to high-level questions." She also talks with her students about why fluency, word-recognition strategies, and high-level thinking are important. Additionally, she has excellent pacing. During this 20-minute small-group lesson, she works on fluency, reviews word-recognition strategies, coaches an individual student while reading and takes a running record, does a phonics lesson with the group, and talks about the story they have just read.

talk about it

✳ When you plan and conduct lessons, how do you stay aware of students who might need additional support?

✳ How do you know which students are ready for more student-directed, less teacher-directed work?

✳ As a group, talk about concerns and goals for making purposes clear and for meeting individual students' needs.

Balancing Teacher and Student Actions

Two interrelated aspects of good reading instruction are teacher direction and student active involvement. Teachers need to maintain a good balance between being front-and-center, telling students information and leading recitations, and providing coaching and feedback as students perform front-and-center in an activity the teacher has structured. In general, very high levels of telling and leading recitations by teachers (e.g., almost all the time) and few instances of coaching and providing feedback are detrimental to students' reading growth (Taylor et al. 2003). Furthermore, effective teachers provide a great deal of scaffolding in which they carefully monitor students' learning and provide just enough support to help students succeed (Pressley et al. 2001).

Expert teaching of reading requires deliberate, daily reflection by a teacher about when she needs to introduce or review new information, strategies, or ideas and when she needs to give students the opportunity to practice using the strategies or information they have learned (Connor et al. 2004). With ongoing, reflective professional development, teachers do modify their balance between direction and support, to the benefit of students and their reading growth (Taylor et al. 2003; Taylor and Peterson 2006a, 2006b).

Expert teachers maximize the amount of time students are actively participating in their learning (e.g., reading on their own instead of listening to someone else read, or writing a reaction to an event in a story). Guthrie and colleagues (2004) found that active, collaborative learning related to the reading of interesting science-oriented texts by third graders and fifth graders enhances their learning, compared with more traditional, teacher-directed instruction covering the same content. Pressley and colleagues (2001) found that in classrooms of effective teachers, students do a great deal of active reading and writing.

What the Research Says: Teacher Stance and Active Pupil Participation

▶ Effective teachers provide scaffolded instruction in the form of modeling, coaching, and providing support and feedback, based on students' needs. They also provide teacher-directed instruction.

▶ Effective teachers reflect on the best times for students to use teacher-directed and student-supported instruction.

▶ Less effective teachers provide primarily teacher-directed instruction.

▶ Students benefit from active participation in learning activities. Teachers have control over the ways in which they structure students' involvement in their learning (e.g., passive versus active involvement).

	Provide scaffolded instruction	Balance teacher-directed and student-supported instruction	Active pupil participation
Connor, Morrison, and Katch (2004)		X	
Guthrie et al. (2004)			X
Pressley et al. (2007)	X		X
Taylor et al. (2003)	X	X	X
Taylor et al. (2007)	X	X	

Some Effective Instructional Approaches

▶ Start with a whole-group lesson, using a text from core material, such as a basal reader. Provide explicit instruction (tell, model, review—teacher-directed stance, passive student involvement) on a comprehension concept (e.g., understanding the difference between a fact and an opinion, understanding what a main idea is), skill or process (making inferences while reading, identifying main ideas, understanding the theme of a story), or strategy (consciously practicing comprehension monitoring or summarizing after reading) related to the text. Coach students (a student-support stance) as they practice (active pupil involvement) the comprehension concept, skill or process, or strategy while reading part of the text. Discuss vocabulary at point of contact in the story, engage in high-level talk about the text during or after reading.

While finishing the story, students (independently, with a partner, or in a small group) engage in and continue to practice comprehension concept, skill/process, or strategy (active pupil involvement). They also engage in high-level talk and/or writing about text.

In guided reading small groups, the teacher continues to work on the comprehension concept, skill/process, or strategy with leveled texts at students' instructional reading level (could be teacher-directed stance with more passive pupil involvement or student support stance with primarily active pupil involvement, depending on teacher's approach).

▶ Teachers need to use a teacher-directed stance frequently in their teaching. This often, by necessity, leads to primarily passive pupil involvement as students listen to you teach or other students respond to questions you ask. However, there may be good times during your teaching to switch to a student-support stance, which also allows for more active pupil responding, as you give students a chance to directly engage in the learning activity you have been talking about. Watch a video of yourself teaching a whole-group and a small-group lesson to see how much of the time you use a teacher-directed versus student-support stance. Think of places you could have used a student-support stance but didn't. Think of ways you could have engaged students in more active pupil responding. After a week or so, watch videos of your teaching again to see if you notice differences in teaching stance and pupil involvement.

Resources for Teacher Stance and Pupil Participation

Connor, C. M., F. J. Morrison, and L. E. Katch. 2004. "Beyond the Reading Wars: Exploring the Effect of Child-Instruction Interactions on Growth in Early Reading." *Scientific Studies of Reading* 8: 305–36.

Pressley, M. 2006. *Reading Instruction That Works: The Case for Balanced Teaching.* 3rd ed. New York: Guilford.

LOOKING INSIDE CLASSROOMS

Nora Johnson begins a whole-group lesson on question-answer relationships (QARs) (Raphael, Highfield, and Au 2006) by providing explicit instruction. Reading the questions that go with a *Weekly Reader* story, she explains when the answer to a question is right there "in the book" and when it is "in my head." "Thinking about whether the answer to a question is 'in the book' or 'in my head' can often help you answer questions better." As students work on the last two questions with a partner, Nora coaches pairs of students as they decide whether their answers are "in the book" or "in my head." Nora maximizes students' active involvement in this lesson by letting them answer questions with a partner (as opposed to taking turns) and label them as "in the book" or "in my head" question-answer relationships.

In another lesson using a *Weekly Reader* story on going to the dentist, Nora keeps students actively involved. "Wilbur had tooth trouble and didn't want to go to the dentist. How many of you are like Wilbur and can remember a time you didn't want to go to the dentist? Share with your partner." After the students share she continues, "One thing I like about the dentist is that when I go, I get a brand-new toothbrush. Thumbs up if you have gotten a new toothbrush at the dentist. How about dental floss? Stickers?" Nora concludes by telling students about the *Weekly Reader* website on teeth, how to use it, and what they will find there.

Sandy Grayson, in her vocabulary lesson in Chapter 2, demonstrates techniques to keep her kindergarteners involved. "Thumbs up," "pair-share," "show me," and "give me a nod" are all actions included in her reading and discussion of the story.

talk about it

* Given the examples from Nora Johnson's and Sandy Grayson's lessons, what are some key attributes of effective teaching?

* What might you do to plan for greater interactivity and participation?

* How might you build in more moments when you can assess not only students' degree of "getting it" but their engagement?

* How often are you and your colleagues consciously using a teacher-directed or student support stance?

* When and why would it be beneficial to break from a teacher-directed lesson and move to students' practice and active involvement?

Motivating Learning and Providing Intellectual Challenge

Going hand in hand with effective pacing and a dynamic flow between teacher and student-led discourse is the concept of motivation. As you embark on improving reading instruction at your school, it's so beneficial—and critical—to engage in a lot of honest talk about what it takes to be a motivating teacher and how to use both content and pedagogy to motivate students to learn. Pressley and colleagues (2003) found that in many primary-grade classrooms there are relatively few challenging activities that engage students in high-level thinking about texts. However, effective teachers introduce many motivating and cognitively challenging learning tasks in their classrooms (Dolezal et al. 2003), including a great deal of high-level talk and writing about text. Effective, motivational teachers also provide many high-quality literature experiences for students and include choice when possible.

In less motivational and less effective classrooms, one tends to find cognitively low-level seatwork activities such as:

▶ Completing workbook pages or other low-level response sheets

▶ Playing phonics, grammar, or vocabulary games

▶ Copying spelling words or sentences out of a story

▶ Listening to stories on tape without any follow-up

▶ Reading books that are too easy

▶ Rereading books more times than is helpful (Pressley et al. 2003; Taylor and Peterson 2006c)

What the Research Says: Motivating Learning Activities

▶ Effective teachers provide lessons and learning activities that engage students in cognitively challenging learning experiences.

▶ Effective teachers regularly provide students with opportunities to learn from high-quality literature and interesting texts.

▶ Less effective teachers often provide low-level activities that are not motivating to their students.

▶ Effective teachers provide students with some choice in terms of activities and materials when possible.

	Cognitively challenging learning experiences	High-quality literature/ interesting texts	Student choice
Bohn, Roehrig, and Pressley (2004)	X		X
Dolezal et al. (2003)	X		
Guthrie et al. (2000)	X	X	
Guthrie et al. (2004)	X	X	X
Pressley et al. (2001)	X	X	
Pressley et al. (2003)	X		
Pressley et al. (2007)	X		
Taylor et al. (2003)	X		
Taylor and Peterson (2006)	X		

Some Effective Instructional Approaches

▶ Engage students in active, high-level talk and writing about texts as much as possible.

▶ Use quality fiction and nonfiction texts as often as possible. Avoid uninteresting texts of mediocre quality as much as possible. Include texts of varying genre and representing many cultures.

▶ Give students frequent opportunities to search for and to learn from information on the Internet.

▶ Give students many opportunities to read and respond orally and in writing to engaging texts in ways that are motivating and challenging.

▶ Give students time every day to read for pleasure from books of their own choosing.

▶ Give students motivating and challenging open-ended response activities during independent work time. Avoid low-level worksheets and repetitive drill activities as much as possible, especially if these activities do little to advance students' reading abilities.

▶ Let students work collaboratively with a partner or small group at least some of the time every day.

▶ Give students some choice in books they read and in learning activities they complete.

Resources for Motivating Learning Activities

Heffernan, L. 2004. *Critical Literacy and Writer's Workshop.* Newark, DE: International Reading Association.

Kelley, M. J., and N. Clausen-Grace. 2007. *Comprehension Shouldn't Be Silent.* Newark, DE: International Reading Association.

Olness, R. 2007. *Using Literature to Enhance Content Area Instruction: A Guide for K–5 Teachers.* Newark, DE: International Reading Association.

Pressley, M. 2006. *Reading Instruction That Works: The Case for Balanced Teaching.* 3rd ed. New York: Guilford.

Pressley, M., S. E. Dolezal, L.M. Raphael, L. Mohan, A. D. Roehrig, and K. Bogner. 2003. *Motivating Primary-Grade Students.* New York: Guilford.

Swan, E.A. 2003. *Concept-Oriented Reading Instruction: Engaging Classrooms, Lifelong Learners.* New York: Guilford.

LOOKING INSIDE CLASSROOMS

In his lesson in Chapter 2, Matthew Thompson provides numerous motivating learning experiences that are intellectually challenging to his students. He coaches them in how to have thought-provoking discussions about the chapter books they are reading. This instruction focuses, in part, on the cooperative aspects of having a group discussion. He also lets the discussion leader choose the student-generated questions the group will talk about. When students work in groups of four at their tables, he lets them choose whether they want to read alone or with a partner and answer questions alone or with a partner. They are to write their own answers to questions, but they also have to discuss their answers cooperatively in their group of four.

In her lesson in Chapter 2, Maggie Voss also provides motivating, challenging learning activities. Students work collaboratively with a partner on a research report on desert animals. They choose the animal they want to study, and they engage in collaborative learning as they work with their partner.

Joan Meyer frequently engages her second graders in motivating activities related to high-level talk and writing about text. Students doing research on oceans get to select several books from a table full of books dealing with the ocean, read the books they've selected, and use a graphic organizer to record facts on a topic of interest. Joan tells the students they will share their ideas later when they meet with her as a group.

MOTIVATING STUDENTS THROUGH HIGH-LEVEL TALK AND WRITING ABOUT TEXT—CLASSROOM EXAMPLES

Effective teachers take the time to model and discuss how to have a rich discussion. It can take weeks and months before students can have high-level conversations on their own, with a high degree of respectful listening and building on one another's ideas. One good way to begin is to use a concrete tool like a sticky note so each student can "hold" their thinking and then add it to the group's conversation. For example, a group of Joan Meyer's students are reading and discussing *Rosie's Story*, a basal selection. Students first read the story on their own, writing interesting words and questions they want to discuss on sticky notes. They also jot down their ideas about how the main character solved her problem and the author's purpose for writing the story.

When Joan calls the group together, she puts their sticky notes up on the board and asks, "How should we act during our discussion?" Students say: "Listen to one another." "Politely agree or disagree and say why." "Talk loud enough." "Don't do all of the talking." Joan praises the students, then asks, "First, what was the author's purpose?" One student offers, "To teach us not to be mean to people." Another student adds, "Maybe the author was teased." Another student says, "I think it is about helping others." They talk about how the story ties into the concept of "being me."

Next Joan asks a question someone has written on a sticky note: "Would you have acted like Rosie?" A student says, "Maybe she could have talked to her mom." Other students share. Joan asks, "Have you ever felt the way Rosie did?" Students answer. Joan concludes, "We have three questions on the board. Later this morning you will be writing an answer to one of these questions. It will be your choice as to which one to answer. We'll discuss them the next time we meet."

Sally Hecht, a third-grade teacher at Edgewood School, uses reciprocal teaching (a cooperative learning technique that actively engages students in their learning, motivates them, and enhances their reading comprehension; see Palincsar and Brown 1986) in a lesson based on her students' science textbook.

She begins, "You might wonder why we are using our science book. Our science book has so much information in it that it can be hard to understand. We will make that information easier to read by using our comprehension strategies. Will you have a science book next year in fourth grade?" Students nod yes. "We are going to work on strategies so you can read it and understand it on your own." Sally begins to read a chapter discussing the environment. She stops to model how to figure out what a ranch is. She asks students for ideas. They offer: "It is kind of like a farm." "It has animals on it."

Sally continues reading. When she gets to the end of the first subsection, she says, "I think I will summarize this part before I go on. When I read, it has to make sense. If I can't summarize and things don't make sense, I need to go back and reread." She continues to summarize subsections. At the end of the section (a page and a half of text), she says, "Now I need to think about what I read in this whole section." Sally holds up a sheet of paper that contains headings under which she will take notes. The first heading is, What Is a Healthy Environment for People? Sally writes, *Food—clean and safe; water; shelter; clean environment; clean air-oxygen.* She continues, "The rest of the chapter is broken up into several more sections. Members of each group of four will talk out loud as they try to summarize their section. Also, talk about things that need clarifying. Then each group will share the summary of their section."

The students move into groups and become very engaged in summarizing their section by reading, talking about things that are confusing, and taking notes. Sally circulates among the groups, coaching and offering feedback.

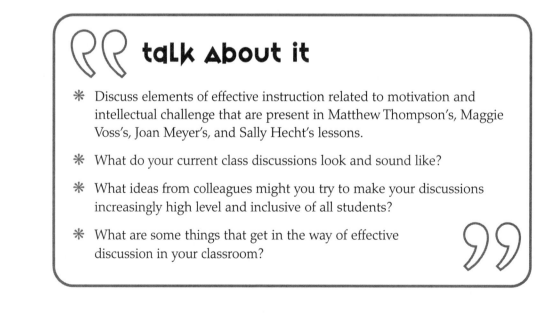

talk about it

❋ Discuss elements of effective instruction related to motivation and intellectual challenge that are present in Matthew Thompson's, Maggie Voss's, Joan Meyer's, and Sally Hecht's lessons.

❋ What do your current class discussions look and sound like?

❋ What ideas from colleagues might you try to make your discussions increasingly high level and inclusive of all students?

❋ What are some things that get in the way of effective discussion in your classroom?

Using Assessments to Evaluate Students' Abilities, Monitor Their Daily Learning, and Differentiate Instruction to Meet Individual Needs

Effective reading teachers continually assess their students' engagement, understanding, and behavior throughout the day. These assessments include checklists and notes based on observations of students' reading abilities as well as schoolwide reading measures that complement district- and state-mandated standardized tests to assess students' reading abilities and progress. Teachers in effective schools also systematically share student assessment data to help them make instructional decisions to improve student performance.

What the Research Says: Use of Assessments to Evaluate Students' Abilities, Monitor Their Daily Learning, and Differentiate Instruction

Effective teachers continually assess their students' engagement, understanding, and behavior throughout the day (Pressley et al. 2003). Also, teachers in effective schools systematically collect and share student assessment data to help them make instructional decisions to improve student performance (Lipson, Mosenthal, Mekkelsen, and Russ 2004; Taylor et al. 2000).

	Regularly monitor students' understanding, engagement, and behavior during the literacy block	Systematically collect and share assessment data to modify instruction and improve student performance
Pressley et al. 2003	X	
Lipson et al. 2004		X
Taylor et al. 2000		X

Some Effective Instructional Approaches

▶ As you listen to students read in guided reading groups or when all students are working on their own, take running records or notes on their decoding accuracy and measure their fluency. Ask them questions about their reading and about vocabulary in their reading, and use a checklist and/or keep notes on their comprehension and vocabulary abilities. Rotate among all students so that you listen to each student read at least once a month.

▶ Share your classroom assessment information with students individually. Also have students self-assess their reading abilities. Help students set goals for growth in their reading abilities.

▶ Share assessment data with colleagues at your grade level at least once a month. Talk about students' collective strengths and weaknesses as well as the reading abilities of struggling readers or other students you are concerned about. Share ideas on changes to your instruction that may be more effective in helping students grow in their reading abilities.

Resources on Assessments

McKenna, M., and S. Stahl. 2003. *Assessment for Reading Instruction*. New York: Guilford.

Paratore, J. R., and R. L. McCormick, eds. 2007. *Classroom Literacy Assessment: Making Sense of What Students Know and Do*. New York: Guilford.

Pressley, M. 2006. *Reading Instruction That Works: The Case for Balanced Teaching*. 3rd ed. New York: Guilford.

Taberski, S. 2000. *On Solid Ground: Strategies for Teaching Reading K–3*. Portsmouth, NH: Heinemann.

LOOKING INSIDE CLASSROOMS

Matthew Thompson records anecdotal notes on individual second graders as he stops by their tables. He listens to students read one by one, coaches them in word-recognition strategies, and asks students questions about their stories. In a notebook with tabs for individual students, he quickly jots down notes on the student's strengths and difficulties related to word recognition, fluency, vocabulary, and comprehension. (See Video 1).

Nora Johnson listens to one of her first graders read during an intervention lesson while the others reread old stories. She takes a running record (records word-recognition errors on a sheet of paper) as the student reads a one hundred–word segment from the story the group read the previous day.

Melissa Norris takes notes on all of her third graders as she listens to them read individually, working with one student a day to limit the time she is pulled away from whole-class or small-group lessons. At the end of a small-group lesson, she keeps one student with her, has the student read, and takes a running record. She also times the reading and asks a few comprehension questions, taking notes on the students' responses. She also talks to the student about the reading before he returns to his seat: "Today, you read seventy-seven words correct per minute, and that is really good. On your first time this year, you were at fifty-five words correct per minute, so you have really moved up. I noticed, though, that you were struggling with your pacing a little, so we'll work on that together. Another thing you can do on your own is reread some of the books in your book box."

❝❝ talk about it

* Discuss the assessments you use to monitor students' learning. Which assessments do you find most useful? Which assessments are required but do not seem that useful to you?

* Discuss the assessments you use to make instructional decisions and to differentiate instruction. How often do you use data to guide your daily lessons?

* Discuss barriers to using data to monitor students' learning and to guide your instruction. ❞❞

Providing Culturally Responsive Instruction

Effective teachers provide culturally responsive instruction by building on students' cultural strengths in the classroom. Effective teachers have high expectations for all students and make connections between students' experiences at home and school. These connections may be made both through the process and the content of instruction (Au 2006).

Relative to process, teachers may want to depart from the typical pattern of individual recitation (teacher initiation, student response, teacher evaluation) and instead allow students to work collaboratively to formulate a response; teachers may also go around the group quickly asking for a brief response from each student. Relative to content, teachers can use multicultural literature, including some works that celebrate students' own cultural heritage and others that introduce them to new cultural perspectives.

What the Research Says: Culturally Responsive Instruction

▶ Effective teachers provide culturally responsive instruction in which they build on their students' cultural strengths.

▶ Effective teachers strive to make connections between students' experiences at home and school.

▶ Effective teachers have high expectations for all students and challenge them with learning experiences that engage them in high-level thinking.

	Connect to students' experiences and build on students' cultural strengths	Maintain high expectations and engage students in high-level thinking
Au (2006)	X	X
Center for Research on Education, Diversity, and Excellence (CREDE) (2002) (review)	X	X
Ladson-Billings (1994)	X	X

Some Effective Instructional Approaches

▶ Use quality fiction and nonfiction texts as much as possible, including texts of varying genres that focus on many cultures and different parts of the world.

▶ Make frequent connections between students' experiences at school and at home.

▶ Build on students' cultural strengths.

▶ Maintain high expectations for all students and challenge them with high-level thinking learning experiences. Engage them in high-level talk and writing about texts that represent a diversity of cultures.

Resources on Culturally Responsive Instruction

Au, K. 2006. *Multicultural Issues and Literacy Achievement.* Mahwah, NJ: Lawrence Erlbaum.

Gaitan, C. D. 2006. *Building Culturally Responsive Classrooms: A Guide for K–6 Teachers.* Thousand Oaks, CA: Corwin.

For a list and review of books for teachers on English language learners, see:

Opitz, M. F., and J. L. Harding-DeKam. 2007. "Understanding and Teaching English-Language Learners." *The Reading Teacher* 60(6): 590–93.

LOOKING INSIDE CLASSROOMS

Matthew Thompson has his second graders read *Justin and the Best Biscuits in the World*, a story about the little-known black cowboys who helped settle the West. Selecting narrative and informational books that represent a wide variety of cultures, including those of students in one's own classroom, is relatively easy, but takes planning.

Two of the teachers we met in Chapter 2 provide extra support in English to their young learners. Angelina Ipson uses "sheltered English" with a group of her students who are new to the United States. She asks them to draw a picture of the word they are learning, *box*, making an outline of a box in the air with her fingers to help them understand her directions. Chuoa Vang speaks in Hmong to a group of her struggling first graders who need more support as they write a sentence about their story.

Before reading a story about Thanksgiving, Benice Daniels, whom we also met in Chapter 2, begins a discussion about culture and traditions by talking about traditional foods served on holidays in her African American culture: greens, sweet potato pie, and macaroni and cheese. She then has students share family traditions related to Thanksgiving: "Now, tell me about a tradition that your family does every year on Thanksgiving." After everyone has shared, Benice and her students discuss how family traditions are different, sometimes inspired by one's cultural background, sometimes not, and yet meaningful and important to individuals.

talk about it

* Discuss practices you use to provide culturally responsive instruction in your classroom.

* What support do you need to be more effective in providing culturally responsive instruction?

Fostering a Positive Classroom Atmosphere

Michael Pressley and his coauthors (2003) have documented that the classrooms of effective teachers in the elementary grades have a very positive atmosphere. Motivating practices include creating an atmosphere of warmth and concern for students, having a positive attitude toward all students, using humor in positive ways, and modeling enthusiasm for learning. Furthermore, effective teachers have excellent classroom management skills, provide effective feedback to students, and foster positive attitudes toward learning in their students.

What the Research Says: Classroom Atmosphere

▶ Effective teachers provide a positive classroom atmosphere.

▶ Effective teachers provide effective classroom management.

▶ Effective teachers provide effective feedback to pupils.

▶ Effective teachers foster positive attitudes toward learning in their students.

▶ Effective teachers foster independence and self-regulation in their students.

▶ Effective teachers promote cooperative learning experiences.

	Positive classroom atmosphere	Effective classroom management	Effective feedback to pupils	Positive attitudes toward learning	Independence and self-regulation	Cooperative learning experiences
Bohn, Roehrig, and Pressley (2004)	X	X			X	X
Dolezal et al. (2003)	X	X		X	X	
Guthrie et al. (2004)						X
Hamre and Pianta (2005)		X		X		
Pressley et al. (2001)	X	X	X	X	X	
Pressley et al. (2003)	X	X	X			
Pressley et al. (2004)	X			X		X
Pressley et al. (2007)	X			X	X	
Taylor, Pressley, and Pearson (2002) (review)		X				

Some Effective Instructional Approaches

▶ Provide a positive classroom atmosphere. Show students that you care about them as individuals; maintain a pleasant classroom setting; display students' work throughout the room; engage in the practices listed here.

▶ Provide effective classroom management. Work with students to establish classroom rules and routinely return to these rules and routines weekly; have students evaluate their success in following classroom rules and routines.

▶ Provide effective feedback to pupils. Praise students, but be sure you are sincere when you offer praise; when you comment on students' work, include constructive feedback and suggestions for the future.

▶ Foster positive attitudes toward learning in your students. Show students things you are excited about as a learner; demonstrate enthusiasm for topics students are learning about.

▶ Foster independence and self-regulation in your students. Give students opportunities to work individually, with a partner, and in a small group and evaluate their success in working in these ways; teach students what to do in lieu of interrupting you when you are with small groups.

▶ Promote cooperative learning experiences. Have students work collaboratively with partners, in small groups within whole groups, in small guided reading groups, and with others during individual work time; teach students how to work well with others—don't talk too much or too little, don't do too much or too little; politely agree or disagree; be a good listener, don't interrupt.

Resources

Manning, M., G. Morrison, and D. Camp. 2009. *Creating the Best Literacy Block Ever.* New York: Scholastic.

Pressley, M. 2006. *Reading Instruction That Works: The Case for Balanced Teaching.* 3rd ed. New York: Guilford.

Pressley, M., S. E. Dolezal, L.M. Raphael, L. Mohan, A. D. Roehrig, and K. Bogner. 2003. *Motivating Primary-Grade Students.* New York: Guilford.

Positive Atmosphere: A Classroom Example

Kathy Little has a very positive atmosphere in her second-grade special education classroom. This is apparent even from her morning message in the lesson we read about in Chapter 2: "Good morning, fantastic readers! Today we'll reread to work on our fluency. We'll use the strategy of monitoring to help us better understand what we read. Have a great day!" She also speaks enthusiastically. However, Kathy is not just a friendly teacher. She holds her students to high standards. She expects students to complete their daily work as well as their homework. Every day she records on her checklist whether they have turned in their homework from the day before. Her students do not want to disappoint her, and almost all of them get their daily work and homework done on time.

Managing the Classroom: A Classroom Example

Well-managed classrooms are the hallmark of effective teachers. Pressley and his coauthors (2003) describe components of effective classroom management, including routines and procedures that minimize disruptions and provide smooth transitions within and between lessons, positive techniques to influence or correct students' behavior, effective extrinsic and intrinsic motivators, appropriate pacing, and structures to foster student self-regulation.

Matthew Thompson has excellent classroom management abilities and creates a very positive classroom atmosphere. At the end of most days, he has a brief class meeting during which he asks students how they think they have behaved that day, based on the rules they have generated as a class. He also teaches his students how to compliment each other. At the end of the student-led discussion described in Chapter 2, he asks his students not only to evaluate how they did in their discussion but also models how to give compliments and prompts them to give compliments to one another. He also teaches his students to offer compliments as well as suggestions when they read other students' writing.

Providing Feedback to Students: A Classroom Example

Teachers in effective classrooms provide encouragement and praise as well as positive feedback (Pressley et al. 2001). They find ways to compliment and encourage their students for their behavior and learning successes. They give specific, constructive feedback to students regularly, providing encouragement and challenging them to think more deeply.

Matthew Thompson provides skillful, constructive feedback to his students at the end of their student-led discussion described in Chapter 2. He asks one student how the student feels he did in the discussion and the student says that he only did so-so. Matthew asks the discussion leader to comment, and the discussion leader offers a positive comment. Matthew offers his own opinion, saying the student was brave when he said he would look back in the book and rethink his answer to a question. Matthew also gives words of encouragement to the shy girl who offered a few ideas during the discussion.

Fostering Positive Attitudes Toward Learning

Effective teachers have high expectations for their students, communicate to students that effort leads to success, encourage independence and responsibility, and foster cooperative learning experiences. Effective teachers also model interest and enthusiasm for their lessons and demonstrate that they are interested in and care about their students.

At a high-poverty school for African American students in an urban area of a large city, in which grade K–12 students, depending on grade level, were performing on average at the forty-seventh to eighty-fifth percentile on standardized tests, teachers made concerted efforts to motivate their students (Pressley et al. 2004). They regularly told students that they could succeed at high levels; they constantly praised students for participating; they interacted with their students in an interested, upbeat manner; and they reminded students that they were in control of their own academic destinies. The teachers at this school also fostered cooperative learning experiences and used tangible rewards to reinforce appropriate behavior and academic achievements.

LOOKING INSIDE CLASSROOMS

Joan Meyer describes her second graders' positive attitudes toward learning. "People who have visited my classroom have remarked over and over again how excited the students are about reading. I work hard to help my neediest students grow but also help the top students soar. All of my students are excited about informational text. They love to discuss books and monitor their own comprehension. They have more ownership of their own learning than my students in the past." Some of this excitement comes from Joan's own enthusiasm for books and for learning. She regularly tells her students about new books she thinks they will enjoy and often mentions things she is learning from books, magazines, the newspaper, and the Internet.

> ❝❝ **talk About it**
>
> Discuss effective practices you use related to the following:
>
> * Positive classroom atmosphere
> * Effective classroom management
> * Constructive feedback to students
> * Positive attitudes toward learning
> * Students' self-reliance as learners
>
> ❞❞

Summary

Much of the research on effective reading instruction in the elementary grades has focused on the content of reading lessons—that is, teaching emergent literacy abilities, including phonemic awareness; phonics; fluency; vocabulary; and reading comprehension. However, a valuable body of research also points to the importance of the many pedagogical decisions that effective teachers make to foster students' reading growth. Effective teachers also develop a motivating, supportive classroom atmosphere that enhances students' reading abilities and achievement. Teaching all children to read well requires excellent reading instruction. Teachers need to remind themselves that materials don't teach, teachers do (Consortium for Responsible School Change 2005).

Time to Collaborate

Launching a Schoolwide Plan

L et's take a moment to recap: When teachers and students engage in a balance of whole-group, small-group lessons, motivating independent learning activities, and experiences with high expectations for students' reading, writing, and thinking about texts, students are on track to become proficient readers. Further, there is a strong motivational aspect to effective teaching. Teachers can bring out the best in children's academic potential when they infuse their classroom culture with practices that provide abundant opportunities for students to participate and feel esteemed and confident. With these things in mind, we turn to the heart of this book: taking these components for success and using them as a basis for a schoolwide reading improvement plan. When teachers collaborate, great things happen for everyone, from administrators, teachers, and support staff to students.

Components of a Schoolwide Reading Program

As you and your colleagues embark on this sustained professional development journey, here are some essential components to developing a cohesive, schoolwide reading program. There are other attributes, of course, but in my experience these are the bedrock ones. (Several of these components are described in more detail in Chapters 5 through 8.)

▶ Collaboration among classroom teachers and resource teachers (e.g., Title I teachers, special education teachers, teachers of English language learners) in whatever delivery model is chosen to provide cohesive, exemplary reading instruction that best meets students' varying needs.

- A significant amount of time is devoted to reading instruction, throughout the grades, during the school day (Taylor et al. 2000).

- A coherent reading program is created through alignment of standards, curriculum, instruction, and assessments.

- A schoolwide assessment plan is in place in which student data is collected and used regularly to inform instruction.

- Interventions to meet the needs of English language learners (ELLs) and other students who are experiencing reading difficulties or who have special needs are available.

- There is collaboration in professional learning and change efforts.

- There are methods of working effectively with parents as partners.

What the Research Says: Effective Schoolwide Practices That Affect Classroom Instruction

- Delivery models, in which classroom and resource teachers work together to provide coherent, exemplary instruction and maximize reading instruction time, affect students' reading growth.

- Time spent on reading instruction is positively related to students' reading growth.

- Effective schools use data from schoolwide assessment systems.

- Effective schools have interventions in place for struggling readers.

- Teachers in effective schools collaborate.

- Effective schools and teachers have strong links to parents.

	Collaborative delivery models and coherent, effective reading program	Maximizing time for reading instruction	Data from schoolwide assessment system	Interventions for struggling readers	Collaboration in professional learning and change efforts	Strong links to parents
Consortium for Responsible School Change (2005) (review)	X				X	
Dolezal et al. (2003)						X
Edwards (2004)						X
Goddard, Hoy, and Hoy (2004)	X				X	
Hiebert and Taylor (1998) (review)				X		
Pressley et al. (2004)			X			
Taylor et al. (2000)	X	X	X	X	X	X
Taylor et al. (2002)	X		X		X	
Taylor and Peterson (2003)	X	X				
Vaughn et al. (2006)	X			X		
Wasik and Slavin (1993) (review)				X		

Resources on Schoolwide Reading Programs and Effective Schools

Allington, R. L., and S. A. Walmsley, eds. 2007. *No Quick Fix: Rethinking Literacy Programs in American's Elementary Schools* (RTI ed.). New York: Teachers College Press.

Christenson, S. L., and S. M. Sheridan. 2001. *Schools and Families: Creating Essential Connections for Learning.* New York: Guilford.

Edwards, P. A. 2004. *Children's Literacy Development: Making It Happen Through School, Family, and Community Involvement.* Boston: Pearson/Allyn & Bacon.

Epstein, J. L., M. G. Sanders, B.S. Simon, K. C. Salinas, N.R. Jansorn, and F.L. van Voorhis. 2002. *School, Family, and Community Partnerships: Your Handbook for Action.* 2nd ed. Thousand Oaks, CA: Corwin.

Morrow, L. M. 2003. *Organizing and Managing the Language Arts Block: A Professional Development Guide.* New York: Guilford.

Resnick, L. B., and S. Hampton. 2009. *Reading and Writing Grade by Grade.* Newark, DE: International Reading Association and National Center on Education and the Economy, University of Pittsburgh.

Reyes, P., J. D. Scribner, and A. P. Scribner, eds. 1999. *Lessons from High-Performing Hispanic Schools.* New York: Teachers College Press.

Slavin, R. E., C. Lake, S. David, and N. A. Madden. 2009. *Effective Programs for Struggling Readers: A Best-Evidence Synthesis.* Baltimore, MD: Johns Hopkins.

Taylor, B. M., and P. D. Pearson, eds. 2002. *Teaching Reading: Effective Schools/ Accomplished Teachers.* Mahwah, NJ: Erlbaum.

Taylor, B. M., D. S. Peterson, M. Marx, and M. Chein. 2007. "Scaling Up a Reading Framework for Prevention and Identification of Students with Reading/ Learning Disabilities." In *Effective Instruction for Struggling Readers K–6*, ed. B. M. Taylor and J. E. Ysseldyke, 216–34. New York: Teachers College Press.

Vaughn, S., J. Wanzek, and J.M. Fletcher. 2007. "Multiple Tiers of Intervention: A Framework for Prevention and Identification of Students with Reading/ Learning Disabilities." In *Effective Instruction for Struggling Readers K–6*, ed. B. M. Taylor and J. E. Ysseldyke, 173–95. New York: Teachers College Press.

Walpole, S., and M. C. McKenna. 2004. *The Literacy Coach's Handbook: A Guide to Research-based Practice.* New York: Guilford.

Putting the Children First

As hard as it is to develop a coherent, schoolwide reading program, it may, inadvertently, be even harder for teachers to keep their students at the forefront of this development effort. That is, when teachers are trying to decide what grade levels should have reading at what times and which resource teacher should work with which classroom teacher at what time and in what manner, it is easy to think about what works best for us as teachers rather than what works best to meet our students' needs. However, research on effective schools has found that teachers in effective schools do continually "put the children first" (Taylor et al. 2002).

What We Know Leads to Success

This reform model has been tried and refined for many years now, so it's nice to be able to draw from the research as I guide you through this school change process. Here, I address the components and detail the data that supports it.

Collaboration on Delivery of Instruction

Valli, Croninger, and Walters (2007) found that resource teachers and instruction aides provide a substantial amount of a student's reading instruction. Thus, the delivery model in which classroom teachers and resource teachers work together to provide reading instruction to accommodate the different needs of students is an important component of a schoolwide reading program and one on which there may not be consensus, even within a grade level. There are strengths and weaknesses in all delivery models, but in one study (Taylor and Peterson 2003) a delivery model in the primary grades in which resource teachers came into the regular classroom (i.e., a push-in model) to provide instruction designed to meet students' varying needs was found to be positively related to reading growth compared with other delivery models. Also, a delivery model in which all students received whole-group reading instruction in their own classroom and small, ability-grouped instruction in a classroom of a teacher other than their own (i.e., a pull-out model) was found to be negatively related to students' reading growth.

At Edgewood Elementary, teachers put the children first when they switched from a pull-out model for special services in which students traveled to another teacher's room for ELL, special education, or Title I reading instruction to a push-in model in which the special teachers come into classroom teacher's rooms to provide additional reading instruction. Teams of teachers, during a daily meeting, planned their day-to-day work, discussed students' progress, and set instructional goals based on learning targets. After they got accustomed to this push-in model supported by common planning, teachers did not want to go back to their pull-out model. A summary of the strength and weaknesses of different delivery models that may help to promote discussion at your school is provided in Chapter 5 in Figure 5–5 under "Whole Group Meeting Conversations."

Time Spent on Reading Instruction

The amount of time devoted to reading instruction is another important component of a schoolwide reading program. One study found that primary-grade students in effective schools received 134 minutes of reading instruction a day, instruction that was separate from writing, spelling, and grammar instruction (Taylor et al. 2000). Thirty-three to 42 percent of this time, depending on the grade level, students were reading. The amount of time spent on reading instruction is related to students' reading growth (Taylor and Peterson 2003; Taylor et al. 2007). Nevertheless, in a recent study teachers reported that they only spent on average about 85 minutes teaching reading in grades 1 through 3 (Chorzempa and Graham 2006).

Joan Meyer from Madina Elementary discusses the importance of the 120-minute block in an interview: "At first parents were appalled that we would spend 120 minutes with reading. Now they are seeing the results. The school board is also supporting us because of our positive results."

Alignment of Standards, Curriculum, Instruction, Interventions, and Assessments

In recent years, district staff, generally speaking, have provided the leadership for standards-based reform in reading, on the heels of state efforts to revise standards and assessments related to reading under No Child Left Behind. However, standards-based reform requires more than alignment of standards, curriculum, instruction, interventions, and assessments if it is to be effective in improving schooling (Cohen and Moffitt 2002). Opportunities for teachers to develop more effective instructional techniques are crucial. One challenge for many teachers is balancing the coverage of content necessary to help students reach state standards and pass required tests without losing sight of the more general goal of teaching students to be competent, motivated readers and independent learners (Gutierrez 2002).

Principals, literacy coordinators, and teachers in the schools introduced in Chapter 1 feel that greater coherence among assessments, curriculum, and instruction is related to students' increases in reading scores. These teachers also say that by working together they have learned to cover the basics and to differentiate instruction yet challenge all students to read, write, and discuss at high levels and become motivated readers.

Collaboration in Professional Learning and School-Based Reading Improvement Efforts

Teachers' perceptions of collective efficacy (Goddard, Hoy, and Hoy 2004)—that is, reaching a goal by pooling efforts and strengths within a school—are related to students' growth in reading (Taylor and Peterson 2006c). Also, perceptions of collective efficacy grow in schools as teachers participate in collaborative professional development, look together at student assessment data, and take on greater leadership roles (Taylor and Peterson 2006b).

Teachers from the Lincoln, Westside, Edgewood, and Madina elementary schools all mention the increases in collaboration in their schools since they began working on school-based reading improvement using the School Change in Reading model (see Chapter 1). Teachers need time and consistent, rewarding opportunities to learn together, to reflect on instruction with other teachers, to plan together, to look at student data in teams, and to celebrate students' and teachers' successes. Processes for making these things happen are discussed in Chapters 5 through 8.

School-Based Reading Reform: Why Now?

With professional learning communities (PLCs) gaining in popularity and teachers' travel budgets waning, school-based reading reform—"revolution from within"—is a very timely concept. There are two essential elements in effective schoolwide reading improvement efforts. The school community needs support for *organizational change* and teachers need support for *individual change* in providing effective reading instruction that attends to students' individual and collective learning needs and reading abilities (Taylor, Raphael, and Au, 2010).

Six recent school-based reading improvement projects have produced significant growth in students' reading achievement based on these intertwined strands of organizational and individual change. They include:

▶ The Standards-Based Change Project. Out of thirty-three high-poverty schools in Hawaii (Au 2005) in Hawaii, those schools that were most successful implementing standards-based change saw greater growth in students reading scores than other schools. Positive results were also seen in Chicago schools (Au, Raphael, and Mooney 2008a).

▶ The Literacy Professional Development Project. In ninety-one elementary schools throughout New Zealand (Timperley and Parr 2007). Students demonstrated twice the expected gain in reading achievement over the two years of the project.

▶ The Acceleration of Achievement in Diverse Schools Project. In seven high-poverty, culturally and linguistically diverse urban schools in New Zealand (McNaughton, MacDonald, Amituanai-Toloa, Lai, and Farry 2006; Lai, M.K., S. McNaughton, M. Amituanai-Toloa, R. Turner, and S. Hsiao 2009). Students in grades 4 through 9 had higher reading achievement than students at comparison schools.

▶ Six Vermont elementary schools (Lipson, Mosenthal, Mekkelsen, and Russ 2004; Mosenthal, Lipson, Torncello, Russ, and Mekkelsen 2004). At least 80 percent of the students in grades 2 and 4 at each of these six schools were performing above the state standards in reading.

▶ A large, diverse, very high poverty elementary school in California (Fisher and Frey 2007), the mean percentage of students in grades 2 through 5 at the proficient or advanced level on the state reading test increased substantially over a six-year period.

▶ The School Change in Reading (SCR) Project. In a study by thirteen high-poverty schools throughout the United States (Taylor, Pearson, Peterson, and Rodriguez 2005) and forty-six moderate- to high-poverty schools in Minnesota (Taylor and Peterson 2007, 2008; Taylor, Peterson, Marx, and Chein 2007). Children at many schools made significant gains in reading comprehension. Students demonstrated greater reading growth in schools that were more successful in implementing the reform than in schools that were less successful (Taylor et al. 2005, 2007).

In all of these projects, teachers and administrators adopted or developed an explicit framework and process for bringing about organizational and individual change that resulted in more effective reading instruction. Factors common to these successful projects are summarized in Table 4–1. For a detailed discussion of these projects and the commonalities across them, see Taylor, Raphael, and Au (2010).

Common Factors Across Six Studies Related to School-Based Organizational and Individual Change Resulting in Effective Reading Instruction

ORGANIZATIONAL CHANGE

Vision, Commitment, and Ownership of Reform Process

- Begin with either an external or internal framework for change.
- Develop a shared internal vision for and ownership of success.
- Commit to a long-term improvement process.
- Make modifications to the improvement process over time.

Leadership

- Designate an onsite teacher leader.
- Ensure that there is principal support and involvement.
- Establish a leadership team.
- Develop shared leadership over time.
- Seek external support.
- Provide ongoing professional development for leadership team members.

Deliberate Use of Data

- Regularly use student data to inform instruction.
- Use common assessments developed by grade level.
- Focus on grade-level and schoolwide literacy standards.
- Regularly use data on classroom instruction and school-level climate and collaboration to inform practice.

Collaborative School Community

- Strive to develop positive school culture and sense of collective efficacy.
- Develop a collaborative vision for teaching, student learning, and professional learning.

INDIVIDUAL CHANGE

Professional Learning and Changes in Teaching

- Have external partners provide some of the professional development on research-based literacy curriculum and instruction.
- Develop school-based learning communities.
- Ensure that professional learning is ongoing, deliberate, and well planned.
- Reflect on practice that is linked to instructional change or modification.
- Tailor professional learning to a school's unique needs.

EFFECTIVE READING INSTRUCTION

Curriculum Coherence and Balanced Instruction

- Teach from a coherent perspective throughout the school.
- Focus on curriculum development and coherence.
- Focus on dimensions of effective instruction.
- Provide balanced reading instruction.

Complex Thinking and Motivating Learning Activities for Students

- Develop strategic readers.
- Focus on high-level thinking.
- Use collaborative learning experiences.
- Focus on motivating student-led, independent learning activities.

Table 4–1. Common Factors Related to School-Based Organizational and Individual Change Resulting in Effective Reading Instruction

Generic reviews of school reform efforts published since 2000 stress similar elements that need to be in place for schools to implement and sustain successful educational reforms (see Borman et al. 2003; Cohen and Moffitt 2002; Datnow and Stringfield 2000; Fink and Brayman 2006; Giles and Hargreaves 2002; Guiney 2002; Jennings 2002; May and Supovitz 2006; McLaughlin and Mitra 2002; Taylor, Raphael, and Au 2010).

Qualities That Bring About Organizational Change

Teachers and administrators need to adopt or develop an explicit framework and process for change that will help them collaborate. Learning to work together as members of a school community is a slow but important process. Organizational interactions and collective understandings must evolve around the schoolwide reading program, use of data, leadership, and school climate in order for the schoolwide reading improvement effort to be successful. (Organizational interactions and collective understandings are explored in more depth in Chapters 5 through 8.)

Everyone shares a vision, a commitment, and ownership of the change process. Teachers and administrators develop a shared vision for literacy improvement. Questions to answer include: *What are we working toward in terms of students' reading and our teaching? Who is going to lead us toward our goals? Who is going to do what? How will we collaborate? How will we evaluate our progress and make adjustments to our improvement process?* The framework for change may come from an external partner or from within the school, and staff members understand that this multiyear process will evolve over time. Also, staff members' ownership of the process develops over time, and commitment to instructional excellence becomes stronger as students' reading scores increase. Teachers develop an increased sense of collective efficacy about their abilities to produce positive changes in students' reading abilities as well as increased ownership of the school's reading program during the years they are involved in reading improvement process.

In the SCR process, teachers improve their understanding of effective reading instruction and engage in collaborative learning experiences to become increasingly effective teachers of reading. To start, at least 75 percent of the teachers and administrators should be willing to undertake a focused reading improvement effort that spans multiple years. Although the SCR model begins with an externally provided change, teachers and administrators will need to develop ownership of a continual process for change. Through workshops and study groups, teachers and administrators learn about and discuss essential elements of successful and sustainable schoolwide reform efforts: leadership, collaboration, ownership, quality professional development, and effective reading instruction. The following table summarizes principles and action steps to develop vision, commitment, and ownership over the change process.

talk About it

* Review the principles and actions on organizational change. Discuss strengths, challenges, and possible first action steps.

Organizational Change: Vision, Commitment, and Ownership

PRINCIPLES	ACTIONS
• Begin with either an external/internal framework for change.	• Agree to develop a deep understanding of effective reading instruction.
• Develop a shared internal vision for and ownership of success.	• Engage in collaborative learning experiences to become increasingly effective teachers of reading.
• Commit to a long-term improvement process.	• Begin with an externally provided or internally developed process for change, like the one described in this book.
• Make modifications to the improvement process over time.	• Develop internal motivation for and ownership of a process of change that is modified over time.

The initiative is guided by strong leadership. Once a school has committed to a reading improvement process, collaborative leadership keeps the reform effort moving forward. The principal and teacher leaders initiate a process of continuous reading improvement. Typically, a key teacher leader serving as coordinator/coach orchestrates the day-to-day activities of the reform effort. An important role of leadership team members is to inspire other teachers to become increasingly engaged in and committed to the school literacy improvement effort. External partners can provide valuable assistance by bringing ideas and support to the reform process as well.

In the SCR process, the leadership team meets about once a month. The members include an effective teacher leader who serves as a literacy coordinator and coach; enthusiastic teacher leaders from various grade levels and special areas; and a supportive principal (Taylor et al. 2005, 2007). The leadership team sets agendas for whole-school meetings to discuss and act upon aspects of the schoolwide reading program. Leadership team members take the lead trying out new professional development techniques, such as video sharing or peer coaching, which are designed to help teachers reflect on practice.

The literacy coordinator visits classrooms regularly to model effective teaching practices, observe, and coach. If possible, each school also receives support from an external consultant who works closely with the literacy coordinator. Principals, leadership team members, literacy coordinators, and external consultants participate in ongoing professional learning to develop their leadership abilities related to the SCR process.

Becky Saunders sums up reading instruction leadership at Edgewood Elementary this way: "The literacy coordinator oversees the SCR process. The principal makes sure the SCR activities and our district standards align. The literacy leadership team deals with more of the nuts and bolts of what is happening in classrooms." Tricia Calahan, Edgewood's principal, adds: "The leadership team is the core group, but leadership really is a collaborative effort among all the teachers."

Organizational Change: Leadership

PRINCIPLES	ACTIONS
• Designate an onsite teacher leader. • Ensure that there is principal support and involvement. • Establish a leadership team. • Develop shared leadership over time. • Seek external support. • Provide ongoing professional development for leadership team members	• The principal, a teacher coordinator/coach, and teacher leaders make up a leadership team and initiate and refine a process of continuous reading improvement. • Leadership team members engage in professional development on leadership. • Leadership team members inspire colleagues to become increasingly engaged in the school literacy improvement effort over time. • Other teachers share leadership roles over time. • A key teacher leader orchestrates the day-to-day activities of the reform effort. • External partners bring ideas and support to the reform process.

❝❞ talk about it

✳ Review the principles and actions in the chart on leadership. Discuss strengths, challenges, and possible first action steps. (You may wish to reread the descriptions of the Edgewood and Westside elementary schools in Chapter 1 for examples of roles and responsibilities of the principal, leadership team, literacy coordinator, and teachers in the SCR process.)

There is ongoing, deliberate use of data. Teachers and administrators regularly use data to improve their reading program and students' reading scores. Student data, teacher data, and school data can be important change agents. Typically, as teachers see students' reading scores rise based on instructional changes, they are motivated to make their teaching practices even more effective. Also, teachers' expectations for students increase as their reading abilities grow.

In the SCR process, teachers and administrators look at data on students' progress in reading, on instruction, and perceptions of school-level collaboration and leadership. Every summer leadership teams use data to identify students' strengths and weaknesses and propose goals for improving practice during the upcoming year. School staff regularly refine their plans to:

▶ Use student reading assessment data.

▶ Identify students who needed reading interventions.

▶ Help teachers make instructional decisions about supplemental learning activities that advance all students at their individual reading levels.

Teachers regularly self-evaluate their instruction or receive feedback on their teaching. This reflection on practice helps them make their instruction even more effective.

As Brenda Heller, the literacy coordinator at Lincoln Elementary, explains, "Teachers are using student assessments on a regular basis to drive their instruction. They bring them to monthly meetings, talk about progress, and talk about students and further interventions they may need."

Organizational Change: Deliberate Use of Data

PRINCIPLES	ACTIONS
• Regularly use student data to inform instruction. • Use common assessments developed by grade levels. • Focus on grade-level and schoolwide literacy standards. • Regularly use data on classroom instruction and school-level climate and collaboration to inform practice.	• School develops a schoolwide plan for looking at, sharing, and using student reading assessment data on an ongoing basis to impact instruction. • School uses common assessments developed by grade levels that attend to grade-level and schoolwide literacy standards. • Teachers look at, share, and use student reading assessment data on an ongoing basis to impact instruction. • Teachers use assessment data to identify students who need reading interventions. • Teachers use assessment data to design supplemental learning activities to challenge students at individual reading levels. • Teachers regularly look at and use feedback on their teaching by themselves or with support from the literacy coordinator to inform their instruction. • Every summer leadership teams identify students' strengths and weaknesses and propose goals for improving practice. • School regularly looks at data on school-level collaboration to improve the reading improvement effort.

talk about it

* Review the principles and actions in the chart on deliberate use of data. Discuss strengths, challenges, and possible first action steps. (You may want to reread the descriptions of the Edgewood and Madina elementary schools in Chapter 1 for examples of deliberate uses of data.)

The school community is collaborative rather than hierarchical or competitive. Schools that successfully improve their literacy instruction are collaborative communities. Teachers teach and learn together, and they play an active role in decision-making related to their schoolwide reading program. These collaborative experiences help teachers and administrators develop ownership and collective efficacy that in turn helps them sustain their ongoing literacy improvement efforts.

In the SCR process, teachers decide how they will work together during reading blocks; develop a scope and sequence across grades for delivery of their reading curriculum; decide what interventions to provide to struggling readers; and decide what to study in their study groups. Teachers report that collaboration in classrooms, at grade-level meetings, and in school-based professional learning contributes to their success in providing effective reading instruction (Taylor, Pearson, Clark, and Walpole 2000; Taylor et al. 2007). Their sense of collective efficacy is positively related to students' reading growths, and it increases over time (Taylor and Peterson 2008).

As Kathy Little, a special education teacher at Lincoln Elementary, explains, "I need study groups because I thrive on the professional conversations. I need to share student work and the videos. I need the whole-group meetings to keep the schoolwide focus."

Organizational Change: Developing a Collaborative School Community

PRINCIPLES	ACTIONS
• Strive to develop positive school culture and sense of collective efficacy. • Develop a collaborative vision for teaching, student learning, and professional learning.	*Teachers and administrators:* • Share instructional data. • Participate in collaborative, school-based professional learning. • Coach and are coached by their peers. • Team with other teachers to provide reading instruction. • Establish consistent reading instruction.

❞❞ talk About it

✳ Review the principles and actions in the chart on collaborative communities. Discuss strengths, challenges, and possible first action steps. (You may wish to reread the descriptions of the Lincoln and Edgewood elementary schools in Chapter 1 for examples of attributes of collaborative school communities.)

Factors That Bring About Individual Change

So often professional development efforts within a school fall by the wayside or don't lead to long-term change because the needs of individual teachers haven't been met. This statement sounds plain as day—but when we look at individual change in Chapter 5, the complexities of what it means to deepen teachers' practice and their belief in themselves as ongoing learners come into high relief. For now, here's an overview of the factors that lead to teacher change.

Professional learning leads to changes in teaching. In schools focusing on improvement in reading instruction, teachers have ongoing, well-planned, relevant professional learning experiences that lead to increasingly effective reading instruction within their classrooms. Teachers learn about research-based literacy curriculum instruction and assessment. They reflect on and work hard to modify their reading instruction based on their ongoing learning. Peer modeling and coaching, self-reflection, and conversations related to reading instruction, curriculum, and assessment also help teachers reflect on their practice. Professional learning sessions are tailored to meet the needs of the teachers and students in the school. Literacy leaders learn how to become increasingly effective agents for change.

In the SCR process, teachers participate in hour-long study groups two or three times a month (Taylor et al. 2005). Professional learning focuses on reflection and change as well as research-based instruction related to emergent literacy, word recognition, vocabulary, comprehension strategies, and high-level thinking abilities. Study group topics are determined by teachers based on their needs and the needs of their students.

Teachers share videotapes or segments of their reading lessons and examples of their students' work in order to improve their practice. In addition, literacy coordinators and external consultants model and coach in classrooms. Teachers use protocols tied to elements of effective reading instruction to help them reflect on their practice.

Estella Butler, the literacy coordinator at Westside Elementary, comments, "Now in year 2 of our improvement process we are showing teachers how to peer-coach using the same model we used in our coaching training. We are beginning by teaching members of the leadership team peer-coaching techniques, and they will then teach others. We are also going to start having leadership team members make classroom visits; later other teachers will do this as another way to learn from one another. Before, our professional learning was all about reading and talking and now it's about action."

Networking with other schools is also valuable. In the Minnesota project (Taylor and Peterson 2007), three times a year teachers across SCR schools attended conferences where they learned from one another, from external partners, and from national literacy experts at roundtables and presentations. Leadership team members across schools met several times a year to learn about effective leadership and sustainability and to share successes and concerns. Literacy coordinators and external consultants met every six weeks to improve their leadership skills and coaching abilities.

As Jane Larson, the literacy coordinator at Madina Elementary, reflects, "Talking with other schools involved in the SCR process at workshops, leadership meetings, and coaching training sessions has been beneficial as a way to learn about similarities and differences across schools and to get ideas from them."

Individual Change: Professional Learning and Changes in Teaching

PRINCIPLES	ACTIONS
• Have external partners provide some of the professional development on research-based literacy curriculum and instruction.	• Participate in professional development on research-based literacy curriculum and instruction provided by external partners.
• Develop school-based learning communities.	• Engage in hour-long study groups tailored to school's needs three times a month.
• Ensure that professional learning is ongoing, deliberate, and well planned.	• Focus on reflection and change in teaching as well as research-based reading instruction.
• Reflect on practice that is linked to instructional change or modification.	• Make research-based changes in reading instruction.
• Tailor professional learning to the school's unique needs.	• Refine practice by sharing videos of your teaching examples of student work.
	• Have literacy coaches model and coach in classrooms.
	• Network with other schools engaged in the SCR process.

talk about it

✳ Review the principles and actions in the chart on professional learning. Discuss strengths, challenges, and possible first action steps. (You may wish to reread the descriptions of the Westside and Madina elementary schools in Chapter 1 and find examples of professional learning that occurs as part of the SCR process.)

Curriculum and Teaching Practices That Produce Effective Literacy Instruction

To help all students achieve at high levels in reading and writing, teachers in successful schoolwide reading improvement efforts develop coherent reading curriculums and provide sound, balanced instruction. They also strive to provide challenging, motivating learning activities for all students.

Teachers embrace curriculum coherence and balanced instruction.

Through their collaborative professional learning, teachers in schools that are committed to reading improvement begin to teach from a more coherent perspective than in the past. They focus on curriculum development and teaching effectiveness rather than on the "correct" use of purchased materials. Teachers focus on balanced reading instruction that covers basic reading skills as well as application of word-recognition and comprehension strategies.

In the SCR process, teachers focus on the content and pedagogy of effective reading instruction as well as on differentiated instruction that meets students' needs. Teachers provide balanced instruction by constantly reflecting on the cognitive engagement teaching model (Taylor et al. 2003). In this model, teachers engage students in high-level talk and writing about text. They balance teaching word recognition and comprehension as basic skills and as strategies applied to texts. They consciously decide when to use direct instruction (e.g., telling) or to provide student support (e.g., coaching) based on students' needs and abilities. They balance learning activities in which students are actively involved (e.g., all students are reading) and more passively involved (e.g., students take turns reading or listen to someone read). Through study groups, teachers develop a common language and learn to use similar teaching strategies related to their reading instruction. These actions help them develop a sense of coherence in their reading program.

As literacy coordinator Anna Berglund reflects, "One thing that's changed is that we have specific names to describe what we are doing. We are much more aware of what's happening at other grade levels and how instruction is building from one grade level to the next throughout the school. Talking about the school reading program gives us a schoolwide perspective of what we are doing to help our students. It breaks down the feelings of isolation, and it gives staff ideas and strategies to make instruction more effective. Learning together builds common language, vision, and goals."

talk about it

* Review the principles and actions in the chart on curriculum coherence and balanced instruction. Discuss strengths, challenges, and possible first action steps.

Curriculum Coherence and Balanced Instruction

PRINCIPLES	ACTIONS
• Teach from a coherent perspective throughout the school.	• Focus on the content and pedagogy of effective, research-based reading instruction.
• Focus on curriculum development and coherence.	• Focus on differentiated instruction matched to students' needs and abilities.
• Focus on dimensions of effective instruction.	• Develop a common language and use similar teaching strategies related to reading instruction.
• Provide balanced reading instruction.	• Provide balanced instruction through cognitive engagement (see Chapters 2 and 3 and Taylor et al. 2003).
	• Use high-level talk and writing about text in addition to more traditional lower-level comprehension activities.
	• Teach word recognition and comprehension as basic skills but also have students apply these strategies to texts.
	• Teach directly (e.g., tell) or support students (e.g., coach) based on students' needs and abilities.
	• Balance active learning activities (e.g., all students read) with more passive learning activities (e.g., students take turns reading, or listen to someone read).

Teachers offer students opportunities for complex thinking and motivating learning activities. To help all students achieve at high levels in reading and writing, effective teachers emphasize reading comprehension, complex thinking, and students' collaborative interactions with text as well as basic skills. They focus on teaching students to be strategic readers and learners. They give students ample opportunities to engage in high-level discussions about text. Students participate in collaborative learning experiences, learn through inquiry, and read widely.

In the SCR process, teachers learn about high-level talk and writing about texts, comprehension strategies instruction, and challenging vocabulary instruction. They engage in self-reflection and talk with other teachers about students' cognitive engagement in their literacy learning (Taylor et al. 2003).

Anna Berglund describes student learning in year 2 of the SCR project: "This year in study groups we focused on comprehension strategy instruction, higher-level questioning, and getting kids to talk to one another about [the] books they were reading. We have seen students deepen their comprehension and their ability to engage in dialogue with other people. Overall we've seen our kids thinking at higher levels than in the past." Melissa Norris, a teacher at Madina Elementary, says about her kindergarten students, "My students are excited about reading books and discussing them with their peers."

Complex Thinking and Motivating Learning

PRINCIPLES	ACTIONS
• Develop strategic readers. • Focus on high-level thinking. • Use collaborative learning experiences.	• Engage students in conversations about theme and character interpretation. • Engage students in student-led discussions. • Provide comprehension strategies instruction. • Provide challenging vocabulary instruction. • Focus on student-led, independent learning activities. • Teach students to work collaboratively with a partner or small group.

talk about it

✳ Review the principles and actions in the chart on complex thinking and motivating learning. Discuss strengths, challenges, and possible first action steps. (You may want to reread the descriptions of the Edgewood and Madina elementary schools in Chapter 1 and find examples of curricular coherence and high-level thinking.)

Summary

Schools can use existing research-validated school improvement models in their own efforts to improve students' literacy abilities. External partners, such as university faculty members or professional development providers, can provide initial knowledge and support. However, the drive and hard work necessary for long-term change must come from within individual schools.

School-based reading improvement needs to be understood and embraced by teachers and must take place in every classroom every day. Successful efforts do not develop from a string of superficial changes but from a positive, collaborative school culture that invites change.

talk about it

* Is your school ready to undertake school-based reading improvement?

* What support will your school need and what changes will need to take place in order for your school to embark on school-based reading improvement?

5

The People Factor

Launching the Meetings and Collaboration

T he most compelling school leaders need good old-fashioned day-to-day plans to affect change. As we know from listening to politicians on the campaign trail, rousing words and lofty goals for student achievement aren't enough. The School Change in Reading (SCR) process (Taylor et al. 2003, 2005) is effective because it details the "dailyness" upon which improvement is built. In this chapter, I share next steps for the who, what, when, where, and why of meetings and professional development activities you'll need to plan. You will discover that it is a *process* you can emulate. It has been years in the making and refining—it works because it respects the local decision making teachers and other staffers need to make in order to develop a reading program that reflects your unique school.

First Step: Share the Vision at a Springtime Presentation to Staff

The ideal season to present a long-term reform initiative is in the spring so there is time to plan to begin the process in the next school year. The principal or literacy leader can share with teachers the general philosophy guiding the approach and help them understand the process. It is important that teachers be introduced to the big ideas underlying effective reading instruction (see Chapters 2 and 3) and the characteristics conducive to effective school improvement (see Chapter 4). Participant roles in the SCR process are listed in Figure 5–1. Copies can be handed out to the teachers attending the meeting at which the reform initiative is initially discussed.

SCR Participant Roles

K–6 Teachers: Responsibilities

Group Work	Work with Specialist	Individual Work	My Notes on the Process
Meet two (or three) times a month in study groups: one to two main topics in reading, and one to two support topics (four to five months each main topic). (See Chapter 7.)	Learn to collect and refine use of progress monitoring data, including running record data and classroom-based comprehension data, to adjust instruction to meet individual students' needs. (See Chapter 6.)	Apply new or refined teaching strategies (from study groups) on a regular basis, take notes on this teaching to share in study groups. Prepare and preview videos of your teaching of new or refined techniques and bring to study groups to share. Collect data (e.g., student work, reading scores) or take notes (reflections/self-evaluation of your teaching) relevant to study group topics.	
Meet three times a year in data retreats to identify students who are above, at, or below grade level and to consider their progress in reading as well as changes in instruction that need to be made to better meet their needs. (See Chapter 6.)	Work with a literacy coordinator, colleague, or outside consultant to become more incisive about evaluating data from your teaching (e.g., observational notes, videos). (See Chapter 6.)	In addition to completing specific Try It Out activities generated by the study groups, continually reflect on how the professional development is changing you as a teacher. What interests you most so far? What do you consider your greatest strengths? Weaknesses? Where else might you go to strengthen your understanding of the study group topics? Other readings? Web resources?	
Meet monthly in grade levels to look at pupil data or work samples and get suggestions from colleagues on how to maximize individuals' or groups' progress. (See Chapter 6.)		Celebrate what you and colleagues are learning and recognize that everyone is being pushed out of their comfort zone. How can you support colleagues? What do you find to be the most effective way of seeing your reading instruction? Feedback from colleagues? Watching videos of your teaching and taking notes?	
	Set up a schedule for the literacy coach to model in your classroom. Have her or him watch you teach in your room and engage in a coaching conversation with him or her later in the day or week (see Chapter 8). By year 2 or 3, when you are familiar with coaching, you may feel ready to peer coach with a grade-level colleague. (See Chapter 8.)	Becoming a more effective reading teacher requires you to understand content and pedagogy and to really know your students as readers and learners. Work at using student data—informal observations as well as formal assessments—and reflect on your teaching to best meet their needs.	
Meet once a month as an entire staff to share findings from study groups, to share data on pupil progress, and to deliberate on schoolwide issues pertaining to school objectives. (More on this in Chapter 5.)			

Catching Schools © 2011 by Barbara M. Taylor (Heinemann: Portsmouth, NH).

continues

Figure 5–1a SCR Participant Roles

SCR Participant Roles, *continued*

Leadership Team: Responsibilities

Principal, Literacy Coordinator, Teachers, External Partners	Additional Roles for Principals	Additional Roles for Literacy Coordinator and External Consultants
Develop an initial plan for deciding upon study group topics and getting people into study groups.	Participate in, be a champion for, and monitor the quality of the SCR process.	Visit classrooms to monitor implementation of new instructional techniques, provide support, and do demonstration teaching.
Keep study groups moving forward. Meet once a month to monitor study group activities, solve problems, and provide guidance to study groups.	Work toward implementing collaborative leadership.	Direct teachers or study groups to relevant resources.
Meet monthly to plan for large group meetings, decide on external partner/expert needs for professional learning sessions or school visits to provide feedback, participate in professional learning activities for leadership team members, and monitor and plan for ongoing SCR activities.	Meet regularly with the literacy coach/coordinator.	Provide feedback on study group action plans, meeting notes, etc. Help teachers reflect on observation data.
Meet as a leadership team to discuss the strengths and weaknesses of your school's current involvement with parents.		Provide oversight to the collection of assessment data on students and to the activities at data retreats in which grade-level teams look at student data and reflect on needed instructional changes.
Devise, implement, and evaluate a plan to develop or improve partnerships with parents.		Work with the staff to determine the extent to which classrooms and the school have balanced, research-based literacy programs and in which curriculum and standards are aligned. Also determine the extent to which the school devotes sufficient blocks of time to reading instruction and has conducive learning environments for students and for teachers.
Beginning in year 2, devise a plan to gradually take over the literacy coordinator's responsibilities, especially if there will be limited, or no, funding for such a position.		Work with the staff to determine the extent to which: • School provides best practices for ELLs. • School has interventions for struggling readers in the earliest grades and for students in other grades as needed.

Figure 5–1b SCR Participant Roles, *continued*

Shortly after this initial meeting (and after teachers' questions have been answered), ask teachers to vote (by ballot) on whether to take on the change process. There should be buy-in by at least 75 percent of the teachers in the school. Without this kind of support, a school is probably not ready to go ahead. If the vote is to move forward, new staff members hired over the summer need to know that by accepting a position at the school they agree to participate in the reading improvement process. For additional readings on schoolwide reading improvement, see the list at end of the chapter.

Key Support Systems

▶ *Study group (PLC) meetings two times a month.* Teachers who teach reading participate in hour-long study groups about two times a month. Some topics are best suited to teachers of one or two specific grades (e.g., phonemic awareness). Other topics work well with teachers at a number of grade levels (e.g., high-level talk and writing about text) and foster cross-grade relationships. Within study groups, teachers learn about and implement research-based reading practices and reflect on and strengthen their reading instruction. Roles for participants in study groups, including rotating leaders, are discussed in Chapter 7.

▶ *Data sharing and data retreats.* Grade-level teachers examine data on students' reading abilities once every four to six weeks and discuss instructional changes that will enhance students' reading growth. Three times a year grade-level teams have half-day data retreats at which they look at growth in students' reading abilities and again talk about instruction, including interventions and supplemental learning activities, that will meet students' needs and challenge and motivate them all. (See Chapter 6 for more about this.)

▶ *Once-a-month whole-group meetings.* In a whole-group meeting, teachers at all grade levels share and discuss data on students' reading abilities, data on reading instruction, and data on school leadership and collaboration as they pertain to their reading program. These data are used to help teachers make changes in their reading instruction and to assess the success of these changes. (See Chapter 6.) They also discuss issues related to the schoolwide delivery of reading instruction, such as the blocks of time devoted to reading instruction and the delivery models used at different grade levels. Examples of activities for whole-group meetings are provided in Chapter 5.

▶ *Teachers, as individuals,* examine data on their students' reading abilities and on their own reading instruction.

▶ *Modeling and coaching.* This begins with support from a literacy coordinator or coach. Over time, teachers learn how to become effective peer coaches and support one another in the use of effective teaching practices. (See Chapter 8.)

▶ *Intervention plans.* Children in grades K–6 who are struggling with reading need extra support. School staff need to consider what interventions are in place and if they are meeting students' needs. Ongoing assessments to help teachers decide which students need reading interventions are discussed in Chapter 6.

▶ *A parent partnership plan.* Successful schools foster partnerships with parents, respect cultural differences, and promote community involvement (Scribner, Young, and Pedroza 1999; Taylor, Pearson, Clark, and Walpole 2000). Schools need to consider how they communicate with parents, discover parents' concerns about their children's education, and decide how they will make parents feel welcome in the school. (See Figure 5–2.) Plans for

Improving Parent Partnerships Plan

Getting Started

a. Meet as a leadership team to discuss the strengths and weaknesses of your school's current involvement with parents. Keep in mind that what is important is the concept of parent partnerships, not simply parent involvement. Survey parents and assess what parents need in order to become more involved in their children's schooling.

b. Devise a plan to develop or improve partnerships with parents. This plan should include ways to communicate regularly with parents, to find out what parents' concerns and needs are for their children, to develop successful at-home reading partnerships in which parents receive support in how to help their students with reading at home in ways they will feel comfortable helping, and to make parents feel welcome in the school.

Maintaining Momentum

c. Ask parents and teachers to evaluate the degree to which the plan for improving partnerships with parents has been successful.

d. Study data from parent feedback or attendance at scheduled events to determine which aspects of the program have been successful and which have not.

Resources on Building Parent Partnerships

Barrera, R., and R. Jimenez. 2002. "Bilingual Teachers Speak About Their Literacy Instruction." In *Teaching Reading: Effective Schools, Accomplished Teachers*, ed. B. M Taylor and P. D. Pearson, 335–60. Mahwah, NJ: Erlbaum.

Christenson, S. L., and S. M. Sheridan. 2001. *Schools and Families: Creating Essential Connections for Learning*. New York: Guilford.

Edwards, P. A. 2004. *Children's Literacy Development: Making It Happen Through School, Family, and Community Involvement*. Boston: Pearson/Allyn & Bacon.

Epstein, J. L., M. G. Sanders, B. S. Simon, K. C. Salinas, N.R. Jansorn, and F. L. van Voorhis. 2002. *School, Family, and Community Partnerships: Your Handbook for Action*. 2nd ed. Thousand Oaks, CA: Corwin.

Goddard, R. D., M. Tschannen-Moran, and W.K. Hoy. 2001. "A Multilevel Examination of the Distribution and Effects of Teacher Trust in Students and Parents in Urban Elementary Schools." *The Elementary School Journal* 102: 3–19.

Scribner, J. D., M. D. Young, and A. Pedroza. 1999. "Building Collaborative Relationships with Parents." In *Lessons from high-performing Hispanic schools,* ed. P. Reyes, J. D. Scribner, and A. P. Scribner, 33–60. New York: Teachers College Press.

Taylor, B. M., P. D. Pearson, K. Clark, and S. Walpole. 2000. "Effective Schools and Accomplished Teachers: Lessons about Primary-Grade Reading Instruction in Low-Income Schools." *Elementary School Journal* 101: 121–65.

Figure 5–2 *Improving Parent Partnerships Plan*

parent involvement that are one-sided (e.g., what can you as a parent do to help us at school?) won't seem like a partnership to parents.

▶ *Staff.* Each school needs to have:

    ▶ A full-time (or at least a half-time) *literacy coordinator* who also serves as a coach.

    ▶ A *leadership team* (suggested make-up follows in the next section).

    ▶ An *external partner/consultant,* if possible, to bring outside expertise and another pair of eyes into the process.

ON TEACHERS' EVOLVING OWNERSHIP

The professional learning sessions from our external partner have been of high quality and very helpful, but now in the third year most of the staff development is internal. We work extraordinarily well together. We are sharing with one another, discussing what we've read, and talking about what we are doing. I've never heard so much discussion about how we're teaching and what we're noticing about the children's learning as I have these past three years. I'm really proud of our staff."

—Matthew Thompson, Lincoln Elementary Teacher

Next Step: Put Together a Leadership Team

The leadership team members should rotate from year to year, but an initial group needs to get the SCR effort started. In most SCR schools, the leadership team is made up of the principal, a lead teacher/literacy coordinator, and three to five other teacher leaders representing different grade levels and resource teacher groups such as special education, ELL, and Title I. As many teachers as possible should feel they have a representative on the leadership team, but the number of members will vary depending on the size of the school.

Because many things require oversight by the leadership team, subgroups may need to deliberate on topics, such as working with new teachers and developing parent partnerships, and report back to the larger group.

The Team's Purposes and Duties

In this section, logistics and roles of the leadership team are discussed. As you will see, the leadership team is a vital group with many responsibilities to get the reform effort up and running as well as moving forward over time in a productive way.

Logistics and Overview

▶ Meet for 45 to 60 minutes, twice a month, during the first year (in subsequent years, once a month is usually sufficient).

▶ Look at data on students, reading instruction, and school climate to plan for whole-group meetings, study groups, and data retreats.

▶ Plan whole-group meetings.

▶ Get study groups started and decide how to help study groups succeed.

▶ Plan for coaching and peer coaching.

▶ Plan data retreats.

▶ Decide how to work with new teachers.

▶ Discuss strategies for developing partnerships with parents.

▶ Reflect on what is working within the school as well as what needs attention in the reform effort (more follows about this).

Roles and Goals

Look at data. The leadership team needs to bring existing school data to the teaching staff so the entire group can set priorities for whole-group meetings and study group sessions. (We'll discuss the tools for assessment more in Chapter 6.) Sources of data important to consider include:

▶ *Student data.* School data, district-mandated data, and state-mandated data on students' reading abilities need to be considered. In addition, teachers need to share their thoughts about particularly problematic areas for their students. (See an example in Figure 5–3. Student data is covered in detail in Chapter 6.)

▶ *Data on teaching.* Before embarking on professional learning in study groups related to effective reading instruction, teachers may want to reflect on their teaching. How to use data on teaching is covered in Chapter 6. The descriptions of instruction in Chapter 6 (Figure 6–2) and the checklists of effective teaching practices (Figures 6–3 and 6–4) will help teachers identify strengths and weaknesses in their classroom reading instruction. Figure 5–4 shows samples of these assessment tools.

▶ *Data on schoolwide collaboration and school climate.* In the SCR process, schools collect data on the degree to which collaboration among all staff members and a positive school climate are developing in the building. The self-study survey (see Figure 6–5) was designed to collect this information. Schools also can use a rubric (see Figure 6–6) to look at the degree to which the SCR process is moving forward effectively.

The form in Figure 5–3 has been used to collect data on students' reading abilities and to help schools take a look at the match between assessment data, core instruction, and interventions and/or supplemental instruction provided to students.

List under regular instruction the programs or materials used and the most important areas of reading being covered by these programs (e.g., list fluency for Read Naturally, a program designed to develop students' fluency). List interventions

Matching Instruction to Data (MINTODA)

Grade _____   Instruction

Regular instruction for all	
Changes to regular instruction and dates	

Grade _____   Indicators of Student's Reading Ability and Interventions/Supplemental Instruction to be Listed Below

	In Need of Reading Intervention	**Making Adequate Progress**	**Performing Above Average**
Fall benchmark scores			
Fall interventions/ supplemental instruction			
Students for fall interventions/ supplemental instruction			
Winter benchmark scores			
Winter/spring interventions/ supplemental instruction			
Students for winter/spring interventions/ supplemental instruction			
Spring benchmark scores			
Students at each level in spring			

Catching Schools © 2011 by Barbara M. Taylor (Heinemann: Portsmouth, NH).

Figure 5–3 Matching Instruction to Data (MINTODA)

Rubric to Describe Classroom Reading Instruction

NOTE: Select the number (1, 2, or 3) that best describes a particular component of your reading instruction in a typical week.

1 Balance in Word Recognition and Comprehension Skill/Strategy Instruction (Taylor 2008; Taylor et al. 2003)

1	2	3
Most of the comprehension and word recognition work that is observed is focusing on the teaching of a skill (e.g., understanding a concept such as main idea, learning a sound that goes with a letter, learning a word meaning). Little or no strategy instruction is observed.	Much of the comprehension and word recognition work that is observed is focusing on the teaching of a skill, but there is some mention of strategy use of a skill as a strategy.	Much of the comprehension and word recognition work that is observed is focusing on the teaching of a strategy (e.g., talk and/or practice about how to use a set of procedures when reading independently to read more successfully). Some skill instruction is observed as well.

Comments:

2 Balance Between Low-Level Questioning/High-Level Questioning (Taylor 2008; Taylor et al. 2003)

1	2	3
Most questions that the teacher is posing or that students are generating are at a lower level of thinking (e.g., students do not have to think very hard to come up with the answer, and there tends to be "one right answer").	Many questions that the teacher is posing or that students are generating are at a lower level of thinking, but some are at a higher level.	Many of the questions that the teacher is posing or that students are generating are at a higher level of thinking (e.g., students do have to think for a while before they come up with the answer, and there tends to be "more than one right answer"). The teacher spends at least as much time or more of time on higher level as lower level questions.

Comments:

3 Teacher Actions: Directed Stance/Student Support Stance (Taylor 2008; Taylor et al. 2003)

1	2	3
Most teacher actions are from a teacher-directed stance (e.g., telling, leading a recitation).	Many teacher actions are from a teacher-directed stance but there is some evidence of a student support stance being used as well.	The teacher has a good balance between using a teacher-directed stance (e.g., telling, leading a recitation) and student support stance (e.g., modeling, coaching, listening, watching, and giving feedback).

Comments: *continues*

Motivational Elementary Reading Instruction Checklist
(influenced by Pressley et al. 2003)

Part 1

Teachers who provide motivational instruction engage in the practices that follow. (This list is not exhaustive. See Pressley et al. [2003] for similar and additional research-based examples of motivational practices as well as practices that undermine motivation.) Reflect on your instruction in general and put a check mark by strengths and select two or more unchecked items as goals for the year. Discuss this checklist with your literacy coach/coordinator or external partner. (This checklist could be tied to reflections on observations or videos prepared for study groups.)

Physical Environment

▸ There are many interesting books in the room and they are easily accessible.

▸ A great deal of student work is displayed in the room.

Classroom Atmosphere

▸ There is a positive, inviting atmosphere in the room; the teacher regularly interacts with her students in a positive manner.

▸ The teacher has high expectations for students and provides regular encouragement for students to meet these high expectations.

▸ The teacher fosters cooperative learning, student independence, and student persistence, and she provides for student choice when possible.

▸ The teacher is interested in and enthusiastic about learning and fosters this interest and enthusiasm in her students.

▸ The teacher values and enjoys her students, and this is apparent to her students.

Classroom Reading Instruction

▸ The teacher focuses on academic work and the value of education.

▸ The teacher provides worthwhile, well-planned, well-organized, and well-taught challenging lessons.

▸ The teacher focuses on students' understanding of and reflection on their learning.

▸ The teacher diligently monitors students' engagement in, understanding of, and behavior related to learning activities.

▸ The teacher structures learning activities that are not too hard or too easy for students and differentiates instruction as needed.

▸ The teacher provides ample opportunities for high-level thinking, including interpretive, critical, and creative thinking; strategy use; and active pupil involvement in learning activities.

▸ The teacher provides effective feedback.

▸ The teacher regularly makes relevant home connections.

Classroom Management

▸ The teacher along with her students establishes, revisits, and expects accountability to classroom rules, routines, procedures, and she fosters students' self-regulation in use of these rules, routines, and procedures.

▸ The teacher makes use of intrinsic rewards that stimulate students.

▸ Teacher praises specific accomplishments.

Observation Recording Form for Elements of Practice for Classroom Reading Instruction

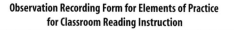

Number of Observation Segments _____

Put an X for each 5-minute segment in which a variable is observed and add comments	Variable (code)	Description
	Whole Class or Large Group (lg)	All of the children in the class (except for one or two or individuals working with someone else), or a group of more than ten children. If there are ten or less in the room, code this as a small group.
	Small Group (sg)	Children are working in two or more groups. If there are more than ten children in a group, call this whole group.
	Phonemic Awareness Instruction (pa)	Students are identifying the sounds in words or blending sounds together (an oral activity). The purpose is to develop phonemic awareness, not letter–sound knowledge.
	Phonics Instruction (phon)	Students are focusing on symbol/sound correspondences, or letter-by-letter decoding, or decoding by onset and rime or analogy, or decoding multisyllabic words. However, this is not tied to decoding of words while reading.
	Word-Recognition Strategies (wrs)	Students are focusing on use of one or more strategies to figure out words while reading, typically prompted by the teacher.
	Lower-Level Text Comprehension (talk or writing about text) (llq)	Students are engaged in talk (m1) or writing (m2) about the meaning of text that is at a lower level of thinking. The writing may be a journal entry about the text requiring a lower level of thinking or may be a fill-in-the-blank worksheet that is on the text meaning (rather than on comprehension skill or vocabulary words).
	Higher-Level Text Comprehension (talk or writing about text) (hlq)	Students are involved in talk (m3) or writing (m4) about the meaning of text that is engaging them in higher-level thinking. This is talk or writing about text that is challenging to the children and is at either a high level of text interpretation or goes beyond the text: generalization, application, evaluation, aesthetic response. Needless to say, a child must go beyond a yes or no answer (e.g., in the case of an opinion or aesthetic response).
	Comprehension Skill Instruction (cskl)	Students are engaged in a comprehension activity (other than a comprehension strategy) which is at a lower level of thinking (e.g., traditional skill work such as identifying main idea, cause-effect, fact-opinion).

continues

Catching Schools © 2011 by Barbara M. Taylor (Heinemann: Portsmouth, NH).

Figure 5–4 *Tools to Use to Reflect on Instruction*

being used with students who are struggling with word recognition and/or fluency. Also, list supplemental instruction being provided to all students in the areas of comprehension and/or vocabulary.

Use the existing school improvement plan. Typically, there is no need to start a school-based reading improvement effort from scratch. If you have already put considerable effort into developing a school improvement plan, weave in aspects of it here. For example, your school improvement plan may include a mandate to improve students' reading scores. You may already have made in-roads on improving students' fluency based on professional development received the previous year, but you are still worried about students' comprehension. This would suggest that a good topic for professional development in the upcoming year would be comprehension strategies instruction or instruction focusing on students' high-level talk and writing about texts.

Schedule and plan large-group meetings. A proposed yearlong schedule for monthly whole-group meetings needs to be presented at an early fall meeting. Monthly whole-group meetings are an important part of a school's reading improvement effort and the professional learning process. These meetings are also important in fostering a collaborative work environment across the school. During whole-group meetings, individual study groups can share what they are learning, a teacher might model a new skill or strategy related to effective reading instruction, teachers can look at or share data, and the entire group can celebrate the successes they are experiencing as a school.

Early on, processes used in the SCR model can be introduced and practiced at whole-group meetings. Processes include learning how to:

▶ collect, record, and use data on a common set of pupil assessments (Chapter 6)

▶ participate in effective data retreats (Chapter 6)

▶ engage in video sharing (Chapter 7)

▶ use the protocol for looking at student work (Chapter 7)

▶ participate in coaching and peer coaching sessions (Chapter 8)

▶ use the protocol for visiting another teacher's classroom (Chapter 8)

▶ use other school improvement processes as the need for them arises

These meetings are also excellent forums for discussing schoolwide issues related to reading instruction. A group may want to react to the work of a subgroup charged with aligning standards, curriculum, and assessments. Or teachers might adjust the school reading program based on schoolwide data. For example, toward the end of a school year, the group might debate ways to restructure time and human resources related to reading instruction to maximize students' success the following year. Figure 5–5 includes topics for whole-group meetings.

Whole-Group Meeting Conversations

Possible Conversations About the School's Current Reading Program

▶ Discuss the strengths and weaknesses of different delivery models and consider possible changes to the delivery models used at different grade levels. (See Figures 5–6 and 5–7.)

▶ Discuss blocks of time and amounts of time for reading instruction at different grade levels and make changes as needed, (See Figures 5–6 and 5–7.)

▶ Establish common planning times for classroom teachers and special teachers of reading who work together to deliver reading instruction to students.

▶ Consider the effectiveness of interventions in place for struggling readers, the research behind these interventions, and possible new interventions to put in place to better meet students' needs.

▶ Consider the recommendations of work groups focusing on curriculum/instruction/assessment coherence in the school reading program (e.g., school, district, and state standards and assessments, Common Core State Standards for English Language Arts led by the Council of Chief State School Officers and the National Governors Association; also see Resnick and Hampton 2009; Hampton and Resnick 2009).

▶ Consider the recommendations of a work group on developing parent partnerships.

Possible Conversations About Deliberate Use of Data
(Also see Chapter 6.)

▶ Agree on times for and activities to engage in during data retreats. (Discussed later. Also see Figure 5–3.)

▶ Three times a year share whole-school data on students' reading progress.

▶ Share data on classroom reading instruction, including changes in practice, that have had a positive impact.

▶ Share data on school-level collaboration and climate and decide how to deal with problem areas.

Possible Conversations About Effective Reading Instruction
(See Chapters 2 and 3 for relevant summaries.)

▶ Share research-based ideas and successes from study groups as well as practical classroom applications.

▶ Learn about a common aspect of reading instruction in a whole-group meeting and agree to apply this in the classroom (e.g., classroom-based assessments in reading, delivering motivating instruction, making good instructional choices from teacher manuals). Additional examples of professional learning activities well suited to whole-group meetings related to effective instruction are provided in Chapter 7).

▶ Share effective independent activities for students while the teacher is working with reading groups.

▶ View and discuss a video of an effective teacher of reading.

▶ Discuss a common support topic that one or more study groups are focusing on (e.g., working effectively with ELLs, techniques for differentiating instruction). Often, all study groups within a school decide to focus on the same support topic for a half-year or full year. More examples of support topics that schools have found to be useful are in Figure 5–8.

Possible Conversations About the Hallmarks of Effective Schools
(Also see Chapter 4.)

▶ View and discuss a video of an effective school. (Principles in Action is one such video; go to www.mcrel.org to order it.)

▶ Discuss an article related to effective schools or effective school improvement (e.g., collective efficacy). (See a list of these articles at the end of the chapter.)

Catching Schools © 2011 by Barbara M. Taylor (Heinemann: Portsmouth, NH).

Figure 5–5 *Whole-Group Meeting Conversations*

Examples of Whole-Group Activities Focusing on the Schoolwide Reading Program

(Activity 1, Examining Literacy Block Delivery Models and Activity 2, Time Spent on Reading Instruction)

Before engaging in Activities 1 and/or 2, teachers should complete the form in Figure 5–7 (also found on DVD) on time spent on reading and delivery model and bring it to the meeting or turn it in to the literacy coordinator prior to the meeting. The form asks teachers to list their daily literacy schedule to get at the amount of time they spend on reading and other aspects of literacy in a day. The form also asks teachers to describe their delivery model (e.g., the way in which they work with resource teachers) and to list the programs/materials they use for reading instruction.

Activity 1: Examining Literacy Block Delivery Models

In a study on schools beating the odds study (Taylor, Pearson, Clark, and Walpole 2000), the most effective schools used a collaborative model for reading instruction in which resource teachers came into the classroom or in one case, students went out of the classroom for an intervention. In the most effective schools, children spent 60 minutes a day in small-group reading instruction, 30 minutes a day in whole-class reading instruction, 30 minutes a day in independent reading, and 15 minutes a day in writing in response to reading.

In Year 1 of the Minnesota REA Project, researchers found further support for this "push-in" delivery model (Taylor and Peterson 2003). In contrast, a "combination" delivery model was found to be negatively related to students' reading growth. Delivery models studied included the following:

▶ Delivery Model 1–In-Class Model with Pull-Out Additional Instruction: Most students received most of their reading instruction from the classroom teacher. Some students went out to a resources teacher for additional instruction.

▶ Delivery Model 2–In-Class Model with Push-In Additional Instruction: Most students received most of their reading

instruction from the classroom teacher. Another classroom teacher or resources teacher came in to the class to work with some students.

▶ Delivery Model 3–Pull-Out, Ability-Grouped Model: Students switched classrooms for a majority of their reading instruction based on ability groups.

▶ Delivery Model 4–Combination Model: Students received at least 50 percent of their reading instruction from the classroom teacher (usually whole-class instruction), but almost all students also left the classroom for ability-grouped instruction (usually for 30–55 minutes).

Specifically, in grade 1, Delivery Model 2 (In-Class Model with Push-In Additional Instruction) was positively related to students' growth in reading comprehension (Gates)*, decoding (Gates), and fluency. Delivery Model 4 (Combination Model) was negatively related to students' growth in comprehension (Gates) and decoding (Gates).

In grades 2 and 3, Delivery Model 2 (In-Class Model with Push-In Additional Instruction) was positively related to students' growth in reading comprehension (Gates). Delivery Model 4 (Combination Model) was negatively related to students' growth in comprehension (Gates), vocabulary, and fluency. Delivery Model 3 (Pull-Out, Ability-Grouped Model) was negatively related to students' growth in comprehension as measured by the maze test. Additionally, more time spent on reading instruction was positively related to growth in vocabulary.

These findings do not tell us that all schools should use Delivery Model 2. However, we do think that schools should reflect on the delivery model(s) they are using and consider whether a different delivery model would serve their children better than the model(s) currently in use. Also, all models have strengths and

continues

---

* Gates-MacGinitie Reading Texts

Catching Schools © 2011 by Barbara M. Taylor (Heinemann: Portsmouth, NH).

Figure 5–6a Examples of Whole-Group Activities Focusing on the Schoolwide Reading Program

Examples of Whole-Group Activities Focusing
on the Schoolwide Reading Program, *continued*

weaknesses, and the weaknesses of any model should be addressed.

Discuss the strengths and weaknesses of Delivery Model 4. Also discuss the strengths and weaknesses of Delivery Model 2. How can the challenges of Delivery Model 2 be overcome?

Potential Strengths and Weaknesses

Delivery Model 1. Most students receive most of their reading instruction from the classroom teacher. Some students go out to a resource teacher for additional instruction.

Strengths: _____

Weaknesses:

▸ Students lose instructional time traveling to and from the resource room. This means struggling students spend less time reading than their more advanced peers.

▸ Communication and collaboration between the classroom teacher and the specialist may not occur.

▸ Instruction may be disconnected or unrelated to the topics, vocabulary, and concepts being worked on in the grade-level classroom.

▸ Skills taught in one location may not be connected to meaningful reading and writing in the other location, making transfer difficult for the students.

▸ Other _____

Delivery Model 2. Most students receive most of their reading instruction from the classroom teacher. One or more resource teachers come in to the class to work with some students:

Strengths: _____

Weaknesses:

▸ Some adults in the classroom may not be working directly with students. (For example, one adult does whole-group instruction while the other adult in the room works with 0–2 students.)

▸ A plan may be selected in which each adult does the same 20-minute lesson with three groups of students rotating among teachers who cover different topics such as reading texts, phonics, comprehension or vocabulary skill sheets, leading to disjointed instruction. Teachers may not differentiate their lesson for the various needs and abilities of the students.

▸ Children may not be reading or writing enough if they are doing isolated word work or phonics only in some of the small groups.

▸ Other _____

Delivery Model 3. Students switch classrooms for a majority of their reading instruction based on ability groups:

Strengths: _____

Weaknesses:

▸ Students lose instructional time traveling to and from their reading groups.

▸ Grade-level, classroom teachers (homeroom teachers) may not see their students for large portions of the school day. This makes it hard to develop a sense of community within the classroom and to integrate the other subject areas into the reading curriculum.

▸ Homeroom teachers may feel that they are not adequately informed on their students' progress in reading, which makes it difficult to communicate to parents during conferences, etc.

▸ Ability groups may be quite large so teachers do whole-group instruction instead of using small groups.

▸ Other _____

continues

Catching Schools © 2011 by Barbara M. Taylor (Heinemann: Portsmouth, NH).

Figure 5–6b Examples of Whole-Group Activities Focusing on the Schoolwide Reading Program, continued

Examples of Whole-Group Activities Focusing on the Schoolwide Reading Program, *continued*

Delivery Model 4. Students receive a portion of their reading instruction from the classroom teacher (usually whole-class instruction), but almost all students also leave the classroom for ability-grouped instruction.

Strengths: _____

Weaknesses:

▸ Students lose instructional time traveling to and from their reading groups.

▸ Communication and collaboration between the homeroom teacher and the reading teacher may not occur.

▸ Ability groups may be quite large so teachers do more whole group instruction instead of using small groups.

▸ Instruction for most students by two teachers in two different locations may be disjointed.

▸ Other _____

Activity 2: Time Spent on Reading Instruction

In a study of schools beating the odds (Taylor, Pearson, Clark, and Walpole 2000), researchers found that teachers in grades 1 through 3 in successful schools spent 134 minutes per day on reading instruction, exclusive of writing, spelling, or the teacher reading aloud to students for literature appreciation. Children in these schools averaged 28 minutes a day on independent reading. In contrast, teachers in less successful schools spent 113 minutes a day on reading and children spent 19 minutes a day in independent reading. Sufficient time spent on reading alone does not guarantee that students will all learn to read well. However, it is an important component of effective reading instruction.

Questions for Reflection

1. How much time are you spending on literacy instruction? Is it enough? If not, what can be done about it? Is it uninterrupted time?

2. Do you notice that you are spending more time or less time on some aspects of literacy instruction than others? Is this too much time? Too little time? What can be done to increase time on aspects of reading that need more attention?

3. As an example of the concern of possibly spending too much time for some students on some components of reading, Taylor et al. (2005) found that in grade 2 through 5 classrooms in which relatively high levels of phonics instruction and practice were observed, children on average showed less growth in reading. The National Reading Panel Report (2000) stated:

The conclusion drawn is that systematic phonics instruction produces the biggest impact on growth in reading when it begins in kindergarten or 1st grade before children have learned to read independently. . . . However, phonics instruction failed to exert a significant impact on the reading performance of low-achieving readers in 2nd through 6th grades. . . . Programs that focus too much on the teaching of letter–sounds relations and not enough on putting them to use are unlikely to be very effective. In implementing systematic phonics instruction, educators must keep the end in mind and ensure that children understand the purpose of learning letter-sounds and are able to apply their skills in their daily reading and writing abilities (2-133, 2-135).

Given these research findings, how much phonics instruction and practice are you providing? Is it all needed in grades 2 and 3 or above?

References

Taylor, B. M., P. D. Pearson, K. Clark., and S. Walpole. 2000. "Effective Schools and Accomplished Teachers: Lessons About Primary Grade Reading Instruction in Low-Income Schools." Elementary School Journal 101(2): 121–66.

Taylor, B. M., and D. S. Peterson. 2003. Year 3 Report of the CIERA School Change Project. Minneapolis: University of Minnesota, Minnesota Center for Reading Research.

Figure 5–6c Examples of Whole-Group Activities Focusing on the Schoolwide Reading Program, continued

Questions on Reading Instruction by Grade Level

Teacher _____ Grade_____

List your general literacy schedule (approximate across classrooms). For example, 9:00–9:30—whole-class reading, 9:30–10:30—guided reading, 10:30–11:00—writer's workshop

*Time Spent on Reading—The average amount of time spent on reading instruction, exclusive of language arts instruction, at a grade level within a school.

**Time Spent on Language Arts—The average amount of time spent on language arts instruction (e.g., writer's workshop, spelling, grammar, handwriting), exclusive of reading instruction, at a grade level within a school.

Indicate which of the following best describes the approach to delivery of reading instruction in your classroom (pick only one).

___ **Delivery Model 1**   *In-Class Model with Pull-Out Additional Instruction*

Most students received most of their reading instruction from the classroom teacher. Some students went out to a resources teacher for additional instruction.

___ **Delivery Model 2**   *In-Class Model with Push-In Additional Instruction*

Most students received most of their reading instruction from the classroom teacher. Another classroom teacher or resources teacher(s) came in to the class to work with some students.

___ **Delivery Model 3**   *Pull-Out, Ability-Grouped Model*

Students switched classrooms for a majority of their reading instruction based on ability groups.

___ **Delivery Model 4**   *Combination Model*

Students received at least 50 percent of their reading instruction from the classroom teacher (usually whole-class instruction), but almost all students also left the classroom for ability-grouped instruction (usually for 30–55 minutes).

___ **Other.** Please describe: _____

_____

_____

List major programs/materials used for reading instruction for grade level in question.

Program/Material   **Used with whom**

Figure 5–7 Questions on Reading Instruction by Grade Level

Get study groups underway. A proposed yearlong schedule for study group sessions, along with proposed study group topics, should also be presented at an early fall whole-group meeting. Therefore, during the summer before the first year of the project or at the very beginning of the school year, the leadership team needs to develop an initial plan for study groups for the upcoming school year. After studying various sources of data, as previously described, the leadership team should generate and circulate a list of possible study group topics to all teachers. At a whole-group meeting, teachers should review the study group plan, look at and discuss data, and add overlooked items to the list of possible study group topics. People should then select their first, second, and third choices for the study groups in which they would like to participate.

Study groups need to focus on substantive topics for extended periods of time (four, five, or six months, or perhaps longer). Teachers need sufficient opportunities to research and discuss selected topics, implement new techniques in their classrooms, and evaluate the impact of these changes over time. (Read the sidebars on this page and Figure 5–8.)

EXCELLENT TOPICS FOR TEACHER STUDY GROUPS

Choose topics carefully! Teachers will talk about and try out instructional ideas for four to six months, so you need to select a topic that is complex and that clearly leads to better reading instruction. In our research (Taylor et al. 2003, 2005, 2007), my colleagues and I found these techniques to be especially helpful in affecting change:

- Learning to ask students high-level questions about what they have read.

- Coaching children to use word recognition strategies as they are reading (e.g., helping students apply phonics to text).

- Teaching comprehension strategies in addition to comprehension skills.

TYPES OF TOPICS THAT ARE LIKELY TO STALL OUT

- **Reading-center activities.** While this is a good topic to cover over lunch or at a grade-level meeting, it isn't rich enough to be sustained over several months, nor is it likely to lead to important changes in reading instruction and in turn to significant gains in students' reading achievement.

- **Leveling trade books in the classroom library.** At first glance this seems sufficiently central to students' reading achievement and complex enough to warrant study over time. Pursuing it in a study group would no doubt improve teachers' ability to match young readers to just-right books, but it would do little to help teachers make substantive changes in the crucial aspects of reading—the "what" and "how" covered in Chapters 2 and 3. Leveling books is perhaps something to work on over the summer, if resources are available.

Possible Study Group Topics and Questions for Evaluating a Potential Topic to Be Studied Over Time in a Study Group

Main Reading Topics

▶ Comprehension Strategies (e.g., comprehension strategy routines, improving inferential comprehension, connecting reading comprehension strategy assessment and instruction)

▶ Comprehension Questioning (e.g., promoting high-level thinking through discussions and writing about text, connecting reading comprehension assessment and instruction focused on high-level thinking)

▶ Vocabulary (e.g., teaching word meanings during and after reading, teaching strategies to learn word meanings, developing students' word consciousness)

▶ Emergent Literacy (e.g., balancing phonemic awareness instruction, phonics instruction, and literature/comprehension instruction, and vocabulary development in kindergarten)

▶ Word Recognition (e.g., balancing explicit phonics instruction and word recognition coaching during reading)

▶ Fluency (e.g., providing varied approaches to fluency instruction in Grades 1–2, deciding who needs explicit fluency practice)

Support Topics (secondary focus during study group work)

▶ Providing motivating instruction

▶ Teaching ELL students effectively

▶ Teaching struggling readers effectively

▶ Conducting useful classroom-based assessments

▶ Developing parent partnerships

Questions for Evaluating the Usefulness of a Potential Study Group Topic

1. Does the technique have research citations? (Also consult the IRA publication, *What Is Evidenced-Based Reading Instruction?*, www.reading.org.)

   a. Yes.

   b. No. Check reference citations very carefully before deciding on whether to study this technique.

2. Check the research support for the actual technique. Is the technique based on research or directly supported by research?

   a. Is the reference citation a research journal article? Yes.

   b. Is the reference citation a textbook or non-research-based journal article? Yes. In this case, this may not be a research-based technique or a directly supported-by-research-based technique. Consult reference citation(s) for further information before deciding on whether to study this technique, or choose another technique to study.

   c. If neither a nor b is selected, you may need to come up with another topic as the one selected may not be a substantial, research-based topic.

3. If the technique is research-based or directly supported by research, is it likely to significantly improve your students' reading ability? Is it worth studying for multiple sessions?

   a. Yes.

   b. No.

You should either have "yes" for question 1 or have determined in question 2 that the technique is based on or directly supported by research. You should have "yes" for question 3. If you have a "no" for question 3, you may wish to consider the topic at a single study group meeting along with a major instructional technique. But first and foremost, you should be studying a substantive technique in a study group that continues for multiple study group sessions.

Catching Schools © 2011 by Barbara M. Taylor (Heinemann: Portsmouth, NH).

Figure 5–8 Possible Study Group Topics and Questions for Evaluating a Potential Topic to Be Studied Over Time in a Study Group

Help study groups succeed. If every study group includes a leadership team member as a participant, study groups that are struggling can be readily identified. Steps to maximize the success of study groups can be discussed and plans to support study groups can be agreed on. Leadership team members should be on the lookout for four types of problems: (1) teachers are not studying major, research-validated topics; (2) teachers are not sticking with topics for a half year or longer; (3) study groups are primarily grade level rather than cross grade; and (4) study group members are not moving beyond discussion to concrete reflection (e.g., sharing videos of their teaching or looking at student work) and action to modify their teaching. (Study groups and ways to maximize their effectiveness are discussed in greater detail in Chapter 7.)

Support new teachers. Leadership team members will need to present an overview of the SCR process (see Chapter 4) and an overview of effective reading instruction (see Chapters 2 and 3) to teachers new to the school. These teachers should understand the process for school-based reading improvement that the school is using and the vision of effective instruction that teachers are working toward. Leadership team members might encourage new teachers to visit classrooms to where research-based instructional techniques are in use.

Develop parent partnerships. Successful schools foster partnerships with parents, respect cultural differences, and promote community involvement (Taylor 2002). To increase parent participation, teachers and administrators need to make parents feel like welcome partners in their children's education. Researched-based books by Christenson and Sheridan (2001), Edwards (2004), and Epstein and colleagues (2002) contain excellent suggestions for developing strong parent partnerships within schools. (Refer back to Figure 5–2.)

Reflect on the school-based reading improvement process. Periodically, the leadership team needs to make sure teachers feel the program for change is worthwhile, intellectually challenging, and impacting classroom instruction. Teachers should be asked what they think is going well and indicate what needs attention to make study groups, whole-group meetings, data retreats, and the improvement effort in general more effective. Figure 5–9 shows a sample feedback form. The rubric shown in Figure 5–10, which can be used to evaluate the extent to which the important components of the improvement process, is discussed further in Chapter 6.

In addition to taking the concrete action steps set out here, leadership team members need to be cheerleaders for the school-based improvement process. They should be the first to step up to the plate and try new reform-related processes such as sharing videos of their teaching, being coached by the literacy coordinator, or coaching their colleagues. They also need to keep conversations related to the reading improvement process positive. *Leadership and Sustainability: System Thinkers in Action,* by Michael Fullan (2005), is a useful resource to help leadership team members better understand their roles as school leaders. With positive language and discussions, a group can move forward. With negative language, it is too easy for a group to get mired in the status quo.

Example of a Feedback Form to Evaluate the Strengths and Challenges of the SCR Improvement Effort

Whole-Group Meetings

What things are going well?

What things are not going well?

What suggestions do you have to make whole-group meetings more effective?

Study Group Meetings

What things are going well?

What things are not going well?

What suggestions do you have to make study group meetings more effective?

Classroom Visits by Peers and Coaching Opportunities

What things are going well?

What things are not going well?

What suggestions do you have to make classroom visits and coaching opportunities more effective?

Data Retreats (three times a year)

What things are going well?

What things are not going well?

What suggestions do you have to make data retreats more effective?

Common Grade-Level Planning Sessions and Data Meetings

What things are going well?

What things are not going well?

What suggestions do you have to make planning sessions and data sharing meetings more effective?

Leadership Team

What things are going well?

What things are not going well?

What suggestions do you have to help make the leadership team more effective?

Other Comments

Catching Schools © 2011 by Barbara M. Taylor (Heinemann: Portsmouth, NH).

Figure 5–9 Example of a Feedback Form to Evaluate the Strengths and Challenges of the SCR Improvement Effort

Additional Responsibilities of the Principal

In addition to serving on the leadership team, the principal needs to participate in whole-group meetings, study groups, and data retreats related to the SCR process. Teachers feel more supported and more positive about the reform effort when their principal is in the thick of it. As Westside Elementary's Angelina Ipson explains, "Our principal, Carla, is very supportive and leads by example. She participates in study groups and even brings a video of herself teaching a group of students. I've never seen a principal open herself to others like that."

Principals need to visit all classrooms regularly. Tricia Calhoun, the principal at Edgewood Elementary, describes her role as an instructional leader thus: "I think principals need to be aware of the instruction that's going on in their schools. I get into classrooms on a regular basis. I know what is happening in our school based on walk-throughs, longer classroom visits, scheduled observations, and formal and informal discussions with teachers."

As principals learn more about effective instruction, they become more comfortable with their role as instructional leaders. Janet Jones, the principal of Lincoln Elementary, says, "I see myself as the instructional leader and manager of daily operations, but with the ultimate responsibility of making sure we provide the best educational programs possible to ensure student success. . . . [The SCR process] has been a really wonderful experience for the staff and for me personally. I now understand what good reading instruction is and how to make it happen."

There will be reluctant teachers in any reform effort, and the responsibility typically falls to the principal to help these teachers become more engaged in the process or at least keep their negative feelings from impacting the positive ideas and work of others. Teacher leaders on the leadership team may also be able to increase reluctant teachers' participation by talking with them about successes they see at the school as a result of the change efforts that are taking place.

Another responsibility of the principal is to build collaborative leadership (Fullan 2005). The literacy coordinator and leadership team members need to feel they share responsibility for the school change effort and the school reading program, not simply taking directions from the principal on the work that needs to get done.

Finally, principals should take advantage of every opportunity to participate in ongoing professional development related to reading instruction and the SCR process. They should meet with other principals who are leading their schools in similar reform efforts. By networking with other administrators, principals can share successes and get ideas about how to solve problems that will most certainly arise during the ups and downs of a multiyear school-based reading improvement effort. Edgewood Elementary Principal Tricia Calhoun comments, "University leadership sessions and

---

School Change in Reading Reform Effort Rubric

Please Note: For most of the reform effort variables, a school receives 1 point if the item is fulfilled at least 80 percent of the time (unless other criteria are specified). The school receives 0 points if the item is fulfilled less than the specified criteria. Put a check mark by each item that is fulfilled, and count up the number of check marks for a total score. In recent SCR schools in Minnesota (n = 23), the mean reform effort score was 7 in year 1 of the SCR process, and 9 in years 2 and 3.

Reform Effort Variables

1. Study group meetings are conducted for 1 hour each week during the school year.

2. Study groups are composed of teachers and specialists across several grade levels.

3. Study group activities cause teachers to reflect on their own instructional practices, and evaluate student work and engagement. (Look for reflection on teaching through video sharing and examining student work on study group meeting notes forms.)

4. Study groups use current research to inform their discussions of instructional methods and practices. ("Using current research" was defined as using research articles and books with substantial numbers of research citations. Additional resources can be counted as "research" if they met the criteria described in the IRA position statement "What Is Evidence-Based Reading Instruction?")

5. Study groups develop action plans that cause teachers to reflect on their own instruction and examine student assessment data. The action plans show that each study group is discussing a substantive topic over time.

6. Study groups have chosen substantive topics that are based on student assessment data and current research on best practices, and they maintain these topics over many months.

7. Schools hold whole-group meetings once a month to look at assessment data, deal with schoolwide issues related to reform, and share across study groups.

8. Schools have specific schoolwide plans for involving parents as partners.

9. Schools have external facilitators who are actively involved with the reform process (i.e., Meet regularly with the internal leadership team to provide expertise and support. Visit classrooms to model lessons, observe, and give feedback).

10. Schools have internal leadership teams that meet for at least 1 hour once a month and play an active role in leadership.

Figure 5–10 School Change in Reading Reform Effort Rubric

teacher institutes have given us a lot of important new information to consider and perhaps try out in our reading lessons. I have also appreciated the time to talk with other principals, get ideas, and hear that others have been facing some of the same challenges I have had."

Coaching and Additional Responsibilities of the Literacy Coordinator

The role of taking the lead and managing the school-based reading improvement process falls to the literacy coordinator. The principal will have many other administrative duties, and leadership team members typically have full-time classroom responsibilities that prevent them from taking on the coordinator's role. Thus, a full- or half-time literacy coordinator is essential to keep whole-group meetings, study group sessions, leadership team meetings, and data retreats not only scheduled and functioning, but moving forward.

At least two-thirds of the literacy coordinator's time should be spent modeling and coaching in classrooms. However, Bean and Zigmond (2006) found that this often doesn't happen. They reported that coordinators in 161 Reading First schools in Pennsylvania spent only five hours a week observing in classrooms, modeling in classrooms, and engaging in coaching conversations with teachers. To be effective at coaching, literacy coordinators need to continually refine their learning related to effective reading instruction and engage in ongoing learning related to coaching and leadership (see Chapter 8).

The literacy coordinator should, in weekly meetings, keep the principal up-to-date on the school's successes and challenges related to the school-based reading improvement process. If the school is able to hire a part-time external consultant to work alongside the literacy coordinator, this person should attend these weekly meetings as well. An external consultant is a valuable colleague with whom the literacy coordinator can brainstorm, plan, and problem solve.

Implementation tips from SCR literacy coordinators and external consultants are presented in Figure 5–11. More support can be subscribed to by going to the School Change in Reading website at www.earlyinterventioninreading.com. Roles of the literacy coordinator related to professional learning through coaching and to changes in teaching are discussed in Chapter 8. (For additional sources of external support, see www.earlyinterventioninreading.com.)

Summary

The SCR process is hard work. But as seen from participant comments, it can be a rewarding experience. Janet Jones, the principal at Lincoln Elementary, exclaims, "I'm almost grieving that [the project is over]. . . . If people put their hearts and souls into something, good things will follow. . . . We're basically going to replicate every piece of the process and continue with the systems we've learned. We are also going to be a demonstration school for other schools in the district so they can learn and we can share with reality and honesty. The project changed the way staff thinks about instruction; it changed relationships in a good way; and it gave everyone confidence, pride, and satisfaction in their work."

Tips for Literacy Coordinators and External Consultants in Schools Using the SCR Process

The following tips are from former literacy coordinators and external consultants who helped the SCR process move forward effectively.

Getting Staff on Board

▶ At a staff meeting early in the school year, ask staff to brainstorm about all the concerns that they have, record this information, and categorize the concerns. Use this information to help address concerns and set priorities for the year. (The self-study survey found in Chapter 6 will give you this information, too.)

▶ Make sure the staff has adequate time to make informed decisions. Allow staff time to talk informally about their commitment to the project.

▶ You need to share specific information about *why* the school is doing this (school needs based on data). Share positive feedback often about what is being done and what is going well. Start with baby steps.

▶ Always begin with need, based on student performance and the self-study survey responses.

▶ Establish trust and rapport by persistently making yourself available to teachers.

▶ Always follow through when you make a promise or commitment to someone. (If you forget a time or two, you will not earn their trust and confidence.)

▶ Begin by building rapport with teachers. Describe your role in the school to the staff—you (the literacy coordinator) are there as a resource and a support, *not* as an evaluator.

▶ Be positive and let teachers know you are there to support them. Remember that change can be scary and is often viewed with fear or anxiety.

▶ "I was in a situation where even though teachers may have had some information about the framework prior to its implementation, their roles in the process were not clear. I'm not even sure that the leadership of the school knew exactly what this was all about or how it would work. It took a long time this year to build trust and understanding."

Establishing a Leadership Team

▶ Try to include representatives from each grade level and the specialists.

▶ Give the leadership team members roles and responsibilities that will allow them to evolve into teacher leaders.

▶ Have each member of the leadership team in a different study group so they can help the groups stay focused and productive.

Setting Priorities

▶ Be aware of your context and players. Know the district's focus areas, the principal's goals, students' needs (as seen in the data), and teachers' practices. Connect these needs with research recommendations.

▶ Provide lots of chocolate!

▶ Use the self-study survey to narrow the focus of our efforts in year 1.

Planning for Large Group Meetings

▶ Carefully plan each session. Have a clear agenda and distribute it to the teachers ahead of time. Keep teachers active. Build in time to reflect. Provide handouts so everyone can focus on the presentation. Review what has been accomplished.

▶ Structure the meeting to allow for maximum interaction. Allow some choice. Make sure all research presented is grounded in the practical. Be sure there is one thing teachers can take with them and try out in their classrooms.

▶ Take time to celebrate! The progress may be small, but a celebration can help to double the growth.

continues

Figure 5–11a *Tips for Literacy Coordinators and External Consultants in Schools Using the SCR Process*

Tips for Literacy Coordinators and External Consultants in Schools Using the SCR Process, *continued*

▶ At the first several whole-group meetings cover the following:

- Protocols for video sharing and sharing student work
- Roles and responsibilities/expectations of study group members
- A sample study group agenda
- Model how to write an action plan and fill in meeting note forms
- Explain to the staff the role of the Leadership Team, Literacy Coordinator, External Consultant (if you have one)

▶ Assign a study group (or ask them to volunteer) to report at each monthly whole-group meeting and have the group members share/model the strategies they have been implementing over time. Promote creativity in the sharing of study group activities. Study groups can share through brief presentations with handouts, poster sessions, and so on. Give them three guiding questions to help them as they plan their presentation:

1. What does the research say about your topic?
2. What examples of this strategy or best practice are you going to share with the whole group?
3. What would be useful for the rest of the staff to know about this topic?

Looking at Data as a School

▶ Reviewing data as a school can really make first efforts at a study topic successful. Choosing a topic that is measurable can give a study group a baseline and a benchmark. Using the data in a graphic form to show change over time is a powerful means to help teachers reflect on the progress their groups made.

▶ Data retreats must be scheduled regularly. At whole-group meetings, encourage teachers to look at data across grades and talk about moving forward as a school.

▶ Ensure that this activity is an ongoing and regular component of action research. Questions to ask:

1. What does it say to us about student performance?
2. What does it say to us about instructional need?
3. Based on the data, what strategies would most significantly impact growth?
4. What professional development is needed in order for teachers to be proficient with these practices?

▶ Use a form to analyze the data looking at four areas:

1. What do you notice about the data?
2. What questions do you have related to this data?
3. What implications does this have for the students and/or teachers?
4. What implications does this data have for the school?

Other Tips

▶ Don't layer this initiative with other major thrusts. When there are too many initiatives in place, progress is slow.

▶ Try to "market" yourself to district personnel. Let them know about the progress the school is making.

Figure 5–11b Tips for Literacy Coordinators and External Consultants in Schools Using the SCR Process, continued

Judy Hunter, the principal at Madina Elementary, comments, "I think this has been an opportunity of a lifetime. I thank the people who selected our school to participate and to learn and grow together. I look forward to sustaining our changes and maintaining our momentum for effective instruction in future years." Melissa Norris, a kindergarten teacher at Madina, says, "Involvement in the SCR process has been a very positive thing for us. It has made us step outside of our comfort zone and take some risks. We have all grown through all aspects of the reform process. I know we can see the growth in our students."

By working together on a school-based reading improvement process over several years, teachers develop a greater sense of collective efficacy in their ability to provide excellent reading instruction to their students. Teachers also develop a greater sense of self-efficacy as teachers of reading who successfully meet individual students' needs and challenge them all. As Lincoln Elementary's Kathy Little comments, "I can say that my personal teaching skills are completely different, in a good way, than what they were five years ago. [As a school], we have seen our staff grow in a way that is outstanding. We have collaboration and dedication and it has been fantastic to grow with one another. I only hope we can keep growing and do so with efforts from everyone."

talk About it

* The School Change in Reading framework focuses on three major goals in which teachers and administrators (a) improve the schoolwide delivery of reading instruction based on local needs and data; (b) work collaboratively to teach reading and reflect on and improve reading instruction through school-based, ongoing professional development; and (c) use research-based knowledge on effective teaching practices, school reform, effective schools, and effective teachers to guide their efforts. Discuss the challenges and benefits of working toward each of these goals.

* Does your school have the necessary administrative and teacher leadership capacity and would you have sufficient teacher buy-in to succeed with a significant schoolwide reading improvement effort such as the one outlined in this chapter?

* Do teachers at your school feel energized by the concept of collaborative, school-based, intellectually stimulating, reflective professional development? Why or why not? If not, what are the barriers?

* Does your school have the "right stuff" to begin on such a reading improvement effort as described in this chapter? What else do people need to know to decide?

Recommended Readings for Implementing a Schoolwide Plan for Reading Improvement

Leadership and School Change

Allington, R. L., and S. A. Walmsley, eds. 2007. *No Quick Fix: Rethinking Literacy Programs in America's Elementary Schools* (RTI ed.). New York: Teachers College Press.

Fullan, M. 2005. *Leadership and Sustainability: Systems Thinkers in Action.* Thousand Oaks, CA: Corwin.

Goddard, R. D., W. K. Hoy, and A. W. Hoy. 2004. "Collective Efficacy Beliefs: Theoretical Development, Empirical Evidence, and Future Directions." *Educational Researcher 33*(3): 3–13.

Hasbrouck, J., and C. Denton. 2005. *The Reading Coach: A How-To Manual for Success.* Boston: Sopris West.

Hawley, W. D., and D. L. Rollie, eds. 2007. *The Keys to Effective Schools: Educational Reform as Continuous Improvement.* 2nd ed. Washington, DC: National Education Association.

Taylor, B. M., D. P. Pearson, D.S. Peterson, and M. C. Rodriguez. 2005. "The CIERA School Change Framework: An Evidence-Based Approach to Professional Development and School Reading Improvement." *Reading Research Quarterly* 40(1): 40–69.

Taylor, B. M., D. S. Peterson, M. Marx, and M. Chein. 2007. "Scaling Up a Reading Framework for Prevention and Identification of Students with Reading/Learning Disabilities." In *Effective Instruction for Struggling Readers K–6,* ed. B. M. Taylor and J. E. Ysseldyke, 216–34. New York: Teachers College Press.

Professional Learning

Hasbrouck, J., and C. Denton. 2005. *The Reading Coach: A How-To Manual for Success.* Boston: Sopris West.

Murphy, C., and D. Lick. 2005. *Whole-Faculty Study Groups: Creating Student-Based Professional Development.* 3rd ed. Thousand Oaks, CA: Corwin.

Walpole, S., and M. C. McKenna. 2004. *The Literacy Coach's Handbook: A Guide to Research-Based Practice.* New York: Guilford.

York-Barr, J., W .A. Sommers, G. S. Ghere, and J. Montie. 2006. *Reflective Practice to Improve Schools: An Action Guide for Educators.* 2nd ed. Thousand Oaks, CA: Corwin.

Assess

● ●

Using Data to Inform Your Practice

*H*ow are the students doing? How are we first-grade teachers doing? How did the
students do on that last assessment, after six weeks with a new focus on explicit
comprehension strategy instruction? Questions like these need to be a part of
how we move forward as a school. The concept of getting more "data-driven" can
seem intimidating or not child centered, perhaps because of the cautionary tales we
all hear about schools that fall into a teach-to-the-test mentality to the point that
engaging effective instruction gets sidelined. In this chapter, I share ideas for schools
to put data at the center of their reform in ways that are constructive, authentic, and
common sense. After all, what practitioner doesn't reflect on the techniques and
materials of his or her trade? Whether surgeon or chef, teacher or carpenter, professionals examine the results of their work in order to do their job well. We have to
help teachers become expert and confident in looking at and evaluating data. In the
School Change in Reading (SCR) process, you learn to look at data at three levels:

▶ student data

▶ teacher data

▶ school data

Teachers and administrators undertaking the SCR process comment that looking at data at these three levels makes it easier for them to recognize just where instructional changes are needed, and then track how these changes impact students' reading abilities. These three lenses help everyone drill down deeper, too, using the collective power of the group to see which students are excelling, which are struggling and why, and what texts and additional support might help them. Getting this highly differentiated look at individual students is worth its weight in gold, because students are less likely to slide by in a sea of data, unsupported as readers. Anna Berglund, the literacy coordinator at Edgewood Elementary, explains, "We are paying more attention to individual student data and the need to differentiate instruction to help individual students. We find that the most frequent assessments impact instruction the most because we can see what students are doing and adjust instruction if we need to. Also, we're being more intentional about choosing materials; we are looking at individual student data and thinking about what types of reading materials specific students need instead of just focusing on a group."

Student Data: Getting Good at Knowing Each Student's Progress

Purposeful use of student data helps teachers become more responsive. They can adjust their instruction to improve student achievement (Hamilton et al. 2009). Teachers have a great deal of data regarding students' reading ability that is collected for district and state purposes. However, a school faculty may also agree to administer additional classroom-based assessments that will help them best determine students' reading progress and diagnose the problems of struggling readers. Sometimes called informal assessments, these are teacher-friendly checklists, rubrics, criteria lists, and activities that can easily be embedded into daily classroom teaching and learning. They help teachers gauge and reflect on the effectiveness of their reading instruction. For example, if a fourth-grade teacher is teaching her students how to summarize informational text, she can use a rubric itemizing the qualities of excellent, good, typical, and poor summaries at the fourth-grade level to evaluate the quality of her students' summaries. If most students' summaries are below grade-level expectations, the teacher can ask herself (and her colleagues) what she might do next to improve students' summarizing abilities.

Augmenting these assessments, teachers need to gather to look across their grades at data—in the sections that follow, I describe how it plays out across the year:

Systematically collect student data three times a year across the school. Effective schools develop schoolwide reading assessment plans in order to use student data productively. In the SCR process, you'll want to collect data at least three times during a school year. This student data is used to identify students who are reading above, at, and below grade level. As a group, look at Figure 6–1 and discuss its features, thinking about how you can adapt it for your school. It shows:

▶ A grade 1 MINTODA (**M**atching **In**struction **to Da**ta) form that teachers can use to look at students' reading growth three times a year and consider what instruction or instructional changes might best move students forward, based on their needs and strengths.

Assessment Plan Used in SCR Schools

1. Use Spring and Fall data to place all students under appropriate categories of the Matching Instruction to Data (MINTODA) Forms.

2. Describe the regular classroom instruction, interventions (as needed), and supplemental instruction (to challenge students at their reading level in vocabulary and comprehension of narrative and informational text) on the MINTODA forms.

3. Turn in to literacy coordinator by mid- to late October.

4. Set a schedule for grade-level meetings to review students' progress. (Meetings at least once a month are recommended.)

5. Set a schedule for three times a year sharing of data by grade level and class on students' progress at whole-group meetings.

   a. November sharing could focus on students' comprehension scores on the district's standardized test from previous spring (below, on, and above grade level based on scores on MINTODA forms) and/or Fall words correct per minute (wcpm) scores in grades 2 and 3 and plans for instruction. Sharing could focus on Fall letter sound scores in kindergarten and fall phonemic awareness scores in grade 1 and plans for instruction (on MINTODA forms).

   b. February sharing could focus on growth in fluency (word correct per minute, wcpm) and plans for instruction.

   c. May sharing could focus on students' growth in standardized reading scores, short answer scores, or summary scores in grades 1 through 3 or phonemic awareness scores in kindergarten. Suggestions for instructional changes for the next school year should be included.

Catching Schools © 2011 by Barbara M. Taylor (Heinemann: Portsmouth, NH).

Figure 6–1 Assessment Plan Used in SCR Schools

Matching Instruction to Data (MINTODA) Form

This form has been used to help schools take a look at the match between assessment data and interventions and/or supplemental instruction provided to students. This is an excellent tool for Response to Intervention work. Sample programs listed here are not being endorsed; they are simply provided as examples.

List under regular instruction the programs or materials used and the most important areas of reading being covered by these programs (e.g., list fluency for Read Naturally, a program designed to develop students' fluency). List interventions being used with students who are struggling with word recognition and/or fluency. Also, list supplemental instruction being provided to all students in the areas of comprehension and/or vocabulary.

Areas of Reading:

PA = Phonemic Awareness

P = Phonics

WR = Word-Recognition Strategies

F = Fluency

V= Vocabulary

CS = Comprehension Strategy

C = Comprehension Skill Practice

HLQ = High-Level Talk and Writing About Text

LLQ = Low-Level Talk and Writing About Text

Students Receiving Extra Support

Ti = Title I

Sp = Special Education

El = ELL

NCE = normal curve equivalent score

Catching Schools © 2011 by Barbara M. Taylor (Heinemann: Portsmouth, NH).

Figure 6–1, continued

Examples of a Completed Matching Instruction to Data (MINTODA) Form

Grade 1 Instruction

Regular instruction for all	**Houghton Mifflin Basal Reader**–All areas of reading **Leveled Texts**–WR, F, LLQ, HLQ **Phonics Library**–P, WR **Trade Books**–C, CS, LLQ, HLQ, V
Changes to regular instruction and dates	

Grade 1 Indicators of Student's Reading Ability and Interventions/Supplemental Instruction Provided

	In need of a systematic early reading intervention program	Making adequate progress in word recognition and fluency; on target (based on spring comp. scores) to pass grade 3 state test)	Performing above average in word recognition and fluency; probably not in need of explicit word ID work extra fluency work (by midyear In top third (national norms) in comprehension
Fall	If 5 or less on PA test. If DIBELS LNF<25 (LNF = letter name fluency)	If scoring more than 7 on PA test in Sept. If DIBELS LNF>=37	If reading at 40–50 words correct per minute (wcpm).
Fall interventions/ supplemental instruction	**Early Intervention in Reading (EIR)**— covers PA, P, WR, F, HLQ, V (for Ti and El students) **Direct Instruction**—covers PA, P (used with Sp students) **Ready Readers**—covers WR, F, LLQ, HLQ (for El and Sp students)	**Read Naturally**—focuses on F	**National Geographic Readers**—deals with V, LLQ, HLQ, CS **Research reports**—focuses on CS, HLQ, V
Students for fall interventions/ supplemental instruction	**Room 12** Tyler T. (Sp) Briana F. (Ti) Joua X. (El) (and others) **Room 16** Ebony P.(Ti) Cynthia B. (Sp) Jamal M. (Ti). (and others) **Room 18** Martin L. (Sp) Todd B. (Ti) (and others)	**Room 12** Arnold G. Sophie L. (and others) **Room 16** Danielle L. Nina Z. Adam B. (and others) **Room 18** Emma A. Joshua Z. (and others)	**Room 12** Noah V. (and others) **Room 16** Tyrese M. Shona F. (and others) **Room 18** Whitney T. (and others)
Winter	If reading at <25 wcpm.	If reading at 40+ wcpm.	If reading at 55–60 wcpm.
Winter/spring interventions/ supplemental instruction	Same as fall PLUS National Geographic Readers—focuses on V, LLQ, HLQ, CS	**Accelerated Reader**—focuses on F, LLQ **National Geographic Readers**—focuses on V, LLQ, HLQ, CS **Research reports**—focuses on CS, HLQ, V	Same as fall PLUS Book Clubs – (chapter books) –focuses on HLQ, V
Students for winter/spring interventions/ supplemental instruction			
Spring	If reading at < 35 wcpm. If at <46 NCE on Gates MacGinitie comprehension test	If reading at 55–60 wcpm by May. If at 45 NCE on Gates comprehension test	If reading at >70 wcpm. If at >58 NCE on Gates comprehension test

- Components of the core instructional program that teachers can share within grades to have a conversation about what components of core materials they are using to effectively cover all aspects of the reading curriculum.

- Interventions and supplemental instruction for high-, average-, and low-ability students that teachers can share to reflect on the appropriateness of the instruction beyond the core program they are providing as well as on students' reading progress. Students who are reading below grade level are then given once-a-month progress monitoring assessments (e.g., number of words read correctly per minute for students in grades 1 through 3).

(A longer version of Figure 6–1, as well as examples from grade 2 and grade 3 MINTODA forms, is presented in Appendix 6–1 on the DVD.)

Look at the data at retreats three times a year. Using the data previously described, teachers participate in data retreats at least three times a year. At these meetings that might last for a half day, teachers at each grade level identify students who are reading above, at, and below grade level in relation to standards and benchmarks developed by the state, district, or school (see Chapter 5; also see Common Core State Standards: English Language Arts, 2010; Hampton and Resnick 2009; Resnick and Hampton 2009). Based on these data, they plan their core instruction, interventions, and supplemental instruction. They also discuss changes in individual students' small-group assignments.

ʃee it iN ActioN

Data Retreat

Grade 2 classroom and resource teachers, the literacy coach, and the principal are meeting for a mid-year morning-long data retreat while substitutes are covering classrooms. To consider the reading progress of students who were below, at, and above grade level in fall, teachers compare fall scores to new reading scores in January. They also talk about the interventions and supplemental instruction that are needed to continue to move students forward. We see a second-grade teacher explaining to the principal the growth he has seen in his lower, average, and above average readers and the instructional strategies he believes have made the most difference. At the end of the retreat, teachers discuss students they are most concerned about and share suggestions regarding new instructional strategies to try next in their lessons with these students.

Attend grade-level meetings and discuss students' needs once a month. At less formal grade-level meetings, held once every four to six weeks, teachers supplement the discussions about students' reading abilities and progress that they have at the more formal data retreats. At these monthly meetings, teachers share data or work samples and ask colleagues for ideas about how to help individuals or groups of students progress. Lincoln Elementary's Kathy Little reports, "Our monthly student progress meetings, where we share reading data on our students, help us focus better on what we're teaching and what modifications are needed to get our students to the next level."

Share student data at whole-group cross-grade-level meetings two or three times a year. After schools have had grade-level data retreats, it is important to share student data at whole-group meetings two or three times a year. This is a good way to review targets and successes regarding students' reading abilities throughout the grade levels. Carla Herrera, the principal at Westside Elementary offers this example: "I think there is a heavier emphasis on vocabulary development across the school based on the data at each grade level showing that our students need help in vocabulary. Also, because we share data across grade levels, all of the grades are collaboratively planning more than in the past, and teachers are more strategic in their lessons based on what students need." A summary of these meeting would look something like this:

Meeting	Purpose	Frequency	Who Goes	Classroom Actions
Data retreats	To look at students' reading progress formal assessments, celebrate successes, discuss interventions for struggling readers, and supplemental instruction for all	Three times a year	Grade-level teams	Adjust instruction
Grade-level meetings	To share students' work or informal assessment data and discuss instructional strategies to meet students' needs	Monthly	Grade-level teams	Adjust instruction
Whole-group meetings	To share data on students' progress, review targets, celebrate successes, share instructional ideas across grade levels, develop coherences across grade levels	Three times a year, after data retreats	All grades	Adjust instruction

Identify and support students requiring systematic reading intervention. All students who struggle with reading and perform substantially below grade level will benefit from systematic reading intervention that may be delivered to a small group of students or one-on-one. Based on data retreat findings, teachers provide struggling readers with the extra support they need to become successful readers. An effective intervention program:

▶ Is research based.

▶ Consists of sound, balanced, fast-paced, engaging instructional routines provided by well-trained teachers or tutors.

▶ Arises from the belief that struggling readers can succeed if they receive effective supplemental instruction to accelerate their learning.

- Provides systematic word recognition instruction, including phonemic awareness (grade 1), letter-by-letter sequential decoding (grades 1 and 2), and other word recognition strategies (grades 1–4).

- Includes repeated or assisted reading for fluency.

- Pays attention to higher-level talk about text (grades K–5) and includes comprehension strategies instruction (grades 2–5).

- Includes regular assessment of pupil progress through progress monitoring and running records.

- Is accomplished in connection with students' parents and other caregivers.

See the following section, Catching Readers, for more on Early Intervention in Reading. See Figure 6–1 and Appendix 6–1 on the DVD for examples. Also see Beginning Reading Programs under What Works Clearinghouse (http://ies.ed.gov/ncee/wwc/) and Slavin et al. (2009) for research-validated interventions.

Identify and support students reading at or above grade level. Students who are reading at or above grade level will benefit from additional instruction and learning activities that supplement their core lessons (e.g., basal readers, guided reading), especially in the areas of comprehension and vocabulary. Teachers should regularly ask themselves, "What am I doing to challenge average and above-average students in comprehension and vocabulary through supplemental activities during independent work?" These may be extensions of basal lessons or entirely different activities. (See Figure 6–1 and Appendix 6–1 on the DVD for examples.)

CATCHING READERS
An Intervention Model That Works

As you read this book, I want you to come away with the strong impression that improving reading instruction schoolwide is as much about advancing our above-average and average readers as it is about addressing those learners at risk of reading failure. Generally speaking, we don't challenge our students intellectually, or find them ideal books, or use their reading ability to encourage them to develop their knowledge and academic capacity to its fullest potential. That said, at the heart of reading reform is reading intervention—in a sense, any reform is intervention in that we are intervening to make things better.

Long before RTI hit the scene and put differentiated teaching in the spotlight, I developed a set of teaching practices for struggling readers called Early Intervention in Reading (EIR). It's been in practice for more than 20 years and in 2010 I created a series of books for teachers called *Catching Readers: Day-by-Day Small-Group Reading Interventions* (Taylor, 2010a, 2010b, 2010c, in press) with volumes for grades K–5. I mention the series here because many of the schools I've worked with find that learning about this intervention model—using it for their professional development focus for a year—was a wonderful way to begin more complex, sweeping schoolwide reading reform. Visit Heinemann.com to learn more about it. Here are some features that make it a worthy schoolwide reform focus for the first year of SCR:

▶ It is effective in increasing the reading abilities of students who need more support to succeed in reading.

▶ It provides students struggling to read with an additional daily opportunity to interact with text in a structured, consistent, and comfortable small-group setting.

▶ It provides teachers with a consistent, clear structure that helps them support these children so they can catch up or keep up with grade-level expectations for reading.

▶ It provides teachers and schools with an intervention model that isn't stigmatizing for children because it uses authentic literature and instructional practices, and is done within the regular classroom—and usually by the classroom teacher.

▶ As shown in the table that follows, EIR dovetails with the effective reading content I address in Chapters 2 and 3.

Teacher Data: Getting Good at Looking at One's Reading Instruction

Deliberate teacher reflection is instrumental to improving reading instruction. To be able to reflect on their instruction, teachers need more than student data—they need tools and platforms that help them see into the mirror of their daily teaching. Videos of their lessons are one source of data. Notes taken by the literacy coordinator or a colleague during classroom visits are another.

Rubrics and checklists. Figure 6–2 is a rubric teachers can use to reflect on and describe their teaching according to elements of effective instruction. When used in school evaluation work, I have found 82 percent inter-rater agreement or better for the various items in the scale. Figure 6–3 includes a checklist of practices that moti-vate students during a lesson and checklist of ways to motivate student action. (Both tools can be found on the DVD.)

Teachers can also use the research-based School Change Classroom Observation Scheme (Taylor et al. 2003) to improve their reading instruction. The purpose of this observation system is to help teachers in grades K–6 analyze their instruction in relation to many of the dimensions of effective reading instruction discussed in Chapters 2 and 3: grouping practices, literacy activities and materials, styles of inter-action, expected student responses to literacy activities, rate of student engagement, and the relationship of teacher practices with growth in student achievement. The categories of practice are defined in Figure 6–4 (also on the DVD).

In a modified version to this observation scheme (one that is more practical for regular use), either you (watching a video of yourself) or an observer (visiting your classroom and writing down what is happening, including what you and children are saying and doing) account for elements of practice during a twenty- to thirty-minute lesson. Every five minutes, you or the observer draws a line across the narrative and records the number of children who appear to be on task. (See Appendix

How EIR Meets the Requirements of Effective Reading Instruction

	Effective Reading Instruction	EIR Lessons
What You Teach (Content)	Explicit phonemic awareness instruction	Sound boxes, writing for sounds in sentence writing
	Systematic phonics instruction	Scope and sequence, making words, writing for sounds in sentence writing, coaching in word-recognition strategies
	Oral reading for fluency	Repeated reading of stories, coached reading with feedback, one-on-one reading with aide or volunteer
	Text-based vocabulary instruction	Discussion of word meanings at point of contact in EIR stories
	Comprehension strategies instruction	Summarizing stories, practicing comprehension monitoring
	Comprehension instruction in the context of high-level talk about text	Coaching for high-level comprehension
How You Teach (Pedagogy)	Application of taught skills and strategies to text	Applying taught skills and strategies to text
	Differentiated instruction	Support is provided by teacher to individual students based on need
	Balance of direct teaching and providing support	Coaching students to use taught skills and strategies as they read EIR stories
	Teaching with clear purpose and good timing	Stating teaching purposes routinely, covering daily steps of each 20-minute lesson at a swift pace
	Active student engagement	All students read, write, talk, share with a partner, engage in word work
	Student engagement in challenging, motivating learning activities	Students read stories that require them to "glue to the print" from the beginning, spend only three days on a story, and move on to new challenges with a new text. EIR stories that are selected are engaging texts
	Developing independent learners	High expectations, releasing responsibility to students, partner work
	Motivating classroom community	Using praise, helpful feedback, demonstrating enthusiasm for learning
Professional Learning	Collaborative learning with a focus on practice	Monthly learning meetings to discuss EIR strategies, successes, and challenges

Catching Schools © 2011 by Barbara M. Taylor (Heinemann: Portsmouth, NH).

Rubric to Describe Classroom Reading Instruction

NOTE: Select the number (1, 2, or 3) that best describes a particular component of your reading instruction in a typical week.

1 Balance in Word Recognition and Comprehension Skill/Strategy Instruction (Taylor 2008; Taylor et al. 2003)

1	2	3
Most of the comprehension and word recognition work that is observed is focusing on the teaching of a skill (e.g., understanding a concept such as main idea, learning a sound that goes with a letter, learning a word meaning). Little or no strategy instruction is observed.	Much of the comprehension and word recognition work that is observed is focusing on the teaching of a skill, but there is some mention of strategy use of a skill as a strategy.	Much of the comprehension and word recognition work that is observed is focusing on the teaching of a strategy (e.g., talk and/or practice about how to use a set of procedures when reading independently to read more successfully). Some skill instruction is observed as well.

Comments:

2 Balance Between Low-Level Questioning/High-Level Questioning (Taylor 2008; Taylor et al. 2003)

1	2	3
Most questions that the teacher is posing or that students are generating are at a lower level of thinking (e.g., students do not have to think very hard to come up with the answer, and there tends to be "one right answer").	Many questions that the teacher is posing or that students are generating are at a lower level of thinking, but some are at a higher level.	Many of the questions that the teacher is posing or that students are generating are at a higher level of thinking (e.g., students do have to think for a while before they come up with the answer, and there tends to be "more than one right answer"). The teacher spends at least as much time or more of time on higher level as lower level questions.

Comments:

3 Teacher Actions: Directed Stance/Student Support Stance (Taylor 2008; Taylor et al. 2003)

1	2	3
Most teacher actions are from a teacher-directed stance (e.g., telling, leading a recitation).	Many teacher actions are from a teacher-directed stance but there is some evidence of a student support stance being used as well.	The teacher has a good balance between using a teacher-directed stance (e.g., telling, leading a recitation) and student support stance (e.g., modeling, coaching, listening, watching, and giving feedback).

Comments: *continues*

Catching Schools © 2011 by Barbara M. Taylor (Heinemann: Portsmouth, NH).

Figure 6–2a Rubric to Describe Classroom Reading Instruction

Rubric to Describe Classroom Reading Instruction, *continued*

4 Student Responding: Active/Passive (Taylor 2008; Taylor et al. 2003)

1	2	3
Most student actions while working with the teacher involve passive responding (e.g., reading turn-taking, oral turn-taking, listening to the teacher or another student talk).	There is some balance in student actions between passive responding (e.g., reading turn-taking, oral turn-taking, listening to the teacher or another student talk) and active responding (e.g., reading, oral responding with a partner, writing, manipulating).	There is a good balance (e.g., almost equal) in student actions involving passive responding (e.g., reading turn-taking, oral turn-taking, listening to the teacher or another student talk) and active responding (e.g., reading, oral responding with a partner, writing, manipulating).

Comments:

5 Instructional Purpose and Pacing (Taylor 2008)

1	2	3
The purposes for many lessons and activities are not readily apparent (e.g., it is not clear why this lesson or this activity is being done with these students, how it will move them forward). Many lessons and activities appear to be moving at a slower pace than necessary.	The purposes for some lessons and activities are clear but not for others. Pacing appears to be appropriate for some lessons and activities but too slow for others.	The purposes for most lessons and activities are clear (e.g., it is clear why this lesson or activity is being done with these students, how it will move them forward). Pacing appears to be appropriate for most lessons and for activities.

Comments:

6 Meeting Individual Needs (Taylor 2007)

1	2	3
Most instruction/activities appear to be very similar for all students (with the exception of having guided reading groups).	Some instruction/activities appear to be different for different students (with the exception of having guided reading groups). It is not necessarily clear on what basis the activities differ.	Many activities appear to be differentiated based on students' reading level and/or interests, etc.

Comments:

continues

Catching Schools © 2011 by Barbara M. Taylor (Heinemann: Portsmouth, NH).

Figure 6–2b Rubric to Describe Classroom Reading Instruction, continued

Rubric to Describe Classroom Reading Instruction, *continued*

7 Providing Motivation and Challenge During Independent (Non-Teacher-Led) Work Time (Taylor 2008)

1	2	3
Teacher does not appear to provide many motivating and cognitively challenging learning tasks during independent work time. Most seatwork activities appear to be at cognitively low levels (beyond independent reading for pleasure).	Teacher provides some motivating and cognitively challenging learning tasks during independent work time (beyond independent reading for pleasure). Some seatwork activities appear to be at cognitively low levels.	Teacher provides many motivating and cognitively challenging learning tasks during independent work time (Pressley et al. 2003). These tasks may include high-level talk and writing about text; high-quality literature experiences for students; student choice when possible. Seatwork activities are not at cognitively low levels.

Comments:

8 Providing a Motivating Classroom Atmosphere (Taylor 2007)

1	2	3
Teacher provides a classroom atmosphere that demonstrates few of the motivating practices identified under rubric description #3 for Item 7 (to the right).	Teacher provides a classroom atmosphere that demonstrates some of the motivating practices identified under rubric description #3 for Item 7 (to the right).	Teacher provides a motivating classroom atmosphere. Motivating practices include creating an atmosphere of warmth and concern for students, having a positive attitude toward all students; using humor in positive ways; holding high standards for students; creating a community of learners; and modeling enthusiasm for learning (Pressley et al. 2003).

Comments:

9 Providing Culturally Responsive Instruction (Taylor 2008)

1	2	3
Teacher provides little evidence of culturally responsive instruction.	Teacher provides some evidence of culturally responsive instruction.	Teacher provides strong evidence of culturally responsive instruction. She may build on students' cultural strengths in the classroom (Au 2006). She may structure interactions that depart from the typical pattern of teacher initiation, student response, teacher evaluation. She may use multicultural literature, including some works that celebrate students' own cultural heritage and others that introduce them to new cultural perspectives.

Comments:

Overall Reflections:

Catching Schools © 2011 by Barbara M. Taylor (Heinemann: Portsmouth, NH).

Figure 6–2c *Rubric to Describe Classroom Reading Instruction, continued*

Motivational Elementary Reading Instruction Checklist
(influenced by Pressley et al. 2003)

Part 1

Teachers who provide motivational instruction engage in the practices that follow. (This list is not exhaustive. See Pressley et al. [2003] for similar and additional research-based examples of motivational practices as well as practices that undermine motivation.) Reflect on your instruction in general and put a check mark by strengths and select two or more unchecked items as goals for the year. Discuss this checklist with your literacy coach/coordinator or external partner. (This checklist could be tied to reflections on observations or videos prepared for study groups.)

Physical Environment

▶ There are many interesting books in the room and they are easily accessible.

▶ A great deal of student work is displayed in the room.

Classroom Atmosphere

▶ There is a positive, inviting atmosphere in the room; the teacher regularly interacts with her students in a positive manner.

▶ The teacher has high expectations for students and provides regular encouragement for students to meet these high expectations.

▶ The teacher fosters cooperative learning, student independence, and student persistence, and she provides for student choice when possible.

▶ The teacher is interested in and enthusiastic about learning and fosters this interest and enthusiasm in her students.

▶ The teacher values and enjoys her students, and this is apparent to her students.

Classroom Reading Instruction

▶ The teacher focuses on academic work and the value of education.

▶ The teacher provides worthwhile, well-planned, well-organized, and well-taught challenging lessons.

▶ The teacher focuses on students' understanding of and reflection on their learning.

▶ The teacher diligently monitors students' engagement in, understanding of, and behavior related to learning activities.

▶ The teacher structures learning activities that are not too hard or too easy for students and differentiates instruction as needed.

▶ The teacher provides ample opportunities for high-level thinking, including interpretive, critical, and creative thinking; strategy use; and active pupil involvement in learning activities.

▶ The teacher provides effective feedback.

▶ The teacher regularly makes relevant home connections.

Classroom Management

▶ The teacher along with her students establishes, revisits, and expects accountability to classroom rules, routines, procedures, and she fosters students' self-regulation in use of these rules, routines, and procedures.

▶ The teacher makes use of intrinsic rewards that stimulate students.

▶ Teacher praises specific accomplishments.

Catching Schools © 2011 by Barbara M. Taylor (Heinemann: Portsmouth, NH).

Figure 6–3a Motivational Elementary Reading Instruction Checklist

Questions to Ask Yourself About Student Motivation
(Part 2)

Complete this form as you watch a video clip of your teaching. For all "no" or "not all" answers ask, "Why are the children not successful with this dimension? What do I need to do differently?" If you share the video in a study group, ask your colleagues for suggestions about what you might do differently.

	Yes	Not All	No	Evidence	Instructional Ideas for the Future
1. Do the students understand the learning activity?					
2. Are the students actively participating?					
3. Are the students working with/interacting with others when the activity is structured for collaboration?					
4. Are the students demonstrating self-reliance?					
5. Are the students demonstrating persistence?					
6. Are the students using strategies?					
7. Are the students thinking at a high level, including interpretive, critical and creative thought, and communicating this thinking through oral and or written responses?					
8. Are the students showing academic enthusiasm for and enjoyment in the current learning activity?					

Catching Schools © 2011 by Barbara M. Taylor (Heinemann: Portsmouth, NH).

Figure 6–3c Questions to Ask Yourself About Student Motivation (Part 2)

Observation Recording Form for Elements of Practice for Classroom Reading Instruction

Number of Observation Segments _____

Put an X for each 5-minute segment in which a variable is observed and add comments	Variable (code)	Description
	Whole Class or Large Group (lg)	All of the children in the class (except for one or two or individuals working with someone else), or a group of more than ten children. If there are ten or less in the room, code this as a small group.
	Small Group (sg)	Children are working in two or more groups. If there are more than ten children in a group, call this whole group.
	Phonemic Awareness Instruction (pa)	Students are identifying the sounds in words or blending sounds together (an oral activity). The purpose is to develop phonemic awareness, not letter–sound knowledge.
	Phonics Instruction (phon)	Students are focusing on symbol/sound correspondences, or letter-by-letter decoding, or decoding by onset and rime or analogy, or decoding multisyllabic words. However, this is not tied to decoding of words while reading.
	Word-Recognition Strategies (wrs)	Students are focusing on use of one or more strategies to figure out words while reading, typically prompted by the teacher.
	Lower-Level Text Comprehension (talk or writing about text) (llq)	Students are engaged in talk (m1) or writing (m2) about the meaning of text that is at a lower level of thinking. The writing may be a journal entry about the text requiring a lower level of thinking or may be a fill-in-the-blank worksheet that is on the text meaning (rather than on comprehension skill or vocabulary words).
	Higher-Level Text Comprehension (talk or writing about text) (hlq)	Students are involved in talk (m3) or writing (m4) about the meaning of text that is engaging them in higher-level thinking. This is talk or writing about text that is challenging to the children and is at either a high level of text interpretation or goes beyond the text: generalization, application, evaluation, aesthetic response. Needless to say, a child must go beyond a yes or no answer (e.g., in the case of an opinion or aesthetic response).
	Comprehension Skill Instruction (cskl)	Students are engaged in a comprehension activity (other than a comprehension strategy) which is at a lower level of thinking (e.g., traditional skill work such as identifying main idea, cause-effect, fact-opinion).

continues

Catching Schools © 2011 by Barbara M. Taylor (Heinemann: Portsmouth, NH).

Figure 6–4a Observation Recording Form for Elements of Practice for Classroom Reading Instruction

Observation Recording Form for Elements of Practice
for Classroom Reading Instruction, *continued*

Put an X for each 5-minute segment in which a variable is observed and add comments	Variable (code)	Description
	Comprehension Strategy Instruction (cstr)	Students are engaged in use of a comprehension strategy that will transfer to other reading and in which this notion of transfer is mentioned (e.g., reciprocal teaching, predicting). If predicting was done, but transfer was not mentioned, this would be coded as cskl.
	Vocabulary Instruction (voc)	Students are engaged in discussing/working on a word meaning(s).
	Reading Text (rdgtxt)	Students are coded as reading (not reading turn-taking).
	Narrative Text (nartxt)	A narrative textbook or narrative trade book was used in the lesson observed.
	Informational Text (inftxt)	An informational textbook or information trade book was used in the lesson observed.
	Teacher-Directed Stance (tds)	The teacher is engaged in telling and/or recitation.
	Student-Support Stance (sss)	The teacher is engaged in modeling, coaching, and/or listening/giving feedback.
	Telling (tell)	The teacher is telling or giving children information, explaining how to do something.
	Recitation (recite)	The teacher is engaging the students in answering questions, or responding, usually low-level q-a-q-a. The purpose primarily appears to be getting the children to answer the questions asked rather than engaging them in a formal discussion or fostering independence in terms of answering questions with more complete thinking.
	Modeling (model)	The teacher is showing/demonstrating the steps of how to do something or how to do a process as opposed to simply explaining it (e.g., a teacher models fluent reading after she models word-by-word readings, and she talks about the difference). A teacher reading her own book as kids are reading would not be coded as modeling since she is not being explicit.

Catching Schools © 2011 by Barbara M. Taylor (Heinemann: Portsmouth, NH).

Figure 6–4b Observation Recording Form for Elements of Practice for Classroom Reading Instruction, continued

Observation Recording Form for Elements of Practice for Classroom Reading Instruction, *continued*

Put an X for each 5-minute segment in which a variable is observed and add comments	Variable (code)	Description
	Coaching (coach)	The teacher is prompting/providing support that will transfer to other situations as students are attempting to perform a strategy or activity or to answer a question. The teacher's apparent purpose is to foster independence to get a more complete action or to help students elaborate on an answer (rather than to simply get a student to answer a question).
	Listening/ Watching/Giving Feedback (lwgfb)	Teacher is listening or watching and giving feedback as students are engaged in activity. Do not code as listening if the listening is only a part of recitation.
	Discussion (discs)	Students engaged in a discussion, which may or may not be led by the teacher, in which formal conventions of a discussion apply; discussion is thought provoking, getting children to express their ideas. Even if led by the teacher, students start to offer their own ideas rather than simply respond to the teacher. Exchange may be t-s-s-s rather than t-s-t-s. This type of discussion is not often observed in the primary grades.
	Active Responding (actvrsp)	Children are engaged in one or more of the following: reading, writing, oral responding, manipulating.
	Passive Responding (psvrsp)	Children are engaged in one or more of the following: reading-turn taking, oral responding-turn taking, listening.
	Time on Task (tot)	At the end of the 5-minute note-taking segment, the observer takes a count of the number of children in the room who appeared to be engaged in the assigned task out of all the children in the room. If a child is quiet, but staring out the window or rolling a pencil on his desk, this is not counted as on task.

Catching Schools © 2011 by Barbara M. Taylor (Heinemann: Portsmouth, NH).

Figure 6–4c *Observation Recording Form for Elements of Practice for Classroom Reading Instruction, continued*

Self-Assessment Questions to Be Used After an Observation

Grouping

▶ To what extent are my students in grades K–5 engaged in small-group as well as whole-group instruction?

Reading Activities

▶ To what extent are my students engaged in higher level in addition to lower level talk or writing about texts they have read?

▶ To what extent am I teaching reading comprehension strategies in addition to reading comprehension skills?

▶ To what extent am I providing effective vocabulary instruction?

▶ Am I providing an appropriate amount of phonemic awareness and phonics instruction?

▶ To what extent am I coaching students in the use of word recognition strategies to figure out unknown words?

▶ To what extent are my students engaged in independent reading?

Reading Materials

▶ To what extent am I using informational text as well as narrative text?

Stance Toward Teaching/Teacher Interaction Style

▶ To what extent am I teaching with a student-support stance (e.g., coaching modeling, watching/giving feedback) in addition to a teacher-directed stance (e.g., telling, recitation)? Am I engaging in too much telling?

Student Responding

▶ To what extent are my students engaged in active versus passive responding?

▶ To what extent are my students on task?

Catching Schools © 2011 by Barbara M. Taylor (Heinemann: Portsmouth, NH).

Figure 6–4d *Self-Assessment Questions to Be Used After an Observation*

6–4 on the DVD for an example of observational notes completed by a kindergarten teacher.) At the end of the observation, you or the observer, using the list of practices in Figure 6–4 as a checklist, indicates what practices were observed during each five-minute segment. Finally, using the questions in Figure 6–4, interpret this data yourself or with help of a colleague (e.g., building literacy coordinator or external partner) in order to enhance the quality of your classroom reading instruction. (For information on the original observation scheme, go to www.earlyintervention inreading.com.)

In the SCR process, teachers receive the set of questions with their observations. They are encouraged to have their literacy coordinator or external facilitator help them make sense of their observations, since these people have received training in how to interpret observations. However, literacy coordinators and external facilitators are asked not to make judgments for teachers.

School Data: Reflecting on Collaboration and the School Climate

In the SCR process, schools collect data on the degree to which effective school-level factors are present in their buildings. The self-study survey in Figure 6–5 is designed to collect this information. Schools also can use a rubric like the one in Figure 6–6 to look at the degree to which the SCR process is being implemented successfully.

Self-study questionnaire. The self-study questionnaire focuses on teachers' perceptions related to the following school-level practices (see Chapter 4 for a review; also see Fullan 2005; Louis and Kruse 1995; Taylor et al. 2000):

- Collaboration among teachers, leadership within the school, and an understanding of the process of school change.

- Ongoing professional development efforts and reflection on teaching.

- Schoolwide decisions about the reading program.

- Elements of effective reading instruction and regular use of assessments to inform instruction.

- Reading interventions in place for struggling readers.

- School-home-community connections.

Appendix 6–5 on the DVD lists the mean scores for all items on the self-study questionnaire for a number of SCR schools, and for one urban elementary school. These data are included so that schools can compare their mean responses to those of other SCR schools as a way to look for strengths and possible areas of concern. (After the first year, comparisons can be made between the means for a school's current year and its means from the previous year for each item of the questionnaire.) As shown in Appendix 6–5, scores on most of the items increased from one year to the next across all schools. This indicates that an increasingly positive school climate is developing at these schools in general.

School Change Self-Study Survey/Questionnaire

Name_____ **School** _____

Grade level(s) if applicable _____

The purpose of this self-study questionnaire is to help your school make decisions about which aspects of the school change framework to focus on during the school year. This questionnaire is focused around the six major categories of the school change project: Effective School Change, Professional Development, Schoolwide Decisions about the Reading Program, Classroom Reading Instruction, Reading Interventions, and School-Home-Community Connections.

5 = strongly agree, 4 = agree, 3 = undecided, 2 = disagree, 1 = strongly disagree

School Change	5 SA	4 A	3 U	2 D	1 SD
1. **Collaboration**—Classroom teachers work with teachers from grade levels above and below their own as well as with non-classroom teachers when planning and making key decisions about benchmarks, curriculum, assessments, and student behavior.					
2. **Collaboration**—Staff works together to create and sustain a culture of continued self-examination and improvement.					
3. **Share vision**—The staff and families have developed a shared vision and redesigned plan to improve students' literacy learning.					
4. **Understanding the process of school change**—Staff understands the basic research on effective school reform.					
5. **Collective focus on student learning**—The staff puts the improvement of students' learning first in its conversations and decision making about reading.					
6. **Trust and rapport**—Members of the school community feel there is a positive, supportive school climate.					
7. **Organizational diagnosis**—Our school regularly collects data, is informed by research, and uses action plans, based on this information, to improve.					
8. **Leadership**—Decision making is shared among teachers, parents, and the principal.					
9. **Leadership**—Leadership is shared between the principal and teachers.					
10. **Stakeholder satisfaction**—Satisfaction surveys are administered on a regular basis and the results used in improvement efforts.					

continues

Catching Schools © 2011 by Barbara M. Taylor (Heinemann: Portsmouth, NH).

Figure 6–5a School Change Self-Study Survey/Questionnaire

School Change Self-Study Survey/Questionnaire, *continued*

Professional Development	5 SA	4 A	3 U	2 D	1 SD
1. Research on teaching and learning is shared among staff members and is used in planning and decision making related to improved reading instruction.					
2. There is a substantial buildingwide commitment to ongoing professional development.					
3. Teachers within the building work together on professional development experiences.					
4. Professional development experiences are reflective, long-term, change-oriented, and extend into the classroom.					
5. There is adequate time and support for meaningful professional development.					
6. Teachers share expertise on various aspects of reading instruction, assessment, and classroom organization.					
Schoolwide Decisions About the Reading Program					
1. Data and research are presented and used in decision making related to reading instruction, assessment, curriculum, and benchmarks.					
2. Improvements come from reallocating resources (e.g., time, personnel) in more productive ways.					
3. The staff put the children first when making decisions about resource allocation (e.g., time for reading instruction, use of personnel to deliver instruction).					
4. We recognize that there are aspects of the school learning environment that hinder student learning and we work to reduce these factors.					
5. The staff is committed to eliminating or reducing those elements of the school reading program that are not the most appropriate for the students' learning or the best use of resources.					

continues

Catching Schools © 2011 by Barbara M. Taylor (Heinemann: Portsmouth, NH).

Figure 6–5b *School Change Self-Study Survey/Questionnaire, continued*

School Change Self-Study Survey/Questionnaire, *continued*

Classroom Reading Instruction	5 SA	4 A	3 U	2 D	1 SD
1. Teachers often reflect on their teaching and discuss problems in their own practice with colleagues.					
2. There is peer pressure to teach well.					
3. I personally have made changes in my classroom as a result of professional development experiences.					
4. I collect or use data on my teaching and track improvements over time based on this data.					
5. I use assessments on my students' reading performance to make changes in the instruction I provide to my students.					
6. I know where to turn and am able to get the help needed if I want to know more about effective instruction and assessment in word recognition, vocabulary, comprehension, and writing.					
7. Teachers use best practices and share responsibility for teaching reading to ELLs, special education students, and struggling readers.					

Reading Interventions for Struggling Readers					
1. The school has a strong system in place to provide research-based reading interventions to struggling readers.					
2. Reading interventions extend beyond first grade to meet the needs of upper elementary students.					
3. The instruction a student receives through reading intervention and classroom reading instruction is coordinated.					

School-Home-Community Connections					
1. The staff is committed to viewing parents as valued partners in the education of their children.					
2. The school reaches out to parents through interviews or focus groups to determine parents' needs and concerns.					
3. The school is successful in bringing parents and community members in to the school.					
4. The school is a welcoming place for parents.					
5. The school successfully communicates with parents about students' progress.					
6. The school provides appropriate support for parents for working with their students at home.					
7. The school is successful in working with community agencies and businesses in support of students' literacy learning.					

Figure 6–5c School Change Self-Study Survey/Questionnaire, continued

School Change in Reading Reform Effort Rubric

Please Note: For most of the reform effort variables, a school receives 1 point if the item is fulfilled at least 80 percent of the time (unless other criteria are specified). The school receives 0 points if the item is fulfilled less than the specified criteria. Put a check mark by each item that is fulfilled, and count up the number of check marks for a total score. In recent SCR schools in Minnesota (n = 23), the mean reform effort score was 7 in year 1 of the SCR process, and 9 in years 2 and 3.

Reform Effort Variables

1. Study group meetings are conducted for 1 hour each week during the school year.

2. Study groups are composed of teachers and specialists across several grade levels.

3. Study group activities cause teachers to reflect on their own instructional practices, and evaluate student work and engagement. (Look for reflection on teaching through video sharing and examining student work on study group meeting notes forms.)

4. Study groups use current research to inform their discussions of instructional methods and practices. ("Using current research" was defined as using research articles and books with substantial numbers of research citations. Additional resources can be counted as "research" if they met the criteria described in the IRA position statement "What Is Evidence-Based Reading Instruction?")

5. Study groups develop action plans that cause teachers to reflect on their own instruction and examine student assessment data. The action plans show that each study group is discussing a substantive topic over time.

6. Study groups have chosen substantive topics that are based on student assessment data and current research on best practices, and they maintain these topics over many months.

7. Schools hold whole-group meetings once a month to look at assessment data, deal with schoolwide issues related to reform, and share across study groups.

8. Schools have specific schoolwide plans for involving parents as partners.

9. Schools have external facilitators who are actively involved with the reform process (i.e., Meet regularly with the internal leadership team to provide expertise and support. Visit classrooms to model lessons, observe, and give feedback).

10. Schools have internal leadership teams that meet for at least 1 hour once a month and play an active role in leadership.

Catching Schools © 2011 by Barbara M. Taylor (Heinemann: Portsmouth, NH).

Figure 6–6 School Change in Reading Reform Effort Rubric

Rubric on implementing the SCR process. In schools implementing the SCR process in the past, notes from study group meetings and action plans, as well as information from interviews, were used to determine which aspects of the SCR process were being implemented within schools. A composite scale was created by which to measure ten aspects of the reform (see Figure 6–6). In three studies (Taylor, Pearson, Peterson, and Rodriguez 2003; Taylor et al. 2007; Taylor and Peterson 2008), it was found that the more elements of the reform a school was implementing, the more that school saw growth in students' reading achievement compared with other schools in the project. The impact of wide-ranging, concentrated reform implementation was especially positive over a two-year period.

In general, most schools using the SCR process in year 2 in a recent study (Taylor et al. 2007):

▶ met weekly in study groups,

▶ met in cross-grade study groups,

▶ were guided by actions plans,

▶ regularly considered research-based practices,

▶ met once a month in a large group to share study group successes and to deal with schoolwide issues related to the reform effort, and

▶ stuck with substantive study group topics over time, effectively used their external partners as a resource, and had effective leadership teams.

▶ Some schools had less success reflecting on instruction in study groups and using data effectively as a school (Taylor and Peterson 2007b).

Summary

Assessment practices play a crucial role in school-based reading improvement projects. The resulting data should be seen as a friend, not an enemy. Teachers need time to collect and collaboratively study pupil performance data with an eye toward modifications to instruction to maximize students' reading progress and success.

Teachers also need to gather data that will help them reflect on and modify their reading instruction, their schoolwide reading program, and the success of their school's reform efforts to maximize students' reading success. However, these important parts of a reading improvement effort often get neglected. I hope the suggestions in this chapter, suggestions that the teachers I work with have come to value highly, give you ideas about how to make all kinds of data your friends.

Idea Swapping

The Vitality of Collaborative Professional Learning

As I've emphasized throughout this book, to improve students' reading, we have to improve ourselves. For this to happen, teachers need to be given the time and the encouragement to reflect on their work. In-depth conversations with colleagues about instruction can do more to bring about reading achievement than the fanciest programs or inspiring inservice, because the ideas take hold from within the school culture. The research-based practices that teachers try are those that teachers know intuitively will fit best with their students and their own next steps in professional development. Reflection on instruction, in-depth conversations with colleagues about teaching, and changes in practice based on these reflections and conversations are at the heart of professional learning but are often missing components in our efforts to improve our students' reading ability.

ABOUT COACHING CONVERSATIONS

Teachers get additional opportunities to debrief on their teaching when they sit down to talk with the literacy coordinator or coach after a classroom visit related to study group topics. The literacy coordinator visits a classroom as a colleague, not an expert, to model a new way to approach a reading lesson or observe the classroom teacher present a reading lesson. These coaching conversations (see Chapter 8) are a powerful way for teachers to reflect on and modify their instructional practices "hot on the heels" of their teaching, when it's fresh in their minds what went well and what aspects of the lesson might have gone better to meet students' needs in reading and to challenge them all.

The Purpose of the Study Groups

Study groups are the key forum for professional development in the SCR process. Some study group topics, like word-recognition instruction or strategies to provide reading interventions, lend themselves to grade-level groups. Other topics, like comprehension strategies, lend themselves to cross-grade groups and enable teachers to build a common language and scope and sequence to teach reading comprehension strategies effectively from one grade level to the next. Ideally, teachers will be in two study groups on different topics, with each study group meeting once a month.

Guided by rotating leaders, with support from a literacy coordinator or coach, and occurring about twice a month throughout the year, teachers learn about research-based practices related to reading instruction, and in between study group sessions, put these practices to work in their daily reading lessons. Each meeting, it often works well to balance debriefing on how the try-the-practice went with discussion of one new aspect of the study group topic to try next. Fellow teachers cheer on the successes and troubleshoot aspects that were challenging, so that each teacher feels empowered to keep refining the practices. They might view videos of their practice, discuss student work samples, and get ideas about instructional next steps in their classrooms.

Reflection on practice is a key element in all study group sessions. Members of study groups reflect on what they are doing and what they might do differently to improve students' reading achievement. Together, using a video sharing or student work protocol, teachers look at their teaching and at student work. This collaboration helps teachers develop a common language, a core set of practices, and most important, a sense of community and trust.

see it in Action

video 3

Comprehension Study Group

In this video clip, teachers from Westside Elementary (see Chapters 1 and 8) begin their study group by sharing their recent experiences with instructional conversations (Goldenberg 1992/1993), a technique that focuses on high-level talk and writing about text as well as comprehension strategies. A second-grade teacher shares his reflections by showing his video. Teachers use the video-sharing protocol to talk about the strengths they observed in the students and the teacher's instruction and they offer suggestions to make future lessons involving instructional conversations even more effective. Next, the group discusses the research article they read on instructional conversations, and they talk about the next techniques they will try when teaching students to use instructional conversations before the next study group meeting. A teacher shares student work on drawing inferences about character traits from an instructional conversation lesson. Teachers use the looking-at-student-work protocol to discuss this student work and offer instructional suggestions for future lessons. Before teachers leave, they take a minute to decide who will assume various roles, like leader, note taker, timekeeper, video sharer, for the next month's study group meeting.

See it in Action

Reading Intervention Study Group

Grade 1 classroom and resource teachers from a suburban school share data and reflections related to the EIR lessons they have been teaching to their first-grade students who are struggling with learning to read (Taylor 2010a). Teachers discuss the transition to independent reading process they have just begun using with their emerging readers. They engage in video sharing, based on a video a teacher has provided of her transition-to-independent reading lesson. Teachers provide a good illustration of the steps of the video-sharing protocol.

The Features of Successful Study Groups

▶ **Action plans are created.** Create action plans that focus on what group members can learn and do to change what and how they teach to improve student learning. Teachers do this together at the start of a series of five or six monthly meetings, or more, on one topic, such as providing reading interventions or teaching comprehension strategies. The plan helps teachers keep track of the goals, the learning activities, and who volunteered to do what (e.g., bring a video to share, bring student work samples, select a research-based article for all to read and discuss). See Figures 7–1 and 7–2.

▶ **The meetings are democratic not hierarchical.** Study group members take turns as the study group leader, timekeeper, and note taker. The note taker records the activities of the meeting. These notes are shared with the leadership team and posted in a central location so that everyone in the school is aware of what the various study groups are doing. See Figures 7–3 and 7–4.

▶ **The conversation must be substantive.** Members need to keep the exchange focused on instruction so they are developing their knowledge of both pedagogy and content, learning research-tested practices that they can use in their classrooms. Concrete examples, including video clips, student work, lesson plans, or research in articles or professional books can be brought to meetings to help teachers envision the content of the lessons under discussion.

▶ **The conversation is action-oriented.** That is, teachers know that they will be trying the practices in their classrooms, so they can participate and ask questions to feel as ready as possible to try new ideas. See Figure 7–5.

▶ **The change in classroom practice is data-driven.** Teachers collect and analyze data over time to assess the effectiveness of the changes they have made in classroom practices. This may be student data such as data shared at data retreats, rubrics, or checklists applied to student performance or work, such as progress monitoring scores. Or it may be data on teaching such as video clips, lesson plans, teacher reflections, self-evaluation checklists (refer back to Figures 6–2 through 6–5), or peer observations.

▶ **Action plans are assessed from time to time.** Teachers also periodically evaluate the effectiveness of study groups. Study group action plans are revisited every four to six weeks and amendments made as needed.

The forms that follow will help you get a sense of how the action plans are used and study groups function. Whole Faculty Study Groups, by Murphy and Lick (2005), has additional useful ideas about conducting study groups within schools.

One Powerful Hour: Sample Study Group Schedule

Because teachers are very busy, the SCR process limits each study group session to an hour. The timekeeper can help the group work efficiently within this time frame. A sample time line for a 60-minute study group meeting might include:

10 minutes: Share reflections on teaching strategies undertaken and data gathered since the last meeting.

10 minutes: Discuss a research article that group members read in preparation for the meeting.

15 minutes: Share a video and use a video-sharing protocol (see Figures 7–6 and 7–7) to discuss instruction related to the study group topic. The purpose of video sharing is to give teachers the opportunity to reflect on and refine teaching by looking at actual teaching.

15 minutes: Look at student work samples and use the looking-at-student-work protocol (see Figure 7–8) to discuss instruction related to the study group topic. As with video sharing, the purpose of looking at student work is to help teachers reflect on and refine instruction.

10 minutes: Decide what is to be done by whom before and at the next meeting.

The conversations in study groups may seem a little formal at first because often teachers are not accustomed to prolonged conversations about practice. However, once teachers become comfortable with talking in depth with colleagues about what they are learning and how they are teaching differently in their classrooms, they become committed members of professional learning communities. Kathy Little, a special education teacher at Lincoln Elementary, reports:

I attribute [changes in my teaching] to study groups, good peer relations, openness to talking with everyone on my team, and collaboration across grade levels. Having a focus during study groups is really improving my teaching; everyone shares their ideas on the same strategies and reflects on changes that need to be made. Our monthly student progress meetings, when we share reading data on our students, help us focus better on what we're teaching and what modifications are needed to get our students to the next level.

Next year when the formal SCR process is over, we definitely want to continue our study groups. This is the norm now and it helps us reflect on and talk about our teaching, bounce ideas off one another, and constructively critique our instruction to help us improve. I need study groups because I thrive on the professional conversations. I need to share student work and the videos. I need the whole group meetings to keep the schoolwide focus. I also need continual access to the latest research.

Study Group Action Plan Form

Study group topic:_____ Support topic:_____

Group name:_____ Date:_____

Leader:_____ Note taker:_____ Grade(s) K 1 2 3 4 5 6

Members present:_____

Members absent:_____

1. Based on your study group's student data, classroom teaching practices, and current research on best practices, what are the specific student needs your study group is addressing?

2. What are the proposed goals for (a) your study group as a whole and (b) how each member will implement instructional change? Be as specific as possible! *Remember the goal is to change or enhance classroom practice to improve student performance in the above area.*

Goals for study groups	Who is responsible?	Resources needed	General timeline/ target dates
a. Study group actions:			
b. Classroom applications:			

3. What data on your own teaching practices (video clips, lesson plans, teacher reflection journals, peer observations) are you collecting (or planning to collect) to see whether your study group goal is making a difference?

4. What student data will you collect to show your study group's impact on student achievement in reading?

5. How is your group making connections to your support topic, to other study groups, or to other professional learning?

6. What are some of your study group's successes or accomplishments so far?

Revised on: _____   _____   _____
                        date   date   date

Catching Schools © 2011 by Barbara M. Taylor (Heinemann: Portsmouth, NH).

Figure 7–1 Study Group Action Plan Form

Example of a Completed Study Group Action Plan Form

Study group topic: _Comprehension strategies_   Support topic: _Parent partnerships_

Group name: _____ Date: _____

Leader: _____ Note taker: _____ Grade(s) K 1 2 3 4 5 6

Members present: _____

Members absent: _____

1. Based on your study group's student data, classroom teaching practices, and current research on best practices, what are the specific student needs your study group is ad dressing?   _Students need to increase their ability to comprehend narrative and informational text while reading with the teacher and independently._

2. What are the proposed goals for (a) your study group as a whole and (b) how will each member implement instructional change? Be as specific as possible! _Remember the goal is to change or enhance classroom practice to improve student performance in the above area._

   Remember the goal is to change or enhance classroom practice to improve student performance in the above area.

Goals for study groups	Who is responsible?	Resources needed	General timeline/ target dates
a. **Study group actions:** _To learn to effectively teach comprehension strategies by sharing videos of our teaching, looking at student work, and reading research. Sustain each strategy in our teaching throughout the year to support reading comprehension. Parent partnerships: Maintain ongoing communication between home and school._	_All members_	_Video camera, research_	_Sept–May_
b. **Classroom applications:** _Model how and when to attend to word meaning while reading, monitor comprehension, summarize the gist of the story, and summarize informational text. Coach students as they use these strategies while reading in whole group, small groups, and independently. Monitor their learning and continue to model but gradually have students take on more responsibility as they learn to use comprehension strategies independently. Parent partnerships: Explain specific strategies to support reading comprehension._	_All members_		_Begin modeling monitoring comprehension and attending to word meaning in Oct–Nov._ _Summarize story Nov–Jan. Summarize informational text Jan–May._

3. What data on your own teaching practices (video clips, lesson plans, teacher reflection journals, peer observations) are you collecting (or planning to collect) to see whether your study group goal is making a difference?   _Participants will take turns sharing a video at each meeting. Study group members will use the video-sharing protocol to facilitate reflection and provide feedback._

4. What student data will you collect to show your study group's impact on student achievement in reading?   _Student summaries of stories and informational text, along with anecdotal teacher notes. We will use rubrics to evaluate the summaries._

5. How is your group making connections to your support topic, to other study groups, or to other professional learning?
   We will continue to coach students to use word-recognition strategies [last year's topic] as students monitor their comprehension monitoring. We will improve our communication with parents [supporting topic] by including information about specific comprehension strategies.

6. What are some of your study group's successes or accomplishments so far?

Revised on: _____   _____   _____
         date   date   date

Catching Schools © 2011 by Barbara M. Taylor (Heinemann: Portsmouth, NH).

Figure 7–2 _Example of a Completed Study Group Action Plan Form_

Taking Study Group Meeting Notes

School: _____ Date: _____ Grade(s) K 1 2 3 4 5 6

Members present: _____

Members absent: _____

Study group topic: _____ Support topic: _____

Before

A | Explain the instructional technique that all members tried prior to coming to the study group and how it impacted students (see section D of your last meeting notes):

During

B Specify the type of reflection your group participated in during the meeting:

	Video Sharing	Student Work	Data	Research	Other
Who					
What				Cite Source:	

Summarize the main points of your reflection (give specific details based on the protocols for video sharing/student work):

C | Explain how your support topic is impacting your instructional practices:

After

D | Describe the instructional technique each member will study and/or apply before the next meeting:

Responsibilities: **video share**: _____ **research**: _____

student work: _____

Next Meeting

E | Date and time of the next meeting: _____ Leader: _____

Note taker: _____ Timekeeper: _____

What questions or concerns do you have for the literacy coordinator or external consultant?

Catching Schools © 2011 by Barbara M. Taylor (Heinemann: Portsmouth, NH).

Figure 7–3 Taking Study Group Meeting Notes

Example of Study Group Meeting Notes

School: _____ Date: _____ Grade(s) K 1 2 3 4 5 6

Members present: _____

Members absent: _____

Study group topic: _Comprehension strategies_____ Support topic: _Parent partnerships_____

Before

A | Explain the instructional technique that all members tried prior to coming to the study group and how it impacted students (see section D of your last meeting notes): *Participants modeled, by talking aloud, how to monitor comprehension and then coached students as they practiced in small-group instruction.*

During

B Specify the type of reflection your group participated in during the meeting:

	Video Sharing	Student Work	Data	Research	Other
Who	Rea/Bill			All members	
What	Talk through how to monitor comprehension while reading/ practice monitoring comprehension with students during a whole-group read-aloud			**Cite Source:** Pressley 2006	

Summarize the main points of your reflection (give specific details based on the protocols for video sharing/student work):

Rea asked for feedback on the clarity of her communication with students as she modeled monitoring comprehension while reading. We noticed she explicitly talked to her students about what the strategy is, why one uses it, how to use it, and when to use it. Bill asked for feedback on how he coached students as they practiced monitoring comprehension with him in a whole-group read-aloud. Many of us agreed that we forget to talk about transfer when we model how to monitor comprehension. We need to tell children why, when, and how to use the strategy. We noted that teaching unfamiliar words within the context of reading is much more effective than teaching a list of vocabulary words—children are much more engaged and are looking for and talking more about unfamiliar words.

C | Explain how your support topic is impacting your instructional practices: *Parents are reinforcing the strategies when reading with their children at home. In conversations with parents we receive feedback about the use of comprehension strategies. We are talking with parents about how to coach their children while reading at home. We notice which children need more coaching in the use of strategies.*

After

D | Describe the instructional technique each member will study and/or apply before the next meeting. Continue with monitoring comprehension.
Also focus on summarizing the gist of the story by talking aloud as we model the use of the strategy.

Responsibilities: **video share:** _Joe/Ann, both doing a talk-aloud_____ **research:** _Pressley 2006_____

student work: _____

Next Meeting

E | Date and time of the next meeting: _____ Leader: _____

Note taker: _____ Timekeeper: _____

What questions or concerns do you have for the literacy coordinator or external consultant?

Catching Schools © 2011 by Barbara M. Taylor (Heinemann: Portsmouth, NH).

Figure 7–4 Example of Study Group Meeting Notes

Evaluating Teachers' Perceptions of Study Groups

1. What has gone well this year in study groups?

2. What do you think are the strengths of the study group process?

3. How have the study group activities impacted your teaching? For example, How has your knowledge of the specific topic deepened? What strategies have you tried? What changes in your classroom teaching are most striking to you? What aspect of your teaching feels the least transformed? In what ways are you more reflective about your teaching practices?

4. What schoolwide changes have taken place as a result of study groups (e.g., professional development, instructional change, building trust and community, improved student reading performance)?

5. What suggestions do you have to improve study group activities for next year? What is needed to develop study groups as learning communities that make a difference? What changes would you suggest? How would these changes be implemented?

6. Who would participate in your ideal study group? For example, mixed grades, grade level?

7. Other comments?

Figure 7–5 Evaluating Teachers' Perceptions of Study Groups

Video-Sharing Protocol

STEP 1. Videotape a lesson segment that is relevant to the study group topic.

Decide on a particular focus ahead of time and edit so the clip is about 5 minutes long. As you view the clip, jot down answers to the following questions before bringing the video to a study group session:

▶ What things related to the study group's focus area were children able to do? What things were going well?_____

▶ What was the teacher doing to help children develop and be successful?_____

▶ What else might the teacher have done to foster development and success?_____

▶ What did you personally learn from watching the video?_____

STEP 2. Share the video at a study group meeting.

▶ Provide one minute of background about the lesson.

▶ Ask the group for help with an aspect of the lesson (if something comes to mind).

▶ View the video with the group.

▶ Have subgroups discuss the video-sharing questions and take notes on:

  • Things the children did well.

  • Things the teacher in the clip did well in getting children to develop and experience success.

  • Suggestions for things that the teacher might have done differently to help the children develop and experience success.

  • Things you personally learned from watching the video segment.

▶ Discuss the video clip as a whole group. The facilitator can ask the video-sharing questions if the teacher featured in the video chooses not to. (Notes from small groups should be given to the teacher featured in the video clip. Teachers appreciate receiving this feedback.)

▶ The teacher featured in the clip can then ask for suggestions related to an aspect of instruction she feels she needs help with.

Catching Schools © 2011 by Barbara M. Taylor (Heinemann: Portsmouth, NH).

Figure 7–6 Video-Sharing Protocol

Multidimensional Video-Sharing Protocol

Dimension of Effective Teaching	Successes of Students and Teacher/Other Comments	Possible Change(s)
High-level questioning		
Strategies (not just skills)		
Support provided by teacher (coaching, modeling, listening/giving feedback)		
Active student response (reading, writing, manipulating, turning to a partner to share)		
Purpose(s)		
Timing		
Teacher actions to get students to where they were in lesson		
Applications to your own classroom		
Other comments or reflections		

Catching Schools © 2011 by Barbara M. Taylor (Heinemann: Portsmouth, NH).

Figure 7–7 Multidimensional Video-Sharing Protocol

Protocol for Examining Student Work

When you look at student work, it is best to have a protocol to follow. Since the focus of the School Change study groups is to use research-based knowledge on effective instruction and to reflect on and improve teaching to increase students' reading achievement, we are recommending a protocol that supports this overall goal. We propose a protocol adapted from the Tuning Protocol (Coalition of Essential Schools) and the Collaborative Assessment Conference protocol (Harvard Project Zero).

1. A facilitator leads the discussion and keeps the group on task.

2. One teacher hands out a few pieces of student work on the same topic from a cross-section of students (e.g., three pieces selected because of a concern you have). The teacher explains the assignment and asks a focusing question. (2 minutes)

3. The group asks clarifying questions. Presenter answers questions. (1–2 minutes)

4. The group examines and describes the work. What skills/strengths are evident? What don't the students know or what aren't the students' able to do? What features of the work stand out, what surprised you? (5–7 minutes)

5. Several areas or skills in need of improvement are identified, and group shares research-based ideas to improve instruction from study group readings. The facilitator may remind the group of the original focusing question of the teacher. (5–7 minutes)

6. The teacher reflects on what she will try to do to improve instruction by speaking to the members' comments or questions (2 minutes). Other members decide on something that they learned from the process that they will implement to improve their instruction as well.

For more on looking at student work, go to www.lasw.org.

Figure 7–8 Protocol for Examining Student Work

Anna Berglund, the literacy coordinator at Edgewood Elementary, says, "There are more opportunities to spend time talking to other people about what they are doing [in their classrooms] during study group meetings and whole-group sessions. The SCR process has given us a structure to work within that leads to productive, reflective discussions about teaching and learning. The processes for reflecting on instruction have given us time to think about what we have been doing and why and have helped us share ideas that have moved our instruction forward."

Also, talking about the school reading program gives us a schoolwide perspective of what we are doing to help our students. It breaks down the feelings of isolation, and it gives staff ideas and strategies to make it more effective. Learning together builds common language and common vision and goals.

Finding Time for Study Groups

Many schools hold study groups after school. In some instances, the principal has limited faculty meetings to once a month to provide time for study groups. Some schools with a later start time have held study groups before school. Others have held study groups during a common planning time. Still other schools accommodate study group meetings with a weekly late start or early release day.

Murphy and Lick (2005) offer many suggestions for ways to incorporate study groups into the school day. Tips from SCR literacy coordinators on finding time for study groups are presented later in this chapter.

Sharing Video Clips and Student Work

Teachers take a little while to warm up to the video sharing, but in time grow to like it a lot. They report that they learn a great deal from reflecting on their own teaching or watching someone else teach and from having a meaningful discussion about instruction.

Teachers start with the Focused Video Sharing Protocol in Figure 7–6. Once they feel successful with this, they transition to the Multidimensional Video Sharing Protocol (Figure 7–7) that gives them the opportunity to look more broadly at effective reading instruction. Looking at student work is an additional activity that allows teachers to refine instruction (see Figure 7–8).

Viewing and discussing a video segment or looking at student work related to the study group topic should take no more than 15–20 minutes. See Figures 7–6 and 7–7 for suggested video sharing steps; keeping a copy of these steps handy will remind you of the questions with which to guide discussions. It works best if people take notes while viewing the video clip so they can remember things they'd like to point out and/or discuss. Video segments of teachers engaged in study groups and video sharing are on the DVD.

Kathy Little, a special education teacher at Lincoln Elementary, reflects, "Sharing videos and student work in study groups has helped me identify strengths and weaknesses in my students and has pointed out areas in which I need to improve professionally." Becky Saunders, a first-grade teacher at Edgewood observes, "I really value study groups and video sharing because of the opportunity to learn from one another. As we watch video clips and talk, we are able to reflect together on what we are doing and whether it's best for students."

Multidimensional Video Sharing

The SCR process stresses reading instruction that maximizes students' cognitive engagement in literacy learning (Taylor et al. 2003). Once teachers feel successful with the focused video-sharing protocol, they can follow an advanced multidimensional video-sharing protocol (see Figure 7–7) that looks more broadly at effective reading instruction. Typically, by year 2 of the SCR process, teachers are ready to look at instruction through this broader lens.

After watching a 7- to 10-minute segment of a videotaped lesson and taking notes in a study group, use the middle column to list student and teacher successes and other comments pertaining to one or more dimensions of effective teaching. Be sure to reflect on what things the children were able to do (what things were going well) and on what the teacher was doing to help the children succeed and become independent. In the right-hand column, list suggestions for possible changes in the lesson or a suggestion for a future lesson.

Generic Plan for a Series of Study Group Sessions

In order to plan a series of sessions, a study group first needs to evaluate their students' needs, as well as their needs as teachers, and decide on a topic. For example, do students need help with and do the teachers in the group need to get better at teaching systematic phonics, comprehension strategies, fluency, vocabulary, or higher-level talk about text? Then the group needs to select a research-based technique (or small set of related techniques) to learn, practice, and refine over four or more monthly sessions.

While searching for research-based techniques to study, the group needs to look at texts or articles that are current and that cite numerous sources. Questions to ask include:

▶ Is the technique validated or directly supported by research?

▶ Is the technique likely to lead to significant improvements in students' reading ability?

▶ Is the technique worth studying over a series of sessions?

Once a specific technique has been selected, the group should choose one book and/or several articles that focus on that particular instructional approach in detail and discuss how to move forward instructionally.

Here's how a series of hourly sessions might play out:

▶ *Session 1.* The group decides, based on students' and teachers' needs, the technique to be studied, assigns what to read before the next session, and develops an action plan. This plan does not have to be final; it can and should be revisited every several sessions and modified if necessary.

▶ *Session 2.* Teachers arrive having read the assigned research-based book or article; they discuss the theory and research behind the technique as well as its implementation in the classroom (20 minutes). They decide as a group how members will implement the technique in their classroom before the next session and perhaps sketch out a tentative lesson plan (25 minutes). Members decide on what to read next (sticking with the same technique, such as comprehension monitoring) before the next session (10 minutes).

▶ *Session 3.* Members discuss what went well and bring up problems or confusions they experienced as they tried out the technique, propose solutions to problems, and clear up confusions (15 minutes). Based on the material they have read, members discuss modifications to how they teach the technique they are studying (20 minutes). The group decides who will bring a video clip to the next study group session and who will bring a sample of students' work related to the technique being studied (10 minutes). The group revisits their action plan (10 minutes).

▶ *Session 4.* The group discusses what went well and problems or confusions they experienced applying the teaching technique (10 minutes). Then, based on their reading and teaching experiences, they propose solutions to problems, clear up confusions, and discuss possible modifications to their teaching (15 minutes). They watch and discuss the video clip a study group member has brought (15 minutes). They use the looking-at-student-work protocol to examine samples of student work that a second study group member has brought (15 minutes). They decide who is going to bring a video clip and who is going to bring student work to the next session (5 minutes).

▶ *Session 5.* Members discuss what went well and problems or confusions they experienced applying the teaching technique (10 minutes). They discuss solutions, clear up confusions, and discuss modifications to their teaching (10 minutes) or decide if the group should now study a new technique (5 minutes). Members, using the focused video-sharing protocol, watch and discuss the video clip brought in by a study group member (15 minutes). Members also use the looking-at-student-work protocol to examine samples of student work brought by another study group member (15 minutes). If the group is sticking with the same technique, they decide who is going to bring a video clip and who is going to bring student work to the next session (5 minutes). If they feel it's time to move on to a related instructional technique (e.g., a different comprehension strategy or high-level talk about text), they decide what to study and read about next (10–15 minutes).

Appendix 7–9 on the DVD contains texts or articles with a strong research base that teachers have found useful when building a general understanding of the theory and research behind good reading instruction in specific areas (e.g., phonics, comprehension strategies). Books and research-based articles on how to teach specific research-based techniques are also provided. The listed resources are only examples, but they may give study group members ideas about the types of research-based books or articles that will be useful in study groups.

Cross-Grade Study Groups

Teachers in effective schools interact both within and across grade levels. Although it is easier for schools to start with grade-level study groups, it is important by midyear to begin moving into some cross-grade study groups. This is one way that teachers can learn to use a common language, teach with compatible techniques, and develop a coherent reading program from grade to grade.

By year 2 of the SCR process, most study groups should be cross grade, not grade level. Also, year 2 study group topics should be different from those addressed in year 1, although teaching practices and reflections will, of course, be built on knowledge and abilities gained in year 1.

Providing Study Group Leadership

As described in Chapter 5, the SCR process depends on leadership from the principal, a literacy coordinator, external consultant (if feasible), and internal leadership team members. This group is responsible for helping study groups move forward successfully. The leadership team looks at the action plans and meeting notes of study groups in order to keep abreast of what study groups are doing and help struggling study groups become more successful. Without support from a leadership team, 20 or 25 percent of the study groups meeting during a given period may be struggling to be productive. Negative voices, teachers not sticking to the group schedule, teachers focusing on what students cannot do as opposed to what support they need, or teachers talking about classroom experiences unrelated to the study group topic are some of the common problems. Study groups who do not feel their meetings are worthwhile need to ask themselves, "What can we do to make this time together more intellectually challenging and useful to our students and to ourselves?"

To help struggling study groups, the leadership team can evaluate their action plans and meeting notes using the following questions (Murphy and Lick 2005, also offer useful suggestions):

▶ Do the topics on the action plan make sense for the grade levels involved?

▶ Are the actions based on research? What is the evidence?

▶ Do the topics have the potential to lead to significant changes in teaching and students' reading achievement?

▶ Is a study group sticking with a topic for a sufficient amount of time?

▶ What other comments or questions may help the group be more successful?

Other questions a leadership team may address include:

▶ Do we have regular meetings to address study groups' progress?

▶ Is every study group represented at this meeting?

▶ What process is in place to give feedback to study groups?

▶ How do study groups share what they are doing and learning?

More Tips for Successful Study Groups

The following suggestions come from SCR literacy coordinators and external consultants on actions they have taken to help teachers have successful study group experiences.

Supporting Study Groups

▶ Remind study groups that it is not necessary to read a research-based article every session. Study groups need to discuss teaching practices from their own classrooms as well as discuss research.

▶ Remind study groups that all members should be studying, trying out, and refining the same set of techniques so they can learn together and provide feedback to one another.

- Have the literacy coordinator, leadership team members, and external consultant meet once a month to review what study groups are doing (via meeting notes and action plans) and strategize ways to help study groups that are "stuck."

- Make action plans and meeting notes public so that everyone learns from what other study groups are doing.

- Have the literacy coordinator and external consultant provide written feedback to study groups.

- Have the literacy coordinator or external consultant visit classrooms to offer support related to teachers' study group topics.

Different Approaches to Scheduling Study Group Meeting Times

- Schedule study groups before or after school.

- Provide release time during the school day or budget money to pay teachers to attend extra meetings after school.

- Have students arrive one hour later one day a week.

- Discontinue most staff meetings and use that time for study groups (communicate information normally shared at staff meetings).

- Arrange schedules so that grade-level study groups can meet during a common planning time.

Other Ideas for Increasing the Effectiveness of Study Groups

- Don't try to do too much too quickly. Narrow the focus of topics and study group activities. Stick with a topic for more than two or three months.

- Establish the time and place for study groups early in the year, make them a priority, and keep them going—make them part of the regular routine.

- Be specific and hands-on with study groups that struggle. They will get off to a better start and become more self-directed later on.

- Periodically remind study group members, if needed, that their goal is improving and changing practice, not just reading and talking.

- Have the principal talk with study group members who are negatively affecting other members in their group.

- Allow group members to develop their own action plans; they will be more motivated to learn, to have a purpose. Provide scaffolding by making suggestions, modeling, finding current research to support their practice, and sharing your expertise.

- Help groups find relevant research-based readings as needed. Keep a file of research articles on best practices.

- Encourage professional growth through praise and the notion that everyone is learning together. No one has all the answers.

Additional Professional Learning in Whole-School Sessions

A number of topics related to effective reading instruction cut across grades and can be effectively covered with the entire staff at whole-group meetings about once every four to six weeks or at other district-scheduled professional learning days.

Classroom-Based Assessments

Teachers throughout a school should use a coordinated set of classroom-based assessments to monitor children's reading that teachers agree are most useful. (Assessments are also discussed in Chapter 6.) How to work through assessment procedures and ways to interpret and make use of the data can be covered in a whole-school meeting. Fluency is probably the easiest dimension of reading to assess because tools for monitoring fluency are readily available (e.g., websites and other products that help teachers assess and interpret students' scores on words read correctly per minute). However, teachers also need to monitor progress in other dimensions of reading. Running records and informal inventories can be used to assess students' word recognition abilities and reading level (Leslie and Caldwell 2010). Rubrics and checklists can be used to assess students' comprehension abilities. Excellent suggestions for classroom-based assessments tied to reading comprehension can be found in Lipson (2007) and Afflerbach (2007).

Motivational Instruction

Motivation is an important dimension of effective reading instruction (Guthrie et al. 2000; Pressley et al. 2003), but it is one that is often overlooked. Teachers in SCR schools use motivational instruction checklists (refer back to Figure 6–3) to reflect on important pedagogical aspects of their instruction related to students' motivation for learning. Often they begin by watching a video of a lesson presented by the literacy coordinator or another effective teacher in a whole-group meeting and discuss dimensions listed on the checklist that they have observed in the lesson. They may also use the checklist on motivational practices in conjunction with the multidimensional video-sharing protocol when reviewing video clips in study groups (refer back to Figure 7–7). Teachers in SCR schools have also found that a discussion of Motivating Primary-Grade Students, by Pressley and colleagues (2003), is a helpful schoolwide activity.

Making Good Instructional Choices from Teachers' Manuals

Effective teachers plan their lessons well and differentiate instruction within these plans to meet students' varied needs (see Chapter 3). Teachers in SCR schools plan lessons and differentiate instruction by thinking aloud as they read through teaching suggestions in teachers' manuals. To get started the literacy coordinator, at a whole-group meeting, may model the process. For example, a literacy coordinator looking at a lesson from a grade 2 teachers manual on a story about a city mouse and a country mouse, might reason:

> The basal says to talk about all six vocabulary words—*cage, content, bottle, wheel, follow,* and *raccoon*—before reading but I think it would be better to talk about these words as we come across them in the story. Students may need context

clues to help them understand some words' meanings. Other words are pretty easy, and I'll just quickly check to see whether they are familiar with them when we come across them in the story. Also, the manual says to do a picture walk before we read, but I think that would give the ending away, so I'll skip it. I think I will have my students who are reading on grade level read the entire six-page story on their own. I'll read the story at the small-group table with my struggling readers. I'll only ask a few of the questions listed for each page of the story because they are mostly low-level questions designed to see whether the students followed the details of the story. By skipping many of these questions, we'll have more time for the questions at the end that focus on story theme and character interpretation.

I've already modeled summarizing a story, so instead of doing the recommended worksheet on summarizing, I'll lead a guided practice on summarizing. I'll have the students as a group generate important parts from the beginning of the story, and then I'll have them, in groups of three, summarize the middle and end of the story by discussing their ideas and writing them down.

I'll teach the phonics lesson on the sounds for /er/, /ir/, and /ur/ to my struggling and average readers, but I think I'll skip it with my above-average readers because they already know this information. I will touch on ways to spell words with the /er/ sound with everyone in our spelling work this week.

Once this is modeled in a whole-group meeting, teachers at grade-level planning meetings can continue to work together to make good instructional choices from the ideas provided in their teacher manuals.

Concluding Thoughts

Often, teachers do not have opportunities to engage in professional learning that is teacher directed, focused on practice, intellectually stimulating, and immediately useful in their daily teaching. Teachers become very enthusiastic about this type of professional learning when they have the opportunity to experience it.

A year after the formal SCR process, which included external support, had ended, teachers at Madina Elementary remained very positive about their ongoing professional learning. A high percentage of the teachers continued to participate regularly in professional learning, inquiry, and reflection. They also regularly asked their colleagues for ideas about how they could improve their teaching. Literacy coordinator Jane Larson reflected, "Through this change process, we have collaborated on reading instruction. Talking with others has led to professional growth for all teachers in our school. It is important to talk with colleagues about instruction and assessments to reflect on your own teaching and make changes." Melissa Norris, a kindergarten teacher, summarized her reaction this way: "Involvement in the SCR process has been a very positive thing for us. It has made us step outside our comfort zone and take some risks. We have all grown through all aspects of the reform process. I know we can see the growth in our students."

talk about it

* Are teachers at your school energized by the idea of participating in collaborative professional development in study groups and whole-group learning sessions?

* What are the barriers, and what can be done to remove them?

* What support is needed to get started?

Research-Based Readings and Resources for Study Groups*

Phonemic Awareness and Emergent Literacy

McCormick, C. E., R. N. Throneburg, and J. M. Smitley. 2002. *A Sound Start: Phonemic Awareness Lessons for Reading Success.* New York: Guilford.

National Reading Panel. 2000. *Report of the National Reading Panel: Teaching Children to Read: Reports of the Subgroups* (NIH Publication No. 00-4754). Washington, DC: National Institute for Child Health and Human Development, National Institutes of Health.

Rog, L. J. 2001. *Early Literacy Instruction in Kindergarten.* Newark, DE: International Reading Association.

Taylor, B. M. (in press a). *Catching Readers: Grade K.* Portsmouth, NH: Heinemann.

Phonics, Word Recognition, and Fluency

Bear, D. R., M. Invernizzi, S. Templeton, and F. Johnston. 2007. *Words Their Way: Word Study for Phonics, Vocabulary, and Spelling Instruction.* 4th ed. Upper Saddle River, NJ: Pearson/Merrill Prentice Hall.

Carnine, D. W., J. Silbert, E. J. Kame'enui, and S. G. Tarver. 2004. *Direct Instruction Reading.* 4th ed. Upper Saddle River, NJ: Pearson.

Johns, J. L., and R. L. Berglund. 2005. *Fluency Strategies and Assessments.* Dubuque, IA: Kendall-Hunt.

Gaskins, I. W., L. C. Ehri, C. Cress, C. O'Hara, and K. Donnelly. 1996. "Procedures for Word Learning: Making Discoveries About Words." *The Reading Teacher* 50: 312–27.

National Reading Panel. 2000. *Report of the National Reading Panel: Teaching Children to Read: Reports of the Subgroups* (NIH Publication No. 00-4754). Washington, DC: National Institute for Child Health and Human Development, National Institutes of Health.

Rasinski, T. V. 2003. *The Fluent Reader: Oral Reading Strategies for Building Word Recognition, Fluency, and Comprehension.* New York: Scholastic.

Samuels, S. J., and A. Farstrup, eds. 2006. *What Research Has to Say About Fluency Instruction.* 3rd ed. Newark, DE: International Reading Association.

Stahl, S. A., and M. R. Kuhn. 2002. "Making It Sound Like Language: Developing Fluency." *The Reading Teacher* 55(6): 582–84.

Taylor, B. M. (2010a). *Catching Readers: Grade 1.* Portsmouth, NH: Heinemann.

———. (2010b). *Catching Readers: Grade 2.* Portsmouth, NH: Heinemann.

———. (2010c). *Catching Readers: Grade 3.* Portsmouth, NH: Heinemann.

Vocabulary

August, D., and C. Snow. 2007. "Developing Vocabulary in English-Language Learners: A Review of the Experimental Research." In *Effective Instruction for Struggling Readers K–6,* ed. B. M. Taylor and J. E. Ysseldyke, 84–105. New York: Teachers College Press.

---

* These research materials are Appendix 7–9 on the DVD.

Baumann, J. F., and E. J. Kame'enui, eds. 2004. *Vocabulary Instruction: Research to Practice.* New York: Guilford.

Beck, I. L., and M. G. McKeown. 2002. "Text Talk: Capturing the Benefit of Read-Aloud Experience for Young Children." *Reading Teacher* 55(1): 10–20.

Beck, I. L., M. G. McKeown, and L. Kucan. 2002. *Bringing Words to Life: Robust Vocabulary Instruction.* New York: Guilford.

Blachowicz, C., and P. Fisher. 2002. *Teaching Vocabulary in All Classrooms.* 2nd ed. Upper Saddle River, NJ: Pearson/Merrill Prentice Hall.

Graves, M. F. 2007. "Conceptual and Empirical Bases for Providing Struggling Readers with Multifaceted and Long-Term Vocabulary Instruction." In *Effective Instruction for Struggling Readers K–6,* ed. B. M. Taylor and J. E. Ysseldyke, 55–83. New York: Teachers College Press.

National Reading Panel. 2000. *Report of the National Reading Panel: Teaching Children to Read: Reports of the Subgroups* (NIH Publication No. 00-4754). Washington, DC: National Institute for Child Health and Human Development, National Institutes of Health.

Comprehension Strategies

Block, C., and M. Pressley, eds. 2002. *Comprehension Strategies: Research-Based Practices.* New York: Guilford.

Duke, N. K., and V. S. Bennett-Armistead. 2003. *Reading and Writing Informational Text in the Primary Grades: Research-Based Practices.* New York: Scholastic.

Kelley, M.J., and N. Clausen-Grace. 2007. *Comprehension Shouldn't Be Silent.* Newark, DE: International Reading Association.

Kletsien, S. B., and M. J. Dreher. 2005. *Informational Text in K–3 Classrooms: Helping Children Read and Write.* Newark, DE: International Reading Association.

Klingner, J. K., S. Vaughn, M. E. Arguelles, M. T. Hughes, and S. A. Leftwich. 2004. "Collaborative Strategic Reading: Real World Lessons from Classroom Teachers." *Remedial and Special Education* 25: 291–302.

National Reading Panel. 2000. *Report of the National Reading Panel: Teaching Children to Read: Reports of the Subgroups* (NIH Publication No. 00-4754). Washington, DC: National Institute for Child Health and Human Development, National Institutes of Health.

Raphael, T. E., K. Highfield, and K.H. Au. 2006. *QAR Now.* New York: Scholastic.

Swan, E. 2003. *Concept-Oriented Reading Instruction: Engaging Classrooms, Lifelong Learners.* New York: Guilford.

Taylor, B. M. (in press b). *Catching Readers: Grades 4/5.* Portsmouth, NH: Heinemann.

Comprehension: High-Level Talk and Writing About Text

Beck, I. L. and M. G. McKeown. 2002. "Text Talk: Capturing the Benefit of Read-Aloud Experience for Young Children." *Reading Teacher* 55(1): 10–20.

Beck, I. L., M. G. McKeown, R.L. Hamilton, and L. Kucan. 1997. *Questioning the Author.* Newark, DE: International Reading Association.

Cunningham, P. M., and D. R. Smith. 2008. *Beyond Retelling: Toward Higher Level Thinking and Big Ideas.* Newark, DE: IRA.

Day, J. P., D. L. Spiegel, J. McLellan, and V. B. Brown. 2002. *Moving Forward with Literature Circles.* New York: Scholastic.

Goldenberg, C. 1992/1993. "Instructional Conversations: Promoting Comprehension Through Discussion." *The Reading Teacher* 46: 316–26.

Kelley, M. J., and N. Clausen-Grace. 2007. *Comprehension Shouldn't Be Silent.* Newark, DE: International Reading Association.

McMahon, S. I. 1997. "Book Clubs: Contexts for Students to Learn to Lead Their Own Discussions." In *The Book Club Connection*, ed. S. I. McMahon and T. E. Raphael, 89–108. New York: Teachers College.

Olness, R. 2007. *Using Literature to Enhance Content Area Instruction: A Guide for K–5 Teachers.* Newark, DE: IRA.

Raphael, T. E., L. S. Pardo, and K. Highfield. 2002. *Book Club: A Literature-Based Curriculum.* 2nd ed. Lawrence, MA: Small Planet.

Raphael, T. R., and S. McMahon. 1994. "Book Club: An Alternative Framework for Reading Instruction." *Reading Teacher* 48(2): 102–16.

Santoro, L. E., S. K. Baker, D.J. Chard, and L. Howard. 2007. The Comprehension Conversation: Using Purposeful Discussion during Read-Alouds to Promote Student Comprehension and Vocabulary. In *Effective Instruction for Struggling Readers K–6*, ed. B. M. Taylor and J. E. Ysseldyke, 109–37. New York: Teachers College Press.

Taylor, B. M. 2010c. *Catching Readers: Grade 3.* Portsmouth, NH: Heinemann.

———. (in press b). *Catching Readers: Grades 4/5.* Portsmouth, NH: Heinemann.

Wood, K. D., N. L. Roser, and M. Martinez. 2001. "Collaborative Literacy: Lesson Learned from Literature." *Reading Teacher* 55(2): 102–11.

Balanced Reading Instruction and Assessment

McKenna, M., and S. Stahl. 2003. *Assessment for Reading Instruction.* New York: Guilford.

Morrow, L. M. 2003. *Organizing and Managing the Language Arts Block: A Professional Development Guide.* New York: Guilford.

Paratore, J. R., and R. L. McCormick, eds. 2007. *Classroom Reading Assessment: Making Sense of What Students Know and Do.* New York: Guilford.

Pressley, M. 2006. *Reading Instruction That Works: The Case for Balanced Teaching.* 3rd ed. New York: Guilford.

Taberski, S. 2000. *On Solid Ground: Strategies for Teaching Reading K–3.* Portsmouth, NH: Heinemann.

Meeting Individual Needs

Au, K. 2006. *Multicultural Issues and Literacy Achievement.* Mahwah, NJ: Erlbaum.

August, D., and T. Shanahan, eds. 2006. *Developing Literacy in Second-Language Learners: Report of the National Literacy Panel on Language-Minority Children and Youth.* Mahwah, NJ: Erlbaum.

Fuchs, D., L. Fuchs, and S. Vaughn, eds. 2008. *Response to Intervention: An Overview for Educators.* Newark, DE: International Reading Association.

Gaskins, I. W. 2004. *Success with Struggling Readers: The Benchmark School Approach.* New York: Guilford.

Lapp, D., D. Fisher, and T. D. Wolsey. 2009. *Literacy Growth for Every Child: Differentiated Small-Group Instruction, K–6.* New York: Guilford.

McCormick, R. L., and J. R. Paratore, eds. 2005. *After Early Intervention, Then What?: Teaching Struggling Readers in Grades 3 and Beyond.* Upper Saddle River, NJ: Pearson.

McCormick, S. 2007. *Instructing Students Who Have Literacy Problems.* 5th ed. Upper Saddle River, NJ: Pearson.

Southall, M. 2009. *Differentiated Small-Group Reading Lessons.* New York: Scholastic.

Taylor, B. M. 2010a. *Catching Readers, Grade 1.* Portsmouth, NH: Heinemann.

———. 2010b. *Catching Readers, Grade 2.* Portsmouth, NH: Heinemann.

———. 2010c. *Catching Readers: Grade 3.* Portsmouth, NH: Heinemann.

———. (in press a). *Catching Readers: Grade K.* Portsmouth, NH: Heinemann.

———. (in press b). *Catching Readers: Grades 4/5.* Portsmouth, NH: Heinemann.

Tyner, B. 2009. *Small-Group Reading Instruction: A Differentiated Teaching Model for Beginning and Struggling Readers.* Newark, DE: International Reading Association.

———. 2009. *Small-Group Reading Instruction: A Differentiated Teaching Model for Intermediate Grade Readers, Grades 3–8.* Newark, DE: International Reading Association.

Vaughn, S., J. Wanzek, and J. M. Fletcher. 2007. Multiple Tiers of Intervention: A Framework for Prevention and Identification of Students with Reading/Learning Disabilities. In *Effective Instruction for Struggling Readers K–6,* ed. B. M. Taylor and J. E. Ysseldyke, 173–95. New York: Teachers College Press.

Walpole, S., and M. C. McKenna. 2009. *How to Plan Differentiated Reading Instruction: Resources for Grades K–3.* New York: Guilford.

The Power of Coaching Conversations

When coaching works, it's very exciting. Think about it—no matter what the endeavor, whether teaching reading, learning to play the flute, or growing a garden in a new landscape, isn't it great to have someone to lean on and learn alongside you? In the School Change in Reading (SCR) process, coaching is carried out with a high degree of peer spirit. And the positive effects are borne out on students, as a body of research shows that literacy coaching supports teachers and contributes to students' gains in reading achievement (Bean, Draper, Turner, and Zigmond 2010; Elish-Piper and L'Allier 2007; Sailors, Lowe, and Sellers 2009).

In this chapter, I share how to set forth a process that puts teachers who are serving in the role of literacy coach or coordinator into classrooms a lot and yet sets a tone to the visits that is collegial rather than formal. In the three-step process, the protocols give everyone a clear process to rely on and are highly respectful of teachers' expertise.

Literacy coaches are respected teachers within their schools who have been selected and released from some, or perhaps all, of their regular teaching responsibilities to provide oversight to the SCR process. They spend part of their day supporting colleagues by first modeling new techniques and then visiting classrooms to watch as colleagues teach new techniques so that the two, teacher and coach, can have a conversation about the practices being implemented. All teachers recognize that the person serving in the literacy coach role is visiting colleagues' classrooms as a peer rather than as an expert. When the coach models something new, she is typically putting herself out there, trying a new technique from a study group first. Later in the day or week, the coach and the teacher use the coaching protocol in Figure 8–1 to talk about what went well and

Peer Coaching Protocol 1

Teacher _____

Coach _____

Date _____

Pre-Classroom Visit Notes (Conference Notes)

Purposes of the Lesson:

Special Area of Focus During Observation (as requested by teacher):

What I Observed

What things related to the lesson's purposes were students doing well?

What things related to the lesson's purposes did the teacher do well?

What other practices or next steps might make the lesson even more effective?

Figure 8–1 Peer Coaching Protocol

discuss suggestions for possible modifications to the coach's modeled lesson. After the coach visits a teacher's classroom to watch a lesson, scheduled follow-up conversations are also key to fostering reflection and ideas for next steps related to the instruction observed during the visit. In this post-visit conversation, the coach asks questions and the teacher who has taught the lesson does most of the talking.

The Coaching Process

At a whole-group meeting before any classroom visits, the teacher serving as the school coach introduces the coaching cycle and explains the three basic steps involved and how each enhances the goal of improving teaching and in turn students' reading. I've found that once teachers have a strong understanding of the cycle, they "jump in with both feet" and appreciate the support of the literacy coordinator.

Step 1: Teacher shares information before a coach's visit. Ideally, the teacher and the coach meet briefly prior to the visit, so the teacher can describe what she's hoping to accomplish in the lesson and give the coach background on students in the class. The teacher might also ask the coach to pay particular attention to one aspect of her teaching that she wonders about, such as her balance of lower- and higher-level questioning or the explicitness of her strategy instruction. However, any dimensions of effective instruction could be discussed during the post-visit conversation as well. If a preview meeting isn't feasible, teachers might email the coach or fill out a quick form that briefly explains the purposes and action steps of the upcoming lesson, students being taught, and materials being used.

Step 2: The coach visits the teacher's classroom. The coach observes the teacher teach a reading lesson, taking notes on a coaching protocol form (see Figures 8–2 and 8–3 and on the DVD). The notes help the coach accurately remember what happened during the lesson. The visits usually last about 30 minutes.

Coaching protocol 1 is the one to use first because it is simpler, more focused, and thus a good place to start. By the second year of the SCR process, schools should switch to using coaching protocol 2 when teachers are ready to reflect on the multiple dimensions and complexity of effective reading instruction. These coaching protocols are later used in peer coaching as well, when teachers (not the school literacy coach) coach each other.

Step 3: The teacher and coach have a follow-up conversation. At a mutually convenient time, the teacher and coach have a conversation about the lesson. (See Video 5 on the DVD.) The coach mainly asks questions and the teacher does most of the talking. The goal of the meeting is for the teacher and the coach, guided by coaching protocol 1 or coaching protocol 2, to identify possible "next steps" the teacher can work toward to make his or her instructional practice even better. The important thing is that the teacher has to feel really free to talk, raise questions, and explore ideas during the conversation. Their conversation might go like this:

Peer Coaching Protocol 2

Dimensions of Effective Teaching	Successes/Other Comments	Possible Changes
Please check the instructional focus of your lesson: _____ HLQ _____ Comprehension _____ Vocabulary _____ Word Recognition/Fluency _____ Emergent Literacy		
_____ **Purpose (state purpose below):** * Was the purpose clearly stated? * How has this lesson helped individual students grow in their literacy abilities?		
_____ **High-Level Questioning** To what extent are the students engaged in higher-level thinking during discussion and writing about text?		
_____ **Explicit Strategy Instruction** To what extent did the teacher teach a reading strategy in addition to reading skills? Did the students understand how this strategy will help them be a better reader and how to use the strategy in the future?		
_____ **Student Support** To what extent did the teacher support students while teaching reading (coaching, modeling, listening, and giving feedback)?		
_____ **Active Responding** To what extent did students respond actively (*i.e., reading, writing, manipulating, partner sharing*) during the lesson?		
_____ **Timing** Did the teacher keep instruction brisk and focused? Were the students on task throughout the lesson?		
_____ **Other** Teacher actions to get students to where they were in the lesson observed. Application to your own classroom: What did you personally learn from observing this lesson that you will transfer to your own classroom? Other comments and reflections/support needed. Teacher actions to get students to where they were in the lesson observed.		

Catching Schools © 2011 by Barbara M. Taylor (Heinemann: Portsmouth, NH).

Figure 8–2 Peer Coaching Protocol 2

Students' Use of Time During Reading Class

Grade _____ Teacher _____ Date _____ **Number of Students** _____

Ability level for emergent literacy/phonemic awareness (el/pa), phonics/word recognition (wr), vocabulary (voc), fluency (fl), comprehension (comp): 3 = good, 2 = average, 1 = low.

Write number that best fits each target student below.

	High student:	Average student:	Low student:
	el/pa ____	el/pa ____	el/pa ____
	wr ____	wr ____	wr ____
	fl ____	fl ____	fl ____
	voc ____	voc ____	voc ____
	comp ____	comp ____	comp ____

Time (in 10-minute segments)	Grouping (whole, small, other)	High Student	Average Student	Low Student
1.		Activity:	Activity:	Activity:
		Comment/question:	Comment/question:	Comment/question:
2.		Activity:	Activity:	Activity:
		Comment/question:	Comment/question:	Comment/question:
3.		Activity:	Activity:	Activity:
		Comment/question:	Comment/question:	Comment/question:
4.		Activity:	Activity:	Activity:
		Comment/question:	Comment/question:	Comment/question:
5.		Activity:	Activity:	Activity:
		Comment/question:	Comment/question:	Comment/question:
6.		Activity:	Activity:	Activity:
		Comment/question:	Comment/question:	Comment/question:

Catching Schools © 2011 by Barbara M. Taylor (Heinemann: Portsmouth, NH).

Figure 8–3 Student's Use of Time During Reading Class

A. Coach thanks the teacher for the opportunity to visit.

COACH: *Thanks for letting me come into your classroom today. I picked up some new ideas.*

B. Coach and teacher clarify lesson purpose.

COACH: *I want to make sure I have your lesson purposes written down correctly. I wrote down. . . . Am I getting this right?*

The teacher elaborates, the coach asks more questions if needed, and teacher and coach keep talking about lesson purposes if needed.

C. Teacher and coach discuss things the students were able to do related to the focus of the lesson.

Teacher offers comments.

Coach (referring to notes): I noticed. . . .

D. Teacher and coach discuss things that went well in the lesson and that helped the students develop and be successful.

Teacher offers ideas.

COACH (REFERRING TO NOTES): *I noticed. . . .*

E. Teacher shares any aspect of the lesson that didn't seem as smooth or effective as she would have liked, and asks the coach for input. The teacher and coach discuss possible changes to the lesson to make it even more effective.

Teacher offers suggestions.

COACH: *One idea I had was. . . . Have you thought about. . . .*

F. Coach and teacher discuss next steps.

COACH: *What would be a "next step" for you in moving your students forward? How can I support you in this goal?*

Teacher responds.

Coach responds and elaborates.

G. Coach offers personal reflections.

COACH: *I want to thank you again for letting me observe today. I learned. . . . I appreciated. . . . I look forward to. . . .*

A Coaching Protocol for Differentiated Instruction

At times, instead of using the SCR coaching protocols to observe a lesson, a coach may observe an entire class period using the students' use-of-time protocol (see Figures 8–3 and 8–4 and on the DVD), highlighting effective activities and jotting down questions about activities that seem less effective. The primary purpose of this longer coaching session is to help classroom teachers look at their reading activities for high-, average-, and low-ability students and reflect on the extent to which these activities meet students' individual needs effectively. For each activity the coach might ask the teacher

Students' Use of Time During Reading Class (completed)

Grade _2_ Teacher _____ Date ___11/15___ Number of Students _19_

Ability level for emergent literacy/phonemic awareness (el/pa), phonics/word recognition (wr), vocabulary (voc), fluency (fl), comprehension (comp):
3 = good, 2 = average, 1 = low.

Write number that best fits each target student below.

High student:	Average student:	Low student:
wr _3_	wr _3_	wr _1_
fl _3_	fl _2_	fl _1_
voc _2_	voc _2_	voc _2_
comp _3_	comp _2_	comp _2_

Time (in 10-minute segments)	Grouping (whole, small, other)	High Student	Average Student	Low Student
1. 9:00–9:10	W	**Activity** Frogs—semantic map	**Activity:** same	**Activity:** same
		Comment/question: Rich vocabulary activity	**Comment/question:** same	**Comment/question:** same
		More active responding?	same	same
2. 9:10–9:20	W	**Activity:** Same as above	**Activity:** Same as above	**Activity:** Same as above
3. 9:20–9:30	S	**Activity:** (with classroom teacher): Outlining Pilgrim story	**Activity:** At center, listening to basal story on tape	**Activity:** (with resource teacher): Filling out basal workbook pages on phonics
9:30–9:40	S	Challenging comprehension activity	Could students read on their own without help	Could students do workbook page on own and teacher coach in word recognition as students read instead?

Catching Schools © 2011 by Barbara M. Taylor (Heinemann: Portsmouth, NH).

Figure 8–4 Example of Students' Use of Time During Reading Class Form

how she felt that activity went (*Any thoughts about this activity? How did you feel this part of your lesson went?*), then offer comments and pose questions he or she jotted down during the observation. SCR teachers like the students' use-of-time protocol because it focuses on students' engagement during whole-group, small-group, and independent activities. It is a challenge to monitor all students during independent activities, and they appreciate a coach's feedback.

Reflections on Classroom Visits and Coaching Experiences

Anna Berglund, the literacy coordinator at Edgewood Elementary, describes the purposes of her modeling and coaching visits this way:

> I work with staff to refine instruction through visits in which I model and coach. The purpose of these visits is to help individual teachers move forward in their instructional practices through guided reflective questioning and constructive feedback. Hopefully, this reflection and support leads to changes in instruction which in turn leads to increased student learning.

Describing Anna Berglund's role, Becky Saunders, a first-grade teacher at Edgewood Elementary, says:

> She helps facilitate our learning. She is a support system for what we are doing in the classroom. She is a source for information we need. She models new practices for us. She encourages and partners with us to move our learning forward. I've appreciated the opportunity to sit down with Anna to talk about things I'm doing or thinking of doing. I like to bounce ideas off her one-on-one. Also, the feedback on what she sees students able to do when she comes to my room or what else I might think about doing is helpful. It has caused me to think about my instruction in different ways and make modifications.

Angelina Ipson, an ELL teacher at Westside Elementary, discusses the value of the coaching she had received from her literacy coordinator, Estella Butler:

> Estella observes in our classrooms and we talk about what we could do better. She pushes us to move forward. If we didn't have her leadership we would not get as far as fast as we do! After she has been in to watch me teach, I find that a lot of her comments simply affirm what I'm doing. She also makes suggestions and encourages us to go out to watch what others in the school are doing. Estella has helped us think and make our conversations about our teaching more academic and more metacognitive.

To learn their techniques, my colleagues and I shadowed and interviewed eight of the most effective literacy coordinators in schools using the SCR process. All of them used coaching protocol 1 or 2 to take notes while they were observing and to guide their questions or comments in follow-up conversations, so they were able to give concrete examples. At these follow-up meetings they elicited the teachers' ideas about what they thought had gone well, what they thought they needed help with, and what they thought they might do next. The teachers identified elements of effective instruction in the modeled or observed lessons and set goals for themselves for future lessons. The literacy coordinators offered suggestions selectively but did not tell teachers what they should or should not do. Coaching conversation starters that SCR literacy coordinators found useful are listed in Figure 8–5 and on the DVD.

Coaching Conversation Starters

Coach

- It was evident that . . .
- As I was listening I felt you were able to . . .
- One thing I thought about when . . .
- I heard you say . . .
- Tell me a little bit about . . .
- You mentioned . . .
- The one piece I would focus on is . . .
- I was wondering about . . .
- What else did you learn as a teacher . . .
- Do you think . . . [coach makes a suggestion]
- Can you think of an area where I could give you some support?
- What will the next lesson look like?
- Looking back, what changes would you make in your lesson?
- Given that your lesson focus was on _____, let's talk about some things that went well . . . and where there may be some ways to improve . . .

Coach's Coach

- Did you feel this conversation brought the teacher to that next place in his or her instruction? How?
- Do you think the teacher was able to identify what went well in his or her lesson and why?
- _____ and _____ would have been good places to stop and talk about _____.
- What did you learn from this coaching session today that will help you . . .
- How might you consider _____ as you think about how to support this teacher getting to this next level?
- As you went into this conversation, what kinds of things were you planning to talk with this teacher about?
- How do you think the conversation you had with the teacher impacted her/his instruction?
- What do you think the teacher learned that will make a difference in his or her teaching?
- Did you as a coach accomplish your goal?
- Do you feel the teacher accomplished her or his goal?
- When do you think you were especially effective as a coach?

Catching Schools © 2011 by Barbara M. Taylor (Heinemann: Portsmouth, NH).

Figure 8–5 Coaching Conversation Starters

Professional Development for Literacy Coordinators

Typically, teachers who assume the literacy coordinator role and who are expected to go into colleagues' classrooms to model and coach have not had formal training on how to do this effectively. As a part of the professional development for coaches in SCR schools, teachers serving in this role learn how to use coaching protocols 1 and 2 (Peterson et al. 2009). Then the professional development coach (e.g., an external partner serving as a coach or Title I teacher at the school) watches the coach-in-training (e.g., the literacy coordinator) have a conversation with a teacher. Together, the two coaches reflect on what has been effective in the coaching conversation and how the coach-in-training can improve his or her questions to guide teachers toward deeper reflection and modifications of practice in the future. In the example that follows, two coaches from Madina reflect on their effectiveness as coaches:

COACH 1 (PROFESSIONAL DEVELOPMENT COACH): *In what ways were you effective in your coaching conversation today?*

COACH 2 (COACH-IN-TRAINING): *I felt I brought up things that helped the teacher think about her questions and whether these did or did not encourage students to give high-level responses. For example, I asked her how she felt when a student answered only "Bad" to her question, "How do you think Sam felt when he showed up for the first day of school as a new student?" Instantly, she said, "I can see why this was not a high-level response. I should have asked him to explain his answer."*

COACH 1: *Was there a part of the coaching conversation that you felt was less successful?*

COACH 2: *I'm not sure I was helpful enough to the teacher on ideas for next steps on high-level questioning.*

COACH 1: *You set up a time to plan a lesson with the teacher. That is a natural time to talk about next steps, so you have another chance. Now, were there some aspects of the teacher's lesson that you hoped would surface in the follow-up coaching conversation? If so, did you feel like you were able to bring these ideas up?*

COACH 2: *Yes, the teacher said she wanted to learn new teaching techniques. So I encouraged her to do more with vocabulary at point of contact in the story as opposed to going over so many words and their meanings before students even read the story. She seemed interested in trying to do this.*

COACH 1: *Was there a valuable example in this lesson that would benefit other teachers?*

COACH 2: *Yes, two things. Because of well-established routines, this teacher was very efficient moving from her whole-group lesson to small-group lessons and independent work. Also, she had motivational independent activities— lots of reading and writing—so her students were very engaged.*

The opportunity for one coach to reflect with another coach on effective practices is an important part of the professional development for coaches and helps them have more robust conversations with teachers that lead to deeper reflection about instruction. Estella Butler, the literacy coordinator at Westside Elementary, describes the value of the coaching training she received from an external partner:

> What I've learned about coaching has really helped me. In the beginning I was in the classroom doing a lot of teaching and modeling myself, and I wasn't really sure how to get teachers to do more of the teaching when I was there. Through the coaching training, I've learned how to divert ownership to the teachers. I have a preobservation conference, go in to observe, and then have a postobservation conference. Following an observation, I question teachers to come up with their own ideas and changes.

ƒee it iN ActioN

Coaching by a Literacy Coach

A group of literacy coaches from different schools meet to hone their coaching abilities. A literacy coach works with a teacher (also a literacy coach herself) who has taught a kindergarten reading lesson. We see the teacher give background on the lesson. She also asks for feedback from the literacy coach on her lesson purposes and for suggestions on how to raise the bar for the students as they read decodable texts in future lessons. After watching a video of the teacher's lesson, the coach asks questions to engage the teacher in a reflective conversation about her teaching. The coach offers a few suggestions related to the teacher's earlier queries about lesson purposes and raising the bar, and she asks what she can do to support the teacher in terms of next steps.

ƒee it iN ActioN

Coaching of a Literacy Coach

In this second clip from the meeting of literacy coaches that we observed in Video 5, a second literacy coach engages in a discussion with the literacy coach whom we saw in action in Video 5. The coach's coach asks questions that get the literacy coach to talk about and reflect on her coaching practices. The coach's coach asks about what went well and what coaching questions seemed to help the teacher of the kindergarten lesson potentially make her teaching even more effective. The coach's coach also offers suggestions to the coach that they then discuss to help the coach make her coaching even more effective in the future.

The Goal: Turn Teachers into Peer Coaches

Once teachers have become comfortable with classroom visits and coaching conversations with their literacy coordinator, the next step is for them to learn how to serve as a peer coach and be coached by a peer. Peer coaching is important because a school may not be able to afford a literacy coordinator indefinitely and more to the point, for reform to happen and be sustained, teachers need to feel elevated into new collaborative roles. Once trained, teachers are ideal for coaching teachers. Getting support, feedback, and suggestions from colleagues motivates them to refine their instruction.

To develop a peer coaching program, the leadership team should first discuss the purposes of a peer coaching program at their school. Once the purposes are set, the leadership team needs to decide how to present the information to the staff.

Teachers must clearly understand the purposes of and procedures for peer coaching to be effective peer coaches. Therefore, before becoming peer coaches, teachers should have had three or more previous coaching sessions with either the literacy coordinator or an external partner across a school year. Before teachers begin peer coaching they should review coaching protocols 1 and 2 (see Figures 8–1 and 8–2), and literacy coordinators should accompany peer coaches on their first series of classroom visits to provide guidance and feedback.

Commenting on the value of peer coaching and classroom visits, Estella Butler, the literacy coordinator at Westside Elementary, says: "We are teaching teachers how to coach their peers using the same coaching model we were taught. We are beginning by teaching members of the leadership team peer coaching techniques and will then teach others. . . . Before, our professional learning was all about reading and talking and now it's about action."

see it iN ActioN

Peer Coaching

A third-grade classroom teacher coaches a second-grade classroom teacher who has taught an EIR lesson to her struggling readers (see Taylor 2010c.) The peer coach has met with the classroom teacher prior to her visit to get information about the upcoming lesson. The peer coach then observes the second grade teacher's lesson while a resource teacher covers her own classroom. After the classroom visit, the two teachers meet to have a conversation about the lesson observed. The peer coach asks questions to help the teacher talk about and reflect on her teaching during the lesson. The peer coach offers several suggestions, including ideas about timing that the teacher had asked the peer coach to focus upon during her visit. At the end of the coaching conversation, the peer coach reflects on what she learned by observing in the second grade teacher's classroom.

Coaching Tips

SCR literacy coordinators and external partners were asked to provide feedback on their coaching experiences. Their suggestions follow. A form used by some SCR literacy coordinators and external consultants to build rapport with teachers is shown in Figure 8–6.

CLASSROOM VISITS

▶ Visiting classrooms is essential so good practices can be discovered and teachers can be encouraged to serve as resources for one another. For example, you might say, "You're really good at asking higher-level questions about the text the children have read. Would you be willing to have other teachers come to watch you do this with a group of children? Or could we videotape you so we could show a clip in a study group?" Classroom visits also help to identify problems that can be discussed with an individual or addressed in a general way in a study group.

▶ An effective strategy is to stop in and ask if there is anything you can do to help, any child that the teacher would like you to read with or observe. Often it is less threatening for teachers at first if they feel you are coming to see a student rather than observe them. Later in the school year when teachers are feeling more comfortable and a high level of trust has been established, teachers ask to be observed and ask for specific suggestions about a problem or instructional strategy.

POSITIVE RELATIONSHIPS

▶ Being present and reliable is very important. Make sure you set a schedule, post it clearly, and stick to it.

▶ Before beginning classroom observations and coaching, build trust with the staff. If they view your relationship as collaborative and supportive (shoulder to shoulder), it will help you when you are in a classroom to observe and coach. Initially, spend quite a bit of time in classrooms assisting teachers with groupings, reading with students, or just being present.

▶ Provide various ways for teachers to ask questions or offer suggestions: post office hours, use a feedback card after staff meetings, email often, and so on.

▶ Be as flexible and accommodating as possible when scheduling coaching opportunities for teachers.

GENERAL SUGGESTIONS

▶ Explain and clarify for the whole staff your role as a literacy coach. Be sure the staff understands the purpose of coaching, observations, walk-throughs, and pre- and postconferences. Distribute information outlining your responsibilities, contact information, and schedule.

▶ Develop active listening skills—do more listening than talking.

▶ Arrive at a strong understanding of the teacher's goals and ideas.

▶ Be confident and be competent. Stay current on reading research.

▶ Ask questions in a nonthreatening way to foster self-reflection. Be able to give constructive feedback beyond praising.

Sample Form for Building Rapport with Teachers

September, 20_____

Teachers at Lincoln Elementary,

Welcome back! We hope you are rested and ready to embark on year 2 of our SCR journey. We are eager to support you as you continue to enhance your literacy instruction using research-based practices. As we begin this new year, we would like to know how best we can support you in your efforts. Please take a few minutes to complete this form and return it to us ASAP so that we can plan the most effective professional development opportunities possible for you.

Thanks!
Literacy Coordinator/External Partner

Name: _____

Grade Level: _____ **Room #:** _____ **Extension #:** _____

Study group topics: _____

Specific strategy I am currently working with: _____

What area of reading instruction would you like to see addressed in professional development sessions?

What is your greatest concern about teaching reading? Why?

What area of reading instruction is of the least concern to you? Why?

Things I would like help with:

_____ Observe and schedule a follow-up visit as I try a new strategy. Help me set goals and give me specific written feedback using the classroom-visit protocol.

_____ Help me/my team with other aspects of teaching.
Please name the area you would like support in:

_____.

_____ Meet with me during my prep time as I plan for reading instruction in making good instructional choices from the core reading program.

Day and time to meet:_____

_____ Help me make sense of my classroom observation data.

Day and time to meet: _____.

_____ Assist me in using assessment data to differentiate instruction.

_____ Team teach and/or model a lesson as I try to implement a new strategy I am learning in my study group.

continues

Figure 8–6a Sample form for Building Rapport with Teachers

Sample Form for Building Rapport with Teachers, *continued*

Please check which strategies you would like modeled:

Emergent Literacy (Phonemic Awareness—K/1 only)

_____ Blending/segmenting

_____ Shared and interactive writing

_____ Sound Boxes

Word-Recognition Strategies

_____ Coaching for word recognition

_____ Making words

_____ Decoding multisyllabic words (grades 2–3)

Fluency

_____ Repeated reading

_____ Assisted reading

Vocabulary

_____ Choosing tier 2 words with student-friendly definitions

_____ Short vocabulary activities (Beck book)

_____ Using read-alouds to teach vocabulary

_____ Text talk

Comprehension Strategies

_____ Asking/answering questions

_____ Summarizing

_____ Making connections

_____ Monitoring comprehension

_____ Visualizing

_____ Summarizing vs. retelling

_____ Drawing inferences

Other

_____ Using informational text

_____ Effective "think-aloud" strategies

_____ Guided reading group instruction

_____ _____

Figure 8–6b, Sample form for Building Rapport with Teachers

- Speak slowly to give the teacher time to make more thoughtful responses.

- Consciously think of your body language.

- Remember that coaching is an ongoing process and does not end with one coaching session—each session builds on the one before.

- Try not to allow coaching conversations to become complaining sessions. Redirect conversations to help teachers become aware of how their decisions impact student learning.

- Start with the teachers who are willing to be coached and have them explain the process to other teachers during a whole-group meeting. This usually helps reluctant teachers come on board.

- Work with a highly regarded teacher early in the school year and ask that teacher to share his or her experiences at a whole-group meeting.

- When you go in to observe, keep the focus on instructional practice, use the protocols, and prioritize needs to target in the reflective coaching conversation following the lesson and in the future.

- Be informed about the teacher before observing/reflecting: What do his or her student assessments look like? What do his or her grade-level observation data reflect? What about the effectiveness of schoolwide reading instruction; does that play a role?

- Affirm the teacher's current knowledge and experience and seek to refine and extend that knowledge through reflective dialogue.

- Build up the teachers you observe by pointing out the positive things you saw. Suggest research that is relevant to something positive or less positive you have observed in the classroom.

- Phrase questions so they are nonthreatening; put the teacher at ease and in control.

- Identify specific examples in the lesson where the teacher was effective.

- Asking questions, paraphrasing, and pausing (wait time) are all important tools. Sometimes waiting for the teacher to process and be reflective is the most powerful tool. Your job as a coach is to help the teacher reflect, analyze, and think about other possibilities.

- If you are uncertain about what a teacher is asking, say, "Tell me more about that."

- Don't feel you have to be the expert and have all the answers but be willing to work with the teacher to find the answers. Ask teachers, "What do you think?" when they approach you with a question.

BEFORE CLASSROOM VISITS

- Make sure teachers have had adequate time to practice the instructional techniques that you plan to observe.

- Share the observation format/framework you will be using during your observation.

- During your preobservation conversation, discuss the areas of instruction the teacher wants you to focus on and provide feedback on. Remind the teacher that you will also be taking notes on other aspects of instruction as well so you can both get a well-rounded view of the instruction.

DURING CLASSROOM VISITS

▶ Say what you will do and then do what you say you will do.

▶ Be unobtrusive; do not interrupt instruction.

▶ Focus your attention on what is happening, not on what your recommendations will be.

▶ Think of questions to ask the teacher to help you understand his or her work better.

AFTER CLASSROOM VISITS

▶ Meet with the teacher to confer, letting the teacher take the lead.

▶ Plan your coaching conversation before the meeting—identify specific feedback relevant to the purpose of the observation. Start with positive comments and then offer suggestions.

▶ Be specific about something you would like the teacher to consider improving, and offer choices about how you can help.

▶ Try to approach postobservation conversations as a working peer eager to assist with problem solving or be a "mirror" to help teachers reflect.

▶ Ask teachers about the benefits they have experienced from coaching conversations.

RELUCTANT TEACHERS

▶ If you have reluctant teachers in your building, a good way to get your foot in the door is to start with a student's use-of-time observation (refer back to Figures 8–3 and 8–4).

▶ Remember that each teacher requires differentiated coaching as determined by his or her students, level of experience, and level of self-reflection.

▶ Some faculty members will at first be suspicious of a literacy coordinator or external coach. Win them over by coming into their classrooms and volunteering to work with a group or with an individual student. Pick out the student who seems to be a particular problem that day and offer to take the student for some reading practice. Coming into a classroom as a helper builds the teacher's trust.

SCHOOL PRINCIPAL SUPPORT

▶ Coaches need the support of the principal. Keep the principal informed and develop professional relationships with administrators.

▶ Meet and talk with the principal to get his or her insights into the strengths of, and opportunities to improve, reading instruction in the building.

▶ Be sure the principal understands the role of "coach" as you will be performing it at the school and explain your role to the teachers who are on the staff. (There are lots of definitions!)

Concluding Thoughts

Reflecting on practice is an important but often overlooked aspect of reading improvement efforts. Students need excellent teachers, but teaching expertly isn't easy. Teachers need to help one another reflect on their reading instruction with an eye toward making it even better. Often, teachers at first are wary about someone coming into their classroom to model and coach. However, teachers become more comfortable with this type of professional learning when they have the opportunity to experience it and see the value of it. Another pair of eyes and someone to talk to about instruction is an excellent way to become the most expert teacher you can be.

talk About it

* Think about your own school. Will teachers feel comfortable with the idea of having a peer serving as a literacy coach or coordinator come into their classroom to model and coach? If not, why not? What are the barriers and how can we get past them?

* Do teachers feel comfortable with the idea of engaging in coaching conversations with the literacy coach? If not, why not?

* What support is needed to get started with coaching?

* Which teachers at each grade level will become peer coaches sooner than later? How can they be trained and cultivated relatively early in the process so that peer-led professional development becomes embedded in the school culture?

A Closer Look at One SCR School

• •

I want to conclude this book with a description of the three-year journey of a diverse urban school that was very successful using the SCR model. I think you will learn more about the SCR process by reading this description. Things were not smooth sailing from the start. It took people time to get better at collaborating and learning together. But by the end of the third year, teachers and administrators had achieved a great deal, for themselves as professionals and for their students.

Westside Elementary, introduced in Chapter 1, is a very diverse, high-poverty school in a large urban school district. Westside has many challenges, but it also has many strengths. The school had many successes during the three years it took part in the SCR program. In year 1, the school, with federal funding, began the SCR reform in grades K–3. The process expanded to grades 4–6 in year 2. Students' reading scores increased slowly but steadily during the three-year period. Westside's story illustrates the challenges, actions, and successes that were a part of the school's journey.

In reading about Westside Elementary, you'll come across some very typical stances having to do with underestimating students' abilities to achieve. I say this not to blame anyone but to emphasize what's so powerful about the candid conversations and professional development are that they expose the understandable presumptions and biases but then gives teachers the effective practices that will help them teach in ways that do turn kids around academically—and turn them around in terms of their perceptions about their students' potential.

Westside's Challenges

In 2007–2008, the third and final year Westside took part in the SCR process, 93 percent of the school's seven hundred K–6 students participated in its subsidized lunch program and 87 percent were English language learners (ELLs). (During the three-year period the number of students at the school had increased from five hundred to seven hundred when another school in the district closed.)

Educating Students from High-Poverty, Diverse Backgrounds

At the beginning of the first SCR year, most teachers at Westside, when asked to name their major challenges, answered that their students were very poor readers, many were ELLs, and a fair number were newcomers to the United States. Many teachers were unsure how to meet the needs of their ELLs. They mentioned behavior problems. They also reported that there was little parent involvement at their school. Some teachers intimated that they had low expectations for their students.

One first-grade teacher reported, "My students have language barriers and limited experiences and knowledge. It is hard to get parents to help—they are either too busy or also non-English speakers. Behavior issues in the classroom are also a challenge." However, by the end of year 3, this teacher was striking a different tone: "My students for the most part are reading a lot better. By the end of last year I only had three kids who were really reading well, but this year I have only three kids who aren't, and they are pretty new to the country." Her perceptions of her own teaching abilities had also changed: "Learning good strategies for teaching reading has been the most valuable aspect of the SCR process to me. When I started teaching, I didn't know how to teach reading effectively, but now I feel like I've gone for a master's program in reading! Before I had a little hodge-podge of ideas, but this program really solidified for me how to teach reading."

At the beginning of year 1, when asked about the main challenges in teaching students to read, a third-grade teacher reported, "Language is a problem for many of my students, as is their economic class, lack of literacy and support in the home, and lack of education they have had before I get them. In recent years, I had to lower my expectations." At the end of year 3, this teacher described her third graders differently: "I think the biggest change is that they now realize that they have to take ownership of their own learning. Some of my students can do it now, and they are not as frustrated. They will go back and reread something to try to find the answer instead of asking me." Talking about parents at the end of year 3, this teacher said, "I have tried to reach more parents on the phone or through email. I feel more confident sharing what is going on with each child. I talked with one mom about the fact that her son needs to be working on certain things at home. I can tell already after just one week that they have been working on these things at home and this is making a big difference."

Staff Changes

There were a fair number of staff changes at Westside during the three years the school participated in the SCR process. One-third of the teachers who were at Westside in year 1 were no longer at the school in year 3. At least six teachers moved from one grade level to another. As principal Carla Herrera pointed out, most of the new teachers at Westside came to the school as inexperienced teachers. "Getting new teachers to the school up to speed on our instructional philosophy of meeting individual needs and providing intellectual challenge as well as learning the research-based techniques that help teachers provide effective reading instruction is a constant challenge."

Bringing Rigor to Whatever Practice You Select

One of the toughest challenges in any reform effort is to select a focused set of instructional beliefs and practices, or methods, and stick with it long enough so that teachers can really do it very well. The effective reading practices recommended in this book, for example, overlay just about any method, whether a school chooses to commit to a reading workshop model or uses a literature basal. The new methods that might get brought into teaching with the SCR process need to be the trigger to fix "old" methods that aren't working—but aren't meant to replace them all. For example, Carla Herrera reported that some teachers had guided reading training that didn't fully train them in how to put it into practice effectively. As a result, the teachers mistakenly had too many small groups of three or four students at a single book level. With the coaching process described in the previous chapter, the literacy coordinator or peer mentor can help adjust the practice, showing teachers the ins and outs of guided reading and its intended purpose. Independent reading, using leveled books, one-to-one conferring, teaching reading strategies—virtually every practice under the sun has the potential to go awry when it becomes too "big" within the literacy block or is seen by leaders as the be-all and end-all solution to teaching reading. Our moms were right—everything in moderation.

That said, in all my years of research and work in schools, I've never gone into a school and said, these teachers are providing too much intellectual challenge. I'm loathe to make generalizations, but one I stand by is that generally speaking, teachers do not give their students enough challenge. That's not the same as pushing them too high and too fast in a test prep kind of way, but what I mean is expecting the most of them in terms of higher-level thinking and writing, discussions, inquiry, high interest, giving them challenging books they'll like, and activities that aren't just coasting. My own notes after spending a morning at the school in the winter of year 1 stated:

> In general, children are not doing enough reading and are not reading hard enough books. For example, many students in grade 1 only have books in their book boxes that contain a small number of words, simple repetitive patterns, and pictures. These are books they can "read" without looking at the print. Also, many teachers have students in groups of two or three based on their guided reading training. As a result, most children are on their own for too long and work on low-level tasks or activities that don't take nearly as long to complete as the time allowed. In one grade 3 classroom, children at their seats spent 15 minutes drawing a picture of their favorite part of a story and writing a sentence or two about it. They could do so much more reading and responding, and be much more excited about their learning, if they were only given the opportunity.

My notes changed substantially across the next two years as I saw many motivating learning activities and many students excited about their learning.

You Can't Do It All at Once

Again, it's crucial to arrive at a group with a vision for reading reform that may involve a few complementary pieces but is focused and manageable. A school can't successfully move forward with more than one major reform effort. For example, Carla commented on a sense of being pulled in too many directions and doing nothing especially well. "Teachers were pulled in too many directions in the past. The district had us involved in guided reading and readers and writers workshop. We were doing responsive classroom. We had a literacy coach because we did not make AYP. We had too many initiatives and different leadership teams for each initiative. Too many people were trying to save us. With the CSR process, we had just one leadership team, one literacy coach, and we felt more in control of our own destiny."

Acknowledge the Stress of New Efforts

Any reform effort is stressful in the first half of the first year. At the beginning of year 1, the third-grade teacher quoted earlier commented, "I am feeling overwhelmed. We have a lot of different things to do for the SCR process along with things from the past. I'm not even sure which curriculum to use anymore."

Westside School also began using a new basal in the first year of SCR reform, which added to teachers' stress. It would have been better if this district decision had been put on hold for a year while the Westside staff became comfortable with the SCR process, a major new initiative in its own right.

Negative Voices

As in most schools implementing schoolwide reform, there were several teachers at Westside who did not want to be involved in the SCR process and whose negative sentiments dragged others down. In the fall of year 1, one teacher said, "Some teachers are overwhelmed and annoyed. I myself am annoyed with all the training so far. There is always something new. Also, we are dropping some of the good things we have done in the past."

Westside's Strengths

A Committed Principal

Westside Elementary was fortunate to have an effective, committed principal. She was a strong advocate for and active participant in SCR reform. She attended study groups herself as often as possible. She led by example, bringing a video of herself teaching a group of kindergarten ELLs to a study group. In the lesson she carefully chose words for blending and segmenting, included higher-level questions about the story, gave students opportunities to respond actively, maintained a brisk pace, and scaffolded her instruction. In the external consultant's opinion, "Her primary objective was to model high expectations for all students, and to challenge a prevalent sentiment among some Westside staff members that English language learners are not ready for some of the rigors of best reading practices as presented in the research."

Carla also had a supportive style of interaction. She praised teachers for their reform efforts and their improvements in reading instruction. She was cheerful, positive, even-tempered, and empathetic, but also committed to change. She listened to teachers' frustrations related to their work and offered support without relinquishing her commitment to improving practice. As the external consultant explained:

> Carla's style was to observe and withhold judgment until a little time had passed in order to reveal any patterns of growth or stagnancy in her staff. She then took time regularly at whole-group meetings to address, in general terms, what she had noticed over the past weeks. This kept staff aware that they were being held accountable for making improvements and at the same time honored them for the hard work they were doing.

Ms. Herrera kept abreast of the reform efforts and helped shape the direction of the reform on a regular basis. She met weekly with the literacy coordinator and external consultant to look at assessment data on students, discuss ways to support teachers, and co-plan monthly whole-group meetings and leadership team meetings.

An Exemplary Literacy Coordinator

Westside Elementary also was fortunate to have a strong, committed literacy coordinator. Estella Butler was respected by her colleagues as an experienced, exemplary teacher. She was also held in high regard by teachers for her knowledge of effective literacy instruction. Additionally, she was an excellent mentor. As the external consultant explained, "Estella modeled lessons for teachers, and then she observed them and engaged them in coaching conversations. She helped them set and accomplish professional goals in the teaching of reading and in the implementation of effective classroom management techniques. She lent a strong voice to the need to improve professional practice and maximize the time devoted to instruction for the students' sake."

Strong, Supportive External Partners

Westside Elementary also had a respected, involved external consultant who helped to keep the reform process moving forward by working closely with the literacy coordinator and the principal. He was an experienced, talented teacher of reading who was appreciated by teachers for the exemplary modeling, coaching, and encouragement he provided.

In addition, faculty members from a nearby university introduced processes for the SCR reform effort. They provided five day-long, research-based professional development workshops on effective reading instruction for all teachers. They held monthly meetings for literacy coordinators and quarterly meetings for principals and leadership team members from a number of schools undertaking SCR reform. Through these meetings school leaders learned new strategies to keep moving the reform effort forward and had the opportunity to network and learn with and from leaders at other SCR schools.

An Involved Leadership Team

Westside Elementary had a committed, involved leadership team. These teacher leaders led by example. They were the first to share videos of their teaching in study groups. They were the first to ask the literacy coordinator to observe in their classrooms and participate in follow-up coaching conversations about their teaching. They were positive, prepared participants in study groups. Most important, they were champions for reform. They were very enthusiastic about reform. They shared information and led discussions at whole-groups meetings, thus reinforcing the impression that meetings and the reform effort belonged to the teachers themselves, not to the literacy coordinator and principal.

Leadership team members planned monthly grade-level meetings at which teachers looked at student data, discussed possible instructional changes, evaluated interventions already in place, and decided when additional interventions were needed. They championed practices such as more extensive, deeper instructional planning within and across grade levels, and they discussed the importance of maximizing teaching time.

Reflecting on the leadership team at the end of the process, the external consultant commented:

> The leadership team met monthly and discussed issues such as school climate, progress toward accomplishing goals set out in action plans, needed reading interventions, the structure of the reading block at different grade levels, and teachers' use of assessment data. All members of the leadership team were positive voices for the reform effort and were effective frontline representatives of the types of changes we were trying to implement. They were the first to volunteer to share videotapes of their teaching or student work samples. They assisted the literacy coordinator and me in communicating with the staff the finer details of the SCR process and the vision for what we were hoping to accomplish next.

Positive Teachers

Westside was very fortunate to have positive teachers who were willing to try new teaching techniques and who put their students first in the decisions they made and the actions they took related to reading instruction. Almost all teachers kept open minds about SCR reform. They were willing to try out new instructional ideas to improve their practice. As the external consultant explained:

> There was a fair degree of discomfort and confusion at the outset of the first year. Emotions ran high as staff came to terms with the demands of video sharing and classroom observations. However, after the first month or so, the discontentment had largely abated. A survey was given to the staff midyear regarding their reactions to the SCR process so far. The results were largely favorable. Most said they felt they were gaining a wider base of knowledge about the teaching of reading and were making informed decisions in their classrooms as a result. Collaboration was first manifested in the cooperative design of lessons among classroom teachers and ELL support staff. Collaboration next occurred on grade-level teams. For example, kindergarten teachers shared results of their phonemic awareness techniques with one another in the lunchroom and hallways as well as in study groups. Ideas were shared

and tried across study groups. By the end of the year, the staff had begun cross-grade discussions related to new instructional techniques and were making instructional adjustments to these techniques in order to make them fit their students' needs.

A Supportive District Liaison

Finally, Westside Elementary had a supportive district liaison. She attended workshops and visited the school at least once a month. She also attended some study groups and whole-group meetings to better understand the SCR process.

Actions and Successes at Westside

The actions taken by the staff at Westside on different aspects of the SCR process across four years follow and are summarized at the end of this section in Figure 9–1. As you can see, they did not do everything all at once, but eased themselves into different parts of the process. However, once they got something started, they kept it going. Hopefully this scope and sequence of actions and successes at Westside will help you set reasonable expectations and bring some order to your own multiyear change process.

Actions and Successes in Year 1

Fall of Year 1

Schoolwide actions and whole-group meetings. At whole-group meetings in the initial three months, the literacy coordinator and external consultant reviewed the roles of leadership team members and all teachers, reintroduced study group processes and protocols, and gave teachers choices related to the study groups in which they would participate. Midway through that first fall, the principal, at a whole-group meeting, gave teachers a pep talk, complimented them on their successes so far, and let them air their concerns. Progress monitoring practices were reviewed at several whole-group meetings and put into place by all teachers. These practices focused on assessing students' fluency through words-read-correctly-per-minute assessments or through other timed measures of emergent literacy for students who were not yet reading independently.

Study groups. By the end of the third month, study groups were running effectively. After a brief period of initial confusion while teachers got used to the concept, they developed a strong sense of ownership. Members of each group regularly contributed video clips of their teaching and brought student work. They read and discussed research articles with professionalism and enthusiasm. As the external facilitator reported in December of year 1, "All study groups are running smoothly. Teachers are using the protocols for video sharing and looking at student work, collegial input is generous and positive, and the general spirit of the study groups is one of an eagerness to learn and to improve. Several staff members have acknowledged that Westside's challenges are great and that the study groups are offering ways to address these needs." The principal, literacy coordinator, and external consultant all remarked at one of their weekly fall meetings that they were impressed with the enthusiasm and preparation that teachers brought to their study groups.

Winter of Year 1

Schoolwide actions and whole-group meetings. At the urging of the principal, effective teaching to maximize students' cognitive engagement (Taylor et al. 2003; see Chapter 2) was stressed at whole-group meetings. Effective and ineffective center activities and independent seatwork activities were called to teachers' attention. Teachers discussed the need for students to have the opportunity to read challenging books on their own and receive differentiated instruction when doing independent seatwork. Teachers talked about the importance of maximizing teaching time and making the best use of every possible minute during reading instruction.

By early winter, the leadership team had set up monthly data meetings at which teachers looked at progress-monitoring data, implemented necessary instructional adjustments, and made sure that struggling readers were receiving appropriate interventions. Teachers also shared new study group techniques with one another at these meetings, and they planned together at a deeper level than in the past to provide maximally effective reading instruction.

In addition to coordinating whole-group and leadership team meetings and study group sessions and getting into classrooms every day, the literacy coordinator and external consultant began to send out a weekly SCR newsletter in December to keep everyone abreast of all that was happening related to the reform effort.

Study groups. Study groups continued to run smoothly. As the external consultant reported:

> Groups seem pretty comfortable with the protocols now, and they are following them when showing videos and student work. The comments I hear are thoughtful and professional. Teachers are citing specific evidence of good practice or techniques from research-based material they have been studying. Teachers are going back and refining their activities (as opposed to doing it once and considering it "done") and slowly incorporating them into routines according to student needs. A few teachers are finding the courage to respectfully rein in the group if a teacher gets them off topic.

Classroom visits and changes to instruction. The literacy coordinator and external facilitator established an ambitious schedule for getting into classrooms frequently to model and to coach. In January the external consultant modeled explicit phonics lessons twice and summarized a story once in the classroom of a new first-grade teacher who was struggling. In addition, he observed and coached one or two other teachers every day he was at the school. Classroom visits were positively received, as can be seen in these comments of the literacy coordinator as she reflected on three postobservation coaching conversation sessions she had in February: "All three teachers found the coaching conversations helpful along with any suggestions I was able to offer. Each was able to articulate an area of strength and an area to improve on."

The literacy coordinator also commented on positive changes in classroom instruction:

Some wonderful changes have been made in a number of classrooms. In kindergarten, I see more explicit teaching of phonemic awareness. Also, there has been a noticeable shift in vocabulary instruction since the beginning of the year based on what teachers are learning in their vocabulary study group. Teachers are focusing more on tier 2 words (Beck, McKeown, and Kucan 2002), even though they were skeptical about doing this with their ELL students. They are teaching richer, higher-level words and talking about the importance of repeatedly using these words with their students. Also, teachers say that they are noticing an impact on behavior as a result of planning more carefully and increasing students' cognitive engagement in their lessons and learning activities. Many teachers have said that some of the new techniques they are learning are becoming routine as they use them on a regular basis.

Spring of Year 1

Study groups. Study groups looked quite different by the end of the first year compared with the fall. Teachers were now engaging in thoughtful discussions about practice. The literacy coordinator described one study group this way: "Teachers were highly interactive in their discussion of the video Alice shared on making words in a first-grade classroom. All teachers shared strengths they noticed and offered a few suggestions on how to make the lesson more challenging."

Grade-level meetings and data meetings. Teachers were planning regularly together at grade-level meetings, something they had not done consistently in the past. Most teams were focusing on how to mesh their new basal reader with what they were learning about effective reading instruction in study groups. Also, teachers were continuing their monthly data meetings. They came to these half-day meetings well prepared with progress-monitoring data and student work samples. They willingly discussed the successes, challenges, and needed changes in their instruction.

Classroom visits to improve instruction. Modeling by the literacy coordinator and external consultant focused on more complex teaching practices than in the fall. The external consultant talked about the modeling he had done in a second-grade classroom:

I was able to prepare, teach, and tape a literature discussion with Jack's students in an adjacent room. The book we were reading was an abridged version of *Frankenstein*. The first day we set norms for discussion, looked at our prior knowledge, and introduced thematic elements of pride/arrogance, remorse, and revenge. Students had numerous misconceptions in their prior knowledge (Frankenstein was the monster, etc.) and were reluctant to challenge or agree with fellow students or me. By the second day, all students had taken big risks in their dialogue with one another, and I was able to facilitate at more of a distance, handing the primary job of questioning to one of the stronger students in the group.

In addition to classroom visits with follow-up coaching conversations, the literacy coordinator and external consultant began using the student's use-of-time protocol when they visited classrooms (see Chapter 8). Leadership team members agreed to participate in this new observation technique first so they could share the experience with other teachers.

Changes in teaching. The literacy coordinator described the significant changes in teaching that she observed in an ELL classroom:

> In Angelina's room the lesson was well-paced and well-balanced, addressing the major elements of reading. The lesson included rereading for fluency, vocabulary instruction on key words from the story, explicit phonics instruction, oral language response to higher-level questions, and some guided sentence writing. It was an excellent example of putting it all together as the year draws to a close.

In the final newsletter of the year, the literacy coordinator and external consultant described the many positive changes they had seen since the fall. They also privately recognized teachers individually for the obstacles they had overcome during the year and the successes they had experienced.

Schoolwide actions and whole-group meetings. By spring, whole-group meetings were led by leadership team members instead of the literacy coordinator and external consultant. At one whole-group meeting in the spring, teachers had a discussion about letting go of old practices. Planning for next year included talk about the best reading interventions to put in place, the best delivery models to use at different grade levels, and how to put 120 minutes of uninterrupted reading instruction in place in all K–3 classrooms.

At the whole-group meeting in May, each teacher came with one positive thing to share about what they had learned during the year related to teaching reading. They also brought one artifact to share that reflected a newly learned instructional technique that helped students make significant progress in word recognition, vocabulary, or comprehension during the year. About the final meeting of the year, the literacy coordinator said, "Teachers' discussion about what they've learned this year was lively and enthusiastic. Several teachers stopped to tell me how much they enjoyed the meeting. They said that it was great to see so much progress as a school and to celebrate their collective efforts."

School collaboration and collective efficacy. During the first year of SCR reform, teachers' perceptions of collaboration and collective efficacy became more positive. On the self-study survey (where 1 = strongly disagree and 5 = strongly agree; see Chapter 6), teachers' mean score went from 3.4 in the fall to 3.9 in the spring regarding the item, "Classroom teachers work with teachers from grade levels above and below their own as well as with non-classroom teachers when planning and making key decisions about benchmarks, curriculum, assessments, and student behavior." Their mean score went from 4.2 to 4.5 regarding the item, "Staff work together to create and sustain a culture of continued self-examination and improvement." Their score went from 3.8 to 4.2 regarding the item, "Our school regularly collects data, is informed by research, and uses action plans based on this information to improve."

Their score went from 4.4 to 4.7 regarding the item, "Leadership is shared between the principal and teachers."

When asked about professional development, teachers' scores on the self-study survey also reflected an increase in positive perceptions related to schoolwide collective efficacy and their professional learning experiences. Teachers' mean score went from 4.1 to 4.6 regarding the item, "Teachers share expertise on various aspects of reading instruction, assessment, and classroom organization." Their mean score went from 4.4 to 4.8 regarding the item, "There is a substantial buildingwide commitment to ongoing professional development." Their mean score went from 3.4 to 4.1 regarding the item, "There is adequate time and support for meaningful professional development."

These positive perceptions about collaboration, collective efficacy, and professional learning were readily apparent to the district office liaison and principal as well. After a visit in May, the district office liaison commented that she was very enthusiastic about the professionalism and positive atmosphere in the study groups she briefly attended. She reported that teachers shared quality videos and student work and were engaged in collegial conversations that were informed, inquisitive, and had high standards.

The principal said she was thrilled with the artifacts and the conversations that took place at the final whole-group meeting. There were several teachers of whom she was particularly proud, including two teachers about whom she had grave concerns in the early part of the year. She also commended the literacy coordinator and external facilitator for their tireless work in getting people on board, managing the study groups, and getting into classrooms to demonstrate and coach.

Teachers' self-efficacy.
Teachers' acknowledgment of improvements in instruction and increases in self-efficacy was apparent from self-study data and teachers' comments. On the self-study survey, when asked about their own reading instruction, teachers' mean score went from 4.6 to 4.8 regarding the item, "I personally have made changes in my classroom as a result of professional development experiences." Their mean score went from 4.3 to 4.6 regarding the item, "I use assessments on my students' reading performance to make changes in the instruction I provide to my students." Their mean score went from 4.4 to 4.7 regarding the item, "I know where to turn and am able to get the help needed if I want to know more about effective instruction and assessment in word recognition, vocabulary, comprehension, and writing."

First-grade teacher Alice White reflected on changes to her teaching during the first year of involvement in SCR reform and discussed the impact of these changes on her students' reading abilities. When asked in May, "Have there been any changes in your reading instruction since the fall?" Alice replied, "There have been a lot of changes. I have learned so much. I am a better teacher, and some of the skills I have struggled with are coming more naturally now."

Second-grade teacher Jody Nilsson talked about changes to her teaching during the year and the impact this had on her students: "I am more focused on what I am doing and where I want the kids to be. I am always thinking of new and better ways to teach. I am more focused on keeping my kids engaged."

When asked about changes in student achievement and engagement that were related to changes in her instruction, Jody answered, "All of my students have made good increases in terms of reading level scores. Also, my kids are more interested in the small-group activities they do without me, and they have better motivation. They are getting better at working with others at their stations."

Fourth-grade teacher Yer Xiong also commented on changes to her reading instruction from fall to spring and the impact of these changes on her students' reading: "Now, I look more at my reading instruction in three pieces: core, supplemental, and intervention, and I make sure each covers a targeted objective. I also am more reflective about my teaching."

When asked about changes she had noticed in students' reading achievement as related to changes she had made in her instruction, Yer replied, "I've seen an increase in the comprehension scores from fall to winter. I've seen students reading more and doing more critical thinking due to my instruction. Also, I'm having to ask them to quit reading in class when they aren't supposed to be—which is actually a good thing."

Students' reading abilities.   Test scores, collected in the primary grades as part of the SCR process, corroborated teachers' comments on the increases they had seen in students' reading abilities during the year. Students in kindergarten went from a mean NCE score on the Peabody Picture Vocabulary Test (PPVT) of 27 in the fall to 30 in the spring. First graders went from a mean PPVT score of 26 in the fall to 28 in the spring, and they went from a mean normal curve equivalent (NCE) score on the Gates MacGinitie Reading Test of 39 in the fall to 41 in the spring. Second graders also saw increases in reading scores. Their Gates MacGinitie comprehension scores went from a mean NCE of 36 in the fall to 38 in the spring; Gates MacGinitie decoding went from a mean NCE of 32 in fall to 36 in spring; Gates MacGinitie vocabulary went from a mean NCE of 35 in fall to 41 in spring. In grade 3, Gates MacGinitie comprehension went from a mean NCE of 28 in fall to 31 in spring; Gates MacGinitie vocabulary went from a mean NCE of 22 in fall to 29 in spring.

Actions and Successes in Year 2

During the second year of SCR reform at Westside, the principal continued to be very supportive of and involved in the reform effort. As in the previous year, she participated in study groups, attended monthly leadership team meetings, and met weekly with the literacy coordinator and external consultant. She scheduled common prep times for teachers at the same grade level so they could collaborate in planning and problem solving, and she also provided time for monthly assessment meetings.

Although not new to the SCR process, the external consultant in year 2, Kathy Sheridan, was new to Westside (the person in this position the previous year went back to full-time teaching). Kathy was an experienced elementary teacher with a strong background in literacy. Like her predecessor, she observed that the literacy coordinator had excellent leadership skills and communicated regularly with the staff. She also observed that the leadership team took leadership roles during monthly-whole group meetings and volunteered first for classroom observations, coaching conversations, and audits of student use of time.

Schoolwide actions and whole-group meetings.   At monthly meetings, teachers always had time to share successes and challenges. As the literacy coordinator reported, "Everyone has positive things to share on literacy instruction and/or student work. It is powerful and moving to have this time at whole-group meetings." Typically, teachers also used response sheets that helped them reflect on their literacy instruction (see Chapter 6) and set goals for themselves for the future. During year 2, the staff at Westside discussed the following topics or engaged in the following activities at whole-group meetings:

▶ Sharing successful independent learning activities in which students were academically and actively involved while the teacher worked with guided reading groups.

▶ Using the advanced video-sharing protocol in study groups.

▶ Viewing several videos focused on pacing and rigor during whole-group lessons.

▶ Selecting or modifying questions in the core reading program and probing to get students to think at a deeper level.

▶ Using the Matching Instruction to Data form (see Chapter 6).

▶ Evaluating study groups and suggesting ways to make them even more effective.

Another schoolwide action focused on increasing efforts to involve parents as partners at the school. Westside had three interpreters available at the school every day and also had a full-time parent coordinator who took the lead on parent communications. During year 2, Westside reestablished a parent site council that met once a month. This was a time for parents to talk with interpreters about what was happening at the school and to offer suggestions. Every Wednesday, parents were welcome to come to the school to have lunch with their child. Every month, Westside held one or more events for families at the school, including open houses, fall and spring conferences, family involvement nights, grade-level homework nights, and family math and literacy nights.

Study groups. Study groups focused on implementing an intervention program, Early Intervention in Reading (Taylor in press, *Catching Readers,* 2010a, 2010b, 2010c, in press a, in press b), in grades K–4. A second set of cross-grade study groups attended by all teachers in grades K–6 focused on improving comprehension by teaching two or more of the following: summarizing using graphic organizers, engaging students in high-level questioning, and engaging students in student-led book club discussions. Kathy Sheridan said, "Study groups at Westside this year were very efficient and well run. Each member came to the group prepared to take on whatever role they were responsible for. Attendance at study groups was good, too. There were not many absences and those who were gone typically had been excused prior to the meeting."

Grade-level meetings and monthly data meetings. Classroom teachers and ELL teachers continued to plan together regularly. At these weekly meetings, made possible because of common prep times, teachers across the school engaged in a plan-implement-reflect-plan cycle that was strongly supported by the principal. Teachers also shared successes and challenges with one another and made changes in their instruction as needed. Teachers at Westside also communicated regularly with one another through email.

Teachers continued to review the most current pupil data in monthly meetings and make team decisions related to student placement in guided reading groups. They also reflected on the effectiveness of the interventions struggling readers were receiving. The principal, literacy coordinator, and external consultant attended these meetings as well.

Interventions. Kindergarten teachers learned how to implement peer-assisted learning strategies (Fuchs and Fuchs 2005) and EIR–K (Taylor 2001). Teachers in grades 1–3 learned how to implement EIR 1–3 in small groups to strengthen their struggling readers' reading abilities.

Coaching and other classroom-visit techniques. The literacy coordinator and external consultant got into classrooms regularly to observe reading instruction and followed up with coaching conversations. They also audited student use of time. (See Figure 8–3.)

Reading instruction and changes in teaching practices. The external consultant described reading instruction at Westside at the end of year 2 this way:

> When the literacy coordinator and I visit first- and second-grade classrooms, we hear students referring to the strategies for decoding words while reading that they have been taught throughout the year. They also have book bins filled with leveled readers, and a fair amount of time each day is devoted to reading. They spend about a third of their reading period in whole-group instruction and two thirds in guided reading groups.
>
> Second- through sixth-grade teachers developed comprehension packets focusing on high-level questioning and comprehension strategies. Packets are differentiated so that varying levels of response are expected based on students' needs and reading levels. Also, students have a rubric to self-evaluate their responses. During guided reading, classrooms have a variety of centers that deal with response to literature, reading and reporting on informational text, and engaging in student-led discussions. These centers operate independently while the teacher is with a guided reading group.

Teacher self-efficacy. Teachers continued to grow in their confidence about being effective teachers of reading. Asked about changes in her reading instruction, third-grade teacher Maria Hernandez commented, "EIR intervention groups have definitely been a useful change, and overall I feel I am better at teaching reading than I was two years ago. I know how to plan reading instruction that directly impacts each kid better than I ever did before. I have solid lessons plans that are good and realistic."

First-grade teacher Alice White reflected:

> I see my kids more engaged, more independent, and learning more than in the past. I'm able to keep the pace moving a bit quicker now. I'm teaching my students routines so they can be independent. I make sure they know what they are learning and why. Also, I'm doing more with nonfiction, and I'm always trying to make independent activities efficient and engaging for students. In fact, my high-achieving kids are doing so well that I need more ideas on what to do with them. This SCR process has challenged us to do many things to improve. It's been hard, but it's a really good thing. I've learned so much about reading in the past few years that I will continue with what I am doing even if the formal SCR process is not in place in a few years.

School collaboration and collective efficacy. At the end of year 2, the literacy coordinator said:

> We have had many successes this year. Teachers are focused on decoding strategies, high-level questioning, coaching, and modeling (as opposed to too much teacher talk), keeping students engaged, and most of all, helping students make gains in reading and feeling confident as learners. All teachers are helping each other with literacy instruction as they implement newly learned strategies from the research. They all have a vested interest in helping kids, they all work together really well, and they support each other. Test scores may not indicate huge gains, but the commitment to change and success is strong. We are looking forward to next school year!

Asked about changes at Westside compared with a year ago, the principal commented:

> Our staff is really, really focused on student achievement and literacy in general. People are more focused on solutions than on problems, which is a shift from prior years. Every child who's falling below grade level is being served in one or more intervention groups, something that is new this year. Additionally, we need more high-level books since we don't have enough. There is a deeper focus on comprehension and vocabulary. Teachers are working hard to make sure that every minute of reading instruction counts for every child.

Students' reading abilities. Although there were about 65 percent more ELL students and 30 percent fewer non-ELL students in grades K–3 at Westside in year 2 than in year 1, test scores, collected in the primary grades as part of funding requirements for SCR implementation, reflected increases in students' reading abilities during the year. Kindergarteners went from a mean NCE PPVT score of 32 in the fall to 37 in the spring. First graders went from a mean NCE PPVT score of 27 in the fall to 28 in the spring and their Gates MacGinitie score went from a mean NCE of 42 to 44. Second graders went from reading 43 words correct per minute in the fall on average to 74 in the spring. Their Gates MacGinitie comprehension scores went from a mean NCE of 35 in the fall to 36 in the spring; Gates MacGinitie decoding went from a mean of 34 in fall to 36 in spring; Gates MacGinitie vocabulary was at a mean of 34 in the fall and spring. In third grade, Gates MacGinitie comprehension was at a mean of 33 in the fall and spring; Gates MacGinitie vocabulary went from a mean of 29 in fall to 34 in spring.

Actions and Successes in Year 3

Leadership. The principal continued to be very supportive of and involved in the SCR process. She regularly attended whole-group, leadership team, and study group meetings. She continued to meet with the literacy coordinator and external consultant once a week. The literacy coordinator and external consultant continued to support teachers with SCR activities. They also continued to get into classrooms to model for new teachers and observe and coach experienced SCR teachers. The leadership team continued to meet monthly and began assuming responsibility for leading whole-group meetings.

Teachers had positive feelings about their school leaders. Katy Holder, a kindergarten teacher, felt supported by her principal. "Carla is very open to ideas, very easily approachable. I think because my kids are learning so much, she's not in here telling me what to do. We meet with her a few times a year to go over data with her and she is always so supportive. If you have a problem with a student, she will lend an ear, and offer ideas and suggestions."

Nora Wendler, a first-grade ELL teacher, commented, "I appreciated the fact that Carla had individual meetings with us. She is open to any concerns or staff development needs. I feel Carla cares about me as a teacher but also personally. I feel I can share what's really on my mind and it won't come back to get me."

Second-grade teacher Jack Lloyd, a member of the leadership team, reflected on the increased involvement of the leadership team. "I think this year, the way that the literacy coordinator and external consultant are releasing responsibility to the leadership team has been really helpful. They are trying to teach the leadership team how to keep all of the pieces of the SCR process going without them."

Whole-group meetings.   Each month a different grade level hosted the whole-group meeting. At each meeting, members shared successes and challenges, especially their positive feelings about student achievement. Teachers evaluated observation data and used rubrics (see Chapter 6) and set future goals for modifications to their instruction. At some whole-group meetings, teachers learned procedures and protocols for peer coaching. At other whole-group meetings, teachers focused on motivation, using ideas and scenarios from the book by Pressley and colleagues (2003; see Chapter 3) to help them discuss motivating/undermining teacher practices and ways to make classrooms more engaging for students.

Study groups.   Teachers continued to engage in thoughtful discussions about practice. Teachers met in cross-grade-level study groups that focused on reciprocal teaching and students' collaboratively sharing written and oral responses to literature. Study groups continued to be very efficient and run well. Members came to their groups prepared to take on whatever role they were responsible for. External consultant Kathy Sheridan reflected, "All groups followed procedures and protocols and allowed time for reflective discussion based on video sharing, professional readings, and student work."

Literacy coordinator Estella Butler commented on the quality of teachers' interactions in study groups and whole-group meetings:

> People are so willing to share ideas and help each other out at study groups with video shares, etc. Teachers are very sensitive with the help they give. We also work well in whole group; teachers share ideas of things that are working well, teachers share student work and help each other think of where to go with certain things. Talking with other teachers about the reading program(s)/instruction in this school is extremely helpful. It's how we learn, it's what we do as a collaborative school.

Fifth-grade teacher Pat Toma stressed the value of study groups:

They are very helpful because we get to hear how other people are teaching. There's not just one way to teach something, so it shows me a variety of ways. Also, doing the videotaping makes me feel comfortable; having teachers watch and give feedback makes me know that what I'm doing is useful and good. I tend to be too hard on myself. Seeing other people teach through the video share has been good too.

First-grade ELL teacher Nora Wendler also stressed the value of study groups:

I brought up that I was having real trouble doing summaries, and the teachers were so nice and so helpful, encouraging and not shaming; we all share our good ideas and know that we have a collegial trust that is so amazing. Study groups, where we get to talk about teaching, don't feel threatening anymore. It's valuable and doesn't feel like it's just another job to do; I think it has really brought our school closer together too.

Grade-level meetings and monthly data meetings. Teachers continued to plan together and communicate regularly. (The principal saw to it that they had common prep times each day.) Also, one ELL teacher was assigned to each grade level so she could be an active member of a grade-level team. Teachers continued to meet once a month to look at student assessment data, place students in appropriate groups, and reflect on the effectiveness of interventions for struggling readers.

Katy Holder stressed the value of grade-level meetings. "We plan together, we work in study groups, we try to help solve each other's problems—offer suggestions about academics and behavior, bounce ideas off each other. Many heads are better than one, and the more you can share and talk with other teachers the better you get."

Estella Butler reflected on teachers' use of data to improve instruction:

The teachers are looking at data more than before the SCR process was in place, and they are using data to focus on what kids need to learn. None of the first graders needed to learn letters in the fall. So the teachers had an aha moment that they needed to start with reading and writing right away. Some of the grade levels are realizing that they are teaching kids, not just a curriculum.

Coaching and other classroom-visit techniques. The literacy coordinator and external consultant continued to get into classrooms regularly to model, coach, and audit students' use of time (see Chapter 8). Teachers were positive about the coaching they experienced.

Third-grade teacher Maria Hernandez said: "I really think that the audits of student use of time by the coaches were valuable because they helped me see what the kids were doing and if they were on task. Also it was helpful to have another brain looking at the same thing. With their expertise the coaches have given me lots of ideas to try."

First-grade ELL teacher Nora Wendler said: "It's been really helpful when coaches come and observe a lesson and give me positives and help me come up with things to work on. It helps me see that I'm on the right track. I really like when I get observed because it's very nonthreatening but is an honest assessment of what I'm doing."

Beginning in November and continuing through February, the literacy coordinator and external consultant also worked with the leadership team members on peer coaching. They observed a leadership team member teach, the literacy coordinator coached the teacher in a follow-up coaching conversation, and the external consultant then coached the literacy coordinator on her coaching. Next, the literacy coordinator taught a lesson, the teacher observed her, and the external consultant coached the teacher on her coaching. This process was repeated one or two times with each leadership team member. In March the leadership team began peer coaching other teachers, with the literacy coordinator or external consultant coaching the leadership team members. In year 4 other teachers would learn how to peer-coach as well. Teachers understood that peer coaching was an important part of the school's sustainability plan.

Changes in teaching. Reading instruction looked quite different at Westside in year 3 compared with year 1. Teachers had modified their teaching practices in the directions suggested by research (see Chapter 2). Across grades K–3, teachers coached students to use word-recognition strategies 28 percent of the time compared with 15 percent of the time in year 1. High-level questioning was observed 19 percent of the time in year 3 compared with 13 percent of the time in year 1. Vocabulary instruction was observed 25 percent of the time (year 3) compared with 20 percent of the time (year 1). Teachers were observed coaching students 31 percent of the time (year 3) compared with 15 percent of the time (year 1). Students were observed reading text 45 percent of the time (year 3) compared with 25 percent of the time (year 1). Students were reading informational text 17 percent of the time (year 3) compared with 7 percent of the time (year 1). They were actively responding to their lessons 40 percent of the time (year 3) compared with 35 percent of the time (year 1). They were on task 94 percent of the time (year 3) compared with 89 percent of the time (year 1).

In addition to these impressive changes, teachers' comments reflected important modifications in their reading instruction and greater satisfaction with this improved instruction.

Jack Lloyd commented, "The whole idea of trying to maximize student instructional time, making every minute count, and the amount of differentiation that we are doing have helped me become better as a teacher. Also, the video sharing and the observation reports have been really helpful. It gives you an idea of what you are good at and what else you need to work on."

Maria Hernandez reflected, "I've learned how to coach kids, by being coached myself. I feel like this year I'm not taking over the book clubs, I'm not the leader anymore, the kids are really in charge. They won't even look at me now, they just look at the leader, which is great."

Dara Strauss, a fourth-grade teacher, said, about changes in her teaching, "I am more comfortable with having kids work on different things and in small groups. I was kind of nervous about differentiation and it has developed on its own a bit, so now I assign different things to different groups and it feels more comfortable that way."

The principal commented on changes in instruction she had seen since the SCR process had begun:

Teachers continue to be more strategic about their planning and looking carefully at what their students need. What felt awkward and cumbersome at the beginning of this model is now becoming more routine. It has unified us, and gotten us to be more reflective about our practice; to be more intentional about our research-based instruction; to open our doors and be more comfortable with peer observation and feedback.

School collaboration and collective efficacy.
The sense of schoolwide collaboration and collective efficacy at Westside grew steadily from year 1 through year 3. On the self-study questionnaire (see Chapter 6), teachers' perceptions related to effective school change, collaboration, and leadership increased from a mean of 3.9 at the beginning of year 1 to 4.4 at the end of year 3 (where 1 = strongly disagree and 5 = strongly agree). Teachers' perceptions about effective professional learning at their school increased from a mean of 4.1 to 4.6. Perceptions about an effective schoolwide reading program increased from 4.3 to 4.4. Perceptions about effective classroom reading instruction at their school and within their own classrooms increased from a mean of 4.3 to 4.6. Perceptions about effective interventions for struggling readers at their school increased from a mean of 3.4 to 4.5.

Teachers' comments also pointed to a strong sense of collaboration and collective efficacy at Westside at the end of year 3.

Jack Lloyd observed, "I think that we are good at being honest and offering constructive criticism. Those people who have been against the SCR process have come to realize that it's a good thing and have helped us to reflect. We have a very collegial atmosphere and people are positive, not whiny. We've had many different reform models here but this is something that is helping us get better."

Maria Hernandez explained, "The study groups have really helped unite all of the grades, because everyone knows what is happening in every area. I've seen lots of programs come in and out, and the SCR process has a sustainability component that is really effective. It has taught us common language and common strategies that will really pay off in the years to come if we can stick with it."

Katy Holder commented, "The whole school is on the same page now. K–6 is doing study groups and there are interventions in the upper grades as well. We have a more unified way of teaching reading through the school."

Nora Wendler explained, "We have a tough population, but shared ways of teaching our students has helped us to be closer as a staff; in every way, people work well together. We have a great way of encouraging each other and we really care about kids." Asked about challenges with the SCR process, Nora said, "Keeping people positive when the going gets rough can be hard. There are some people who can be negative and they bring others down, so staying positive can be a challenge."

Students' reading abilities.
When we take a look at students' reading scores, it is important to keep in mind that Westside is a school in which 93 percent of the students participated in its subsidized lunch program and 87 percent were English language learners (ELLs). Although there were about 100 percent more ELLs and 50 percent fewer non-ELLs in grades K–3 at Westside in year 3 than in year 1, test scores in year 3 reflected increases in students' reading abilities during the year, and teachers were very proud of and encouraged by these gains. Kindergarteners went from the eighth to twenty-first percentile on average on the PPVT (Peabody Picture Vocabulary Test) from fall to spring. First graders went from the sixteenth to the twenty-fourth percentile on this vocabulary test. Their mean score on a standardized reading test (Gates MacGinitie) went from the fortieth percentile to forty-second percentile from fall to spring. Second graders went

from reading 42 words correct per minute in the fall on average to 70 in the spring. Their mean comprehension on the Gates MacGinitie Reading Test comprehension scores went from the twentieth to twenty-third percentile from fall to spring. In grade 3, students' mean comprehension score on the Gates MacGinitie went from the twenty-sixth percentile to thirty-third percentile from fall to spring, and their mean score in vocabulary went from the sixteenth to the twenty-fourth percentile. By comparison, students at the end of grade 3 in year 1 were at the eighteenth and sixteenth percentiles in comprehension and vocabulary on average.

Teachers acknowledged that students still have a long way to go in terms of reading growth. Nonetheless, they were pleased with the good growth they had seen in students' reading abilities.

Katy Holder exclaimed, "I have seen great gains in what my kindergarteners know, in all aspects! Every time I assess them, it amazes me! The kids that might not have made such great gains at the first conferences have now made huge gains toward the end of the year. The kids who are shy always seem to shock me in a good way!"

Amy O'Connor, a third-grade teacher, reflected, "I don't know if it's necessarily my instruction, but I feel like my kids are better readers in general and I feel it's been SCR reform that has pushed them to higher levels. Also, I have seen the comprehension of struggling readers in EIR groups improve and therefore their reading has improved."

Nora Wendler commented:

The kids are really flying now that they have been in the EIR program. Since the beginning of the year they are reading, using strategies, and doing all of the things that I have taught them. Before they weren't sure what to do with connections, now they make great connections throughout every lesson. They make predictions, ask good questions, and know when their reading breaks down. Some were nonreaders and now they are reading at a level 12! It's neat to see them becoming more independent and applying their skills.

Sustainability in year 4. At the end of year 3, the principal, literacy coordinator, and teachers shared their thoughts about sustaining the SCR process without the support of the external consultant or university staff members. Principal Carla Herrera reported, "Study groups for all grades will continue video sharing; the leadership team will continue to meet monthly; we will maintain the position of a literacy coordinator with our own funds; we will continue to build in opportunities for teachers to peer coach and reflect together on their practices."

Estella Butler, the literacy coordinator, elaborated, "In year 4, we will have study groups, whole-group meetings, continue to look at data, and continue to study the research. We're going to try to keep it the same way this year and hopefully in the years to come."

Third-grade teacher Amy O'Connor said, "We have taken the framework and made it our own. It was a great outline and I feel that we have a meaty reading program that will really help our kids to become better readers."

Kindergarten teacher Katy Holder explained, "I know we will continue with study groups, try to do a lot of the same testing, and continue 120 minutes of reading time in the primary grades. I don't plan on changing anything, but I still hope to make it even better each year."

Second-grade teacher Jack Lloyd, a member of the leadership team, said, "We're planning to continue the study group model, twice a month instead of three times a month. As for the video sharing, everyone is on board with that."

Fifth-grade teacher Pat Toma commented, "We want to keep study groups going, keep the communication lines open. We want to keep doing the video sharing, keep getting feedback from each other."

First-grade ELL teacher Nora Wendler explained:

> We still want to deliver high caliber instruction; still work in study groups, focus on high-level questioning, be collaborative, work together, all of the good things that come out of the SCR process. We still want to assess and know where our kids are. I'm excited to start peer coaching, which the other ELL teacher and I are going to be doing; just taking what we know about good teaching and helping each other. I think that we can now take the knowledge that we have and focus on doing what we know really well.

Second-grade teacher Alice White observed, "The SCR process is not so much a program but more a way of teaching and it works! I think it will be good to still have a literacy coach to model things if we get stuck; to continue with study groups; to keep doing what we are doing and not throw away any parts of it because it's good work that we are doing."

Results

I visited Westside in the spring of year 4 and talked with the principal and literacy coordinator about the success of their sustainability plans related to the SCR process. The principal commented:

> We are sticking with it all in year 4. We have study groups twice a month and use the protocols regularly. We still have 120 minutes of reading instruction in the primary grades, 90 minutes in the intermediate grades. We put our resources where are priorities are. We still have Estella full-time as a literacy coordinator, and we have a half-time coach for grades 4–6. Most important, we have a fantastic group of teachers.

Estella Butler, the literacy coordinator, added, "We are looking at our instruction, data on our teaching, taking suggestions form one another. Teachers want to get keep getting better!"

Clearly, the staff at Westside was sustaining the SCR process a year after external support had ended. By year 4, the SCR process had become their SCR process as they continued to work together to improve their instruction and to provide the best reading instruction possible to meet the diverse needs of their very diverse student body.

Actions and Successes at Westside Elementary School

Fall of Year 1

Schoolwide actions and whole-group meetings

- roles reviewed
- study group processes and protocols reintroduced
- progress monitoring practices reviewed

Study groups

- running effectively by end of three months

Winter of Year 1

Schoolwide actions and whole-group meetings

- focus is on maximizing students' cognitive engagement
- effective center and independent seatwork activities considered
- challenging books and differentiated instruction for independent seatwork
- focus on maximizing teaching time
- monthly data meetings
- weekly SCR newsletter

Study groups

- continuing to run smoothly
- members comfortable with the protocols
- teachers refining their activities and slowly incorporating them into routines

Classroom visits and changes to instruction

- coach getting into classrooms frequently to model and coach
- classroom visits positively received
- positive changes in classroom instruction: more explicit teaching of phonemic awareness; vocabulary instruction focusing on unfamiliar, high-utility words; planning more carefully and increasing students' cognitive engagement

Spring of Year 1

Schoolwide actions and whole-group meetings

- lead by leadership team members
- letting go of old practices
- focus on best reading interventions put in place
- focus on best delivery models for different grade levels
- 120 minutes of uninterrupted reading instruction in all K–3 classrooms, 90 minutes in grades 4–6
- enthusiastic discussions about what was learned and students' progress

Study groups

- thoughtful discussions about practice
- highly interactive discussion of video clips

Grade-level meetings and data meetings

- regular planning regularly at grade-level meetings
- mesh new basal lessons with effective reading instruction
- discussion of successes, challenges, and needed changes in instruction

Classroom visits to improve instruction

- modeling by coach focused on more complex teaching
- regular classroom visits with follow-up coaching conversations
- use of students' use-of-time protocol

continues

Catching Schools © 2011 by Barbara M. Taylor (Heinemann: Portsmouth, NH).

Figure 9-1a Actions and Success at Westside Elementary School

Actions and Successes at Westside Elementary School, *continued*

Changes in teaching

▶ significant changes in teaching reported by LC: well-paced, well-balanced in addressing the major elements of reading

School collaboration, collective efficacy, self-efficacy

▶ perceptions of collaboration and collective efficacy increasing

▶ district office liaison enthusiastic about the professionalism and positive atmosphere in the study groups

▶ teachers' acknowledgment of improvements in instruction and increases in self-efficacy

Actions and Successes in Year 2

Schoolwide actions and whole-group meetings

▶ principal very supportive of and involved in the reform effort

▶ excellent leadership and communication by literacy coordinator

▶ leadership team running whole-group meetings

▶ regular sharing of successes and challenges

▶ teachers setting goals for themselves

▶ sharing of successful independent learning activities

▶ focus on pacing and rigor during whole-group lessons

▶ selecting or modifying questions in the core reading program and probing to get students to think at a deeper level

▶ comfortable with the Matching Instruction to Data form

▶ evaluating study groups and suggesting ways to make them even more effective

▶ increasing efforts to involve parents as partners at the school

Study groups

▶ using the advanced video-sharing protocol

▶ focus on implementing an intervention program: Early Intervention in Reading (Catching Readers series, Heinemann)

▶ cross-grade study groups on improving comprehension, high-level questioning, and engaging students in student-led book club discussions

Grade-level meetings and monthly data meetings

▶ grade level teams continue to plan together regularly

▶ share successes and challenges with one another and made changes in their instruction as needed

▶ review current pupil data in monthly meetings and make team decisions related to student placement in guided reading groups

▶ reflection on the effectiveness of interventions

Coaching and other classroom-visit techniques

▶ coach and external consultant visiting classroom regularly with follow-up coaching conversations

▶ use of students' use-of-time protocol

Reading instruction and changes in teaching practices

▶ increased time each day devoted to reading

▶ one-third of reading period in whole-group and two-thirds in guided reading groups

▶ centers in grades 2–6 focused on response to literature, reading and reporting on informational text, engaging in student-led discussions

continues

Catching Schools © 2011 by Barbara M. Taylor (Heinemann: Portsmouth, NH).

Figure 9-1b Actions and Success at Westside Elementary School

Actions and Successes at Westside Elementary School, *continued*

Teacher self-efficacy

- continued growth in confidence teaching reading: plan reading instruction that directly impacts each kid better; realistic, solid lessons plans; kids more engaged, more independent, and learning more; lesson pace better; independent activities more efficient and engaging

School collaboration and collective efficacy

- all teachers helping each other with literacy instruction
- all have a vested interest in helping kids
- commitment to change and success is strong
- greater focus on solutions than problems
- deeper focus on comprehension and vocabulary
- focus on making every minute of reading instruction count for every child

Actions and Successes in Year 3

Leadership

- principal very supportive of and involved in the SCR process
- continued release of responsibility to the leadership team
- focus on leadership team keeping all of the pieces of the SCR process going without formal literacy coordinator

Whole-group meetings

- hosted each month by different grade-level
- members share successes and challenges
- set future goals for modifications to instruction
- learn procedures and protocols for peer coaching
- focus on motivation

Study groups

- continued thoughtful discussions about practice
- cross-grade-level study groups focused on reciprocal teaching; students' collaboratively sharing written and oral responses to literature
- very efficient and run well
- teacher evaluations stress the value of study groups

Grade-level meetings and monthly data meetings

- continuing to plan together and communicate regularly
- common prep times each day
- continuing to meet monthly to look at student assessment data, place students in appropriate groups, reflect on the effectiveness of interventions for struggling readers
- focus on teaching kids, not just a curriculum

Coaching and classroom visits

- literacy coordinator and external consultant continue to get into classroom regularly to model, coach, and audit student use of time
- teachers positive about the coaching
- leadership team members first and then other teachers learn how to engage in peer coaching

Changes in teaching

- reading instruction looks quite different in year 3 compared to year 1: more coaching students to use word-recognition strategies; more high-level questioning; more and more effective vocabulary instruction; more coaching in general; more reading by students; more active; greater time on task
- maximizing student instructional time
- making every minute count

continues

Catching Schools © 2011 by Barbara M. Taylor (Heinemann: Portsmouth, NH).

Figure 9-1c Actions and Success at Westside Elementary School

- more differentiation based on what their students need
- more reflection on practice
- more comfortable opening doors, engaging in peer observation and feedback

School collaboration and collective efficacy

- sense of schoolwide collaboration and collective efficacy grew steadily from year 1 through year 3
- very collegial atmosphere and people positive
- common language and common strategies, whole school is on the same page now
- closer as a staff; in every way, people work well together, encouraging each other, all really care about kids; see good growth in students' reading abilities

Sustainability in year 4

- leadership team continues to meet monthly
- full-time literacy coordinator/coach for grades K–3, half-time coach for grades 4–6 using school funds
- monthly whole-group meeting
- looking at instruction, data on teaching, taking suggestions from one another to keep getting better
- study groups for all grades twice a month
- continuing with video sharing
- continuing to use all protocols
- focus on research
- 120 minutes of reading instruction in the primary grades, 90 minutes in the intermediate grades
- data retreats take place three times a year

Figure 9-1d Actions and Success at Westside Elementary School

Conclusion

School-based reading improvement that goes on for multiple years, as it must, is not an easy process. Teachers and administrators have to work hard at collaborating and learning together. Giving up old instructional practices and putting new, or refined, ones in place can be stressful, but it can also be energizing. Most teachers I have had the good fortune to work with on the SCR process and to learn from over multiple years have truly become more effective teachers of reading in schools with more effective reading programs. Most important, staff members at these schools take great pride in the reading progress they have seen in their students over this multiyear reading improvement journey. I hope this book gives you useful ideas and inspiration as you are embarked on your school's similar journey.

For more support, go to www.earlyinterventioninreading.com. Best wishes, and thank you for the important work you do for your students.

References

Adams, M. J. 1990. *Beginning to Read: Thinking and Learning About Print.* Cambridge, MA: MIT Press.

Afflerbach, P. 2007. *Understanding and Using Reading Assessment K–12.* Newark, DE: International Reading Association.

Allington, R. L., and S. A. Walmsley, eds. 2007. *No Quick Fix: Rethinking Literacy Programs in American's Elementary Schools* (RTI ed.). New York: Teachers College Press.

Anderson, N. A. 2007. *What Should I Read Aloud?* Newark, DE: International Reading Association.

Au, K. H. 2005. "Negotiating the Slippery Slope: School Change and Literacy Achievement." *Journal of Literacy Research* 37(3): 267–88.

———. 2006. *Multicultural Issues and Literacy Achievement.* Mahwah, NJ: Lawrence Erlbaum.

Au, K. H., T. E. Raphael, and K. C. Mooney. 2008a. "Improving Reading Achievement in Elementary Schools: Guiding Change in Time of Standards." In *The Administration and Supervision of Reading Programs,* 4th ed., eds. S. B. Wepner and D. S. Strickland, 71–89. New York: Teachers College Press.

———. 2008b. "What We Have Learned About Teacher Education to Improve Literacy Achievement in Urban Schools." In *Improving Literacy Achievement in Urban Schools: Critical Elements in Teacher Preparation,* ed. V. Chou, L. Morrow, and L. Wilkinson, 159–84. Newark, DE: International Reading Association.

August, D., and T. Shanahan, eds. 2006. *Developing Literacy in Second-Language Learners: Report of the National Literacy Panel on Language-Minority Children and Youth.* Mahwah, NJ: Lawrence Erlbaum.

Barrera, R., and R. Jimenez. 2002. "Bilingual Teachers Speak About Their Literacy Instruction." In *Teaching Reading: Effective Schools, Accomplished Teachers,* ed. B. M. Taylor and P. D. Pearson, 335–60. Mahwah, NJ: Lawrence Erlbaum.

Barrett, J. 1988. *Animals Should Definitely Not Wear Clothing.* New York: Aladdin.

Baumann, J. F., and B. S. Bergeron. 1993. "Story Map Instruction Using Children's Literature: Effects on First Graders' Comprehension of Central Narrative Elements." *Journal of Reading Behavior* 25(4): 407–37.

Baumann, J. F., J. V. Hoffman, A. M. Duffy-Hester, and J. M. Ro. 2000. "The First R, Yesterday and Today: U.S. Elementary Reading Instruction Practices Reported by Teachers and Administrators." *Reading Research Quarterly* 35: 338–77.

Baumann, J. F., and E. J. Kame'enui. 2004. *Vocabulary Instruction: Research to Practice.* New York: Guilford.

Bean, R., J. Draper, G. Turner, and N. Zigmond. 2010. "Reading First in Pennsylvania: Achievement Findings After Five Years." *Journal of Literacy Research* 42(1): 5–26.

Bean, R., and N. Zigmond. 2006. Professional Development Role of Reading Coaches In and Out of the Classroom. Paper presented at the International Reading Association Conference, Chicago, IL, May.

Bear, D. R., M. Invernizzi, S. Templeton, and F. Johnston. 2007. *Words Their Way: Word Study for Phonics, Vocabulary, and Spelling Instruction.* 4th ed. Upper Saddle River, NJ: Pearson/Merrill Prentice Hall.

Beck, I. L. 2006. *Making Sense of Phonics: The Hows and Whys.* New York: Guilford.

Beck, I. L., and M.G. McKeown. 2002. "Text Talk: Capturing the Benefit of Read-Aloud Experience for Young Children." *The Reading Teacher* 55(1): 10–20.

Beck, I. L., M. G. McKeown, and L. Kucan. 2002. *Bringing Words to Life: Robust Vocabulary Instruction.* New York: Guilford.

Beck, I. L., M. G. McKeown, C. Sandora, L. Kucan, and J. Worthy. 1996. "Questioning the Author: A Year-Long Classroom Implementation to Engage Students with Text." *The Elementary School Journal* 96(4): 385–414.

Beck, I.L., M.G. McKeown, R.L. Hamilton, and L. Kucan. 1997. *Questioning the Author: An Approach for Enhancing Student Engagement with Text.* Newark, DE: International Reading Association.

Bergman, J. L. 1992. "SAIL: A Way to Success and Independence for Low-Achieving Readers." *The Reading Teacher* 45(8): 598–602.

Biemiller, A., and C. Boote. 2006. "An Effective Method for Building Meaning Vocabulary in Primary Grades." *Journal of Educational Psychology* 98: 44–62.

Blachowicz, C., and P. Fisher. 2000. "Vocabulary Instruction." In *Handbook of Reading Research, Volume III*, ed. M.L. Kamil, P.B. Mosenthal, P.D. Pearson, and R. Barr, 503–24. Mahwah, NJ: Lawrence Erlbaum.

Blachowicz, C., and P. Fisher. 2002. *Teaching Vocabulary in All Classrooms.* 2nd ed. Upper Saddle River, NJ: Pearson/Merrill Prentice Hall.

Block, C., and M. Pressley, eds. 2002. *Comprehension Strategies: Research-Based Practices.* New York: Guilford.

Bogner, K., L. Raphael, and M. Pressley. 2002. "How Grade 1 Teachers Motivate Literate Activity by Their Students." *Scientific Studies of Reading* 6(2): 135–65.

Bohn, C. M., A. D. Roehrig, and M. Pressley. 2004. "The First Days of School in the Classrooms of Two More Effective and Four Less Effective Primary-Grades Teachers." *The Elementary School Journal* 104: 271–87.

Borman, G. D., G. M. Hewes, L.T. Overman, and S. Brown. 2003. "Comprehensive School Reform and Achievement: A Meta-Analysis." *Review of Educational Research* 73: 125–230.

Brown, R., P. B. El-Dinary, M. Pressley, and L. Coy-Ogan. 1995. "A Transactional Strategies Approach to Reading Instruction (National Reading Research Center)." *The Reading Teacher* 49: 256–58.

Camilli, G., S. Vargas, and M. Yurecko. 2003. "Teaching Children to Read: The Fragile Link Between Science and Federal Education Policy." *Education Policy Analysis Archives* 11 (15, May).

Carnine, D. W., J. Silbert, E. J. Kame'enui, and S. G. Tarver. 2004. *Direct Instruction Reading.* 4th ed. Upper Saddle River, NJ: Pearson.

Chorzempa, B. F., and S. Graham. 2006. "Primary-Grade Teachers' Use of Within-Class Ability Grouping in Reading." *Journal of Educational Psychology* 98: 529–41.

Christensen, C. A., and J. A. Bowey. 2005. "The Efficacy of Orthographic Rime, Grapheme-Phoneme Correspondence, and Implicit Phonics Approaches to Teaching Decoding Skills." *Scientific Studies of Reading* 9: 327–49.

Christenson, S. L., and S. M. Sheridan. 2001. *Schools and Families: Creating Essential Connections for Learning.* New York: Guilford.

Cohen, D. K., and S. L. Moffitt. 2002. "Standards-Based Reform and the Capacity Problem." In *Miles to Go: Reflections on Mid-Course Correction for Standards-Based Reform.* Pew Forum on Standards-Based Reform. Bethesda, MD: Education Week Press.

Common Core State Standards: English Language Arts. 2010. National Governors Association Center for Best Practices (NGA Center) and the Council of Chief State School Officers (CCSSO). www.corestandards.org.

Connor, C. M., F. J. Morrison, and L. E. Katch. 2004. "Beyond the Reading Wars: Exploring the Effect of Child-Instruction Interactions on Growth in Early Reading." *Scientific Studies of Reading* 8: 305–36.

Consortium for Responsible School Change. 2005. *Description of Common Findings Across Multiple Studies on School Change in Reading.* St. Paul, MN: University of Minnesota, Minnesota Center for Reading Research.

Center for Research on Education, Diversity, and Excellence (CREDE). 2002. *Five Standards for Effective Pedagogy,* from http://crede.berkeley.edu/.

Cunningham, P. M. 2009. *Phonics They Use: Words for Reading and Writing.* 5th ed. Boston: Pearson.

Cunningham, P. M., and D. R. Smith. 2008. *Beyond Retelling: Toward Higher Level Thinking and Big Ideas.* Newark, DE: International Reading Association.

Datnow, A., and S. Stringfield. 2000. "Working Together for Reliable School Reform." *Journal of Education for Students Placed at Risk* 5(1–2): 183–204.

Day, J. P., D. L. Spiegel, J. McLellan, and V.B. Brown. 2002. *Moving Forward with Literature Circles.* New York: Scholastic.

Dolezal, S. E., L. M. Welsh, M. Pressley, and M. M. Vincent. 2003. "How Nine Third-Grade Teachers Motivate Student Academic Engagement." *Elementary School Journal* 103: 239–67.

Duffy, G. G., L. R. Roehler, E. Sivan, G. Rackliffe, C. Book, M.S. Meloth, et al. 1987. "Effects of Explaining the Reasoning Associated with Using Reading Strategies." *Reading Research Quarterly* 22(3): 347–68.

Duke, N. K., and V. S. Bennett-Armistead. 2003. *Reading and Writing Informational Text in the Primary Grades: Research-Based Practices.* New York: Scholastic.

Edwards, P. A. 2004. *Children's Literacy Development: Making It Happen Through School, Family, and Community Involvement.* Boston: Pearson/Allyn & Bacon.

Ehri, L. 1991. "Development of the Ability to Read Words." In *Handbook of Reading Research, Volume II,* ed. R. Barr, M. L. Kamil, P. B. Mosenthal, and P. D. Pearson, 383–417. New York: Longman.

Elish-Piper, L, and S. L'Allier. 2007. "Does Literacy Coaching Make a Difference? The Effects of Literacy Coaching on Reading Achievement in Grades K–3 in a Reading First District." Paper presented at the annular meeting of the National Reading Conference, Austin, Texas.

Englert, C. S., T.V. Mariage, C. M. Okolo, C.A. Courtad, R. K. Shankland, K. D. Moxley, A. Billman, and N. Jones. 2007. "Accelerating Expository Literacy in Middle Grades: The ACCEL Project." In *Effective Instruction for Struggling Readers K–6,* ed. B. M. Taylor and J. E. Ysseldyke, 138–72. New York: Teachers College Press.

Epstein, J. L., M. G. Sanders, B. S. Simon, K. C. Salinas, N. R. Jansorn, and F. L. van Voorhis. 2002. *School, Family, and Community Partnerships: Your Handbook for Action.* 2nd ed. Thousand Oaks, CA: Corwin.

Fink, D., and C. Brayman. 2006. "School Leadership Succession and the Challenges of Change." *Educational Administration Quarterly* 42(1): 62–89.

Fisher, D., and N. Frey. 2007. "Implementing a School-Wide Literacy Framework: Improving Achievement in an Urban Elementary School." *The Reading Teacher* 61(1): 32–43.

Foorman, B. R., and J. Torgesen. 2001. "Critical Elements of Classroom and Small-Group Instruction Promote Reading Success in All Children." *Learning Disabilities Research and Practice* 16: 203–12.

Foorman, B. R., C. Schatsneider, M.N. Eakin, J. M. Fletcher, L. C. Moats, and D. J. Francis. 2006. "The Impact of Instructional Practices in Grades 1 and 2 on Reading and Spelling Achievement in High Poverty Schools." *Contemporary Educational Psychology* 31: 1–29.

Fuchs, D., and L. S. Fuchs. 2005. "Peer-Assisted Learning Strategies: Promoting Word Recognition, Fluency, and Reading Comprehension in Young Children." *The Journal of Special Education* 39: 34–44.

Fuchs, D., L. S. Fuchs, and S. Vaughn, eds. 2008. *Response to Intervention: A Framework for Reading Educators.* Newark, DE: International Reading Association.

Fullan, M. 2005. *Leadership and Sustainability: Systems Thinkers in Action.* Thousand Oaks, CA: Corwin.

Gaitan, C. D. 2006. *Building Culturally Responsive Classrooms: A Guide for K–6 Teachers.* Thousand Oaks, CA: Corwin.

Gajria, M., A. K. Jitendra, S. Sood, and G. Sacks. 2007. "Improving Comprehension of Expository Text in Students with LD: A Research Synthesis." *Journal of Learning Disabilities* 40: 210–25.

Galda, L., B. Cullinan, and L. Sipe. 2009. *Literature and the Child.* 7th ed. Belmont, CA: Thomson/Wadsworth.

Gaskins, I.W. 2004. *Success with Struggling Readers: The Benchmark School Approach.* New York: Guilford.

Gaskins, I. W., L. C. Ehri, C. Cress, C. O'Hara, and K. Donnelly. 1996. "Procedures for Word Learning: Making Discoveries About Words." *The Reading Teacher* 50: 312–27.

Gersten, R., D. Compton, C. M. Connor, J. Dimino, L. Santoro, S. Linan-Thompson, and W. D. Lilly. 2009. *Assisting Students Struggling with Reading: Response to Intervention and Multi-Tier Intervention in the Primary Grades.* IES: Washington, DC: What Works Clearinghouse, NCEE 2009-4045, http://ies.ed.gov/ncee/wwc/.

Gersten, R., L. S. Fuchs, J. P. Williams, and S. Baker. 2001. "Teaching Reading Comprehension Strategies to Students with Learning Disabilities: A Review of Research." *Review of Educational Research* 71(2): 279–320.

Giles, C., and A. Hargreaves. 2002. "The Sustainability of Innovative Schools as Learning Organizations and Professional Learning Communities." *Educational Administration Quarterly* 42(1): 124–56.

Gajria, M. A., K. Jitendra, S. Sood, and G. Sacks. 2007. "Improving Comprehension of Expository Text in Students with LD: A Research Synthesis." *Journal of Learning Disabilities,* 40(2): 210–225.

Goddard, R.D., W.K. Hoy, and A.W. Hoy. 2004. "Collective Efficacy Beliefs: Theoretical Developments, Empirical Evidence, and Future Directions." *Educational Researcher* 33(3): 3–13.

Goddard, R. D., M. Tschannen-Moran, and W. K. Hoy. 2001. "A Multilevel Examination of the Distribution and Effects of Teacher Trust in Students and Parents in Urban Elementary Schools." *The Elementary School Journal* 102: 3–19.

Goldenberg, C. 1992/1993. "Instructional Conversations: Promoting Comprehension Through Discussion." *The Reading Teacher* 46: 316–26.

Graves, A. W., R. Gersten, and D. Haager. 2004. "Literacy Instruction in Multiple-Language First-Grade Classrooms: Linking Student Outcomes to Observed Instructional Practice." *Learning Disabilities Research & Practice* 19: 262–72.

Graves, M. F. 2007. "Conceptual and Empirical Bases for Providing Struggling Readers with Multifaceted and Long-Term Vocabulary Instruction." In *Effective Instruction for Struggling Readers K–6*, ed. B. M. Taylor and J. E. Ysseldyke, 55–83. New York: Teachers College Press.

Guiney, E. 2002. "A Modest Proposal: Work on the Right Problem in the Right Way." In *Miles to Go: Reflections on Mid-Course Correction for Standards-Based Reform*, Pew Forum on Standards-Based Reform. Bethesda, MD: Education Week Press.

Gunn, B., K. Smolkowski, A. Biglan, C. Black, and J. Blair. 2005. "Fostering the Development of Reading Skill Through Supplemental Instruction: Results for Hispanic and Non-Hispanic Students." *The Journal of Special Education* 39: 66–85.

Guthrie, J. T., A. Wigfield, and C. VonSecker. 2000. "Effects of Integrated Instruction on Motivation and Strategy Use in Reading." *Journal of Educational Psychology* 92: 331–41.

Guthrie, J.T., A. Wigfield, P. Barbosa, K. C. Perencevich, A. Taboada, M. H. Davis, et al. 2004. "Increasing Reading Comprehension and Engagement Through Concept-Oriented Reading Instruction." *Journal of Educational Psychology* 96: 403–23.

Gutierrez, C. 2002. "The Kid Is Not a Car! Teaching and Learning for Young Lives Need to Drive Standards and Accountability." In *Miles to Go: Reflections on Mid-Course Correction for Standards-Based Reform*, Pew Forum on Standards-Based Reform. Bethesda, MD: Education Week Press.

Hacker, D. J., and A. Tenant. 2002. "Implementing Reciprocal Teaching in the Classroom." *Journal of Educational Psychology* 94: 699–718.

Hamilton, L., R. Halverson, S. S. Jackson, E. Mandinach, J. A. Supovitz, and J. C. Wayman. 2009. *Using Student Achievement Data to Support Instructional Decision Making.* IES: Washington, DC: What Works Clearinghouse, NCEE 2009-4097 http://ies.ed.gov/ncee/wwc/.

Hampton, S., and L. B. Resnick. 2009. *Reading and Writing with Understanding.* Washington, DC: National Center on Education and the Economy.

Hamre, B. K., and R. C. Pianta. 2005. "Can Instructional and Emotional Support in the First-Grade Classroom Make a Difference for Children at Risk of School Failure?" *Child Development* 76(5): 949–67.

Hasbrouck, J., and C. Denton. 2005. *The Reading Coach: A How-to Manual for Success.* Boston: Sopris West.

Hawley, W. D., and D. L. Rollie, eds. 2007. *The Keys to Effective Schools: Educational Reform as Continuous Improvement.* 2nd ed. Washington, DC: National Education Association.

Heffernan, L. 2004. *Critical Literacy and Writer's Workshop.* Newark, DE: International Reading Association.

Hiebert, E. H., and B. M. Taylor. 1998. "Beginning Reading Instruction: Research on Early Interventions." In *Handbook of Reading Research, Volume III*, ed. M. L. Kamil, P. B. Mosenthal, P. D. Pearson, and R. Barr, 455–82. Mahwah, NJ: Lawrence Erlbaum.

Jennings, J. 2002. "Early Victories, Serious Challenges." In *Miles to Go: Reflections on Mid-Course Correction for Standards-Based Reform*, Pew Forum on Standards-Based Reform. Bethesda, MD: Education Week Press.

Johns, J. L., and R. L. Berglund. 2005. *Fluency Strategies and Assessments.* Dubuque, IA: Kendall-Hunt.

Juel, C., and C. Minden-Cupp. 2000. "Learning to Read Words: Linguistic Units and Instructional Strategies." *Reading Research Quarterly* 35: 458–92.

Kelley, M. J., and N. Clausen-Grace. 2007. *Comprehension Shouldn't Be Silent.* Newark, DE: International Reading Association.

Kletsien, S. B., and M. J. Dreher. 2005. *Informational Text in K–3 Classrooms: Helping Children Read and Write.* Newark, DE: International Reading Association.

Klingner, J. K., S. Vaughn, M. E. Arguelles, M. T. Hughes, and S. A. Leftwich. 2004. "Collaborative Strategic Reading: Real World Lessons from Classroom Teachers." *Remedial and Special Education* 25: 291–302.

Knapp, M. S. 1995. *Teaching for Meaning in High-Poverty Classrooms.* New York: Teachers College Press.

Koskinen, P. S., and I. H. Blum. 1986. "Paired Repeated Reading: A Classroom Strategy for Developing Reading Fluency." *The Reading Teacher* 40: 70–75.

Kuhn, M. R., P. J. Schwanenflugel, R. D. Morris, L.M. Morrow, D. G. Woo, et al. 2006. "Teaching Children to Become Fluent and Automatic Readers." *Journal of Literacy Research* 38: 357–87.

Kuhn, M. R., and S. A. Stahl. 2003. "Fluency: A Review of Developmental and Remedial Practices." *Journal of Educational Psychology* 95: 3–21.

Ladson-Billings, G. 1994. *The Dreamkeepers: Successful Teachers of African American Children.* San Francisco, CA: Jossey-Bass.

Lai, M. K., S. McNaughton, M. Amituanai-Toloa, R. Turner, and S. Hsiao. 2009. "Sustained Acceleration of Achievement in Reading Comprehension: The New Zealand Experience." *Reading Research Quarterly*, 44(1): 30–56.

Lapp, D., D. Fisher, and T. D. Wolsey. 2009. *Literacy Growth for Every Child: Differentiated Small-Group Instruction, K–6.* New York: Guilford.

Leslie, L., and J. Caldwell. 2010. *Qualitative Reading Inventory, 5th edition.* Upper Saddle River, NJ: Allyn and Bacon/Pearson.

Lipson, M. 2007. *Teaching Reading Beyond the Primary Grades.* New York: Scholastic.

Lipson, M. L., J. H. Mosenthal, J. Mekkelsen, and B. Russ. 2004. "Building Knowledge and Fashioning Success One School at a Time." *The Reading Teacher* 57(6): 534–42.

Little, J. 2002. "Professional Communication and Collaboration." In *The Keys to Effective Schools,* ed. W. Hawley, 51–66. Thousand Oaks, CA: Corwin.

Louis, K. S., and Kruse 1995. *Professionalism and Community in Schools.* Thousand Oaks: Corwin.

Lovett, M. W., S. L. Borden, L. Lacerenza, J. D. Frijters, K. A. Steinbach, and M. DePalma. 2000. "Components of Effective Remediation for Developmental Reading Disabilities: Combining Phonological and Strategy-Based Instruction to Improve Outcomes." *Journal of Educational Psychology* 92: 263–83.

MacGinitie, W. H., R. K. MacGinitie, K. Maria, and L.G. Dreyer. 2000. Gates MacGinitie Reading Tests (4th ed.). Itasca, IL: Riverside.

Manning, M., G. Morrison, and D. Camp. 2009. *Creating the Best Literacy Block Ever.* New York: Scholastic.

Martinez, M., N. Roser, and S. Strecker. 1998/1999. "I Thought I Could Be a Star: A Reader's Theater Ticket to Fluency." *The Reading Teacher* 52(4): 326–37.

Mathes, P. G., C.A. Denton, J. M. Fletcher, J. L. Anthony, D. J. Francis, and C. Schatschneider. 2005. "The Effects of Theoretically Different Instruction and Student Characteristics on the Skills of Struggling Readers." *Reading Research Quarterly* 40: 148–82.

May, H., and J. A. Supovitz. 2006. "Capturing the Cumulative Effects of School Reform: An 11-Year Study of the Impacts of America's Choice on Student Achievement." *Educational Evaluation and Policy Analysis* 28(3): 231–57.

McCormick, C. E., R. N. Throneburg, and J. M. Smitley. 2002. *A Sound Start: Phonemic Awareness Lessons for Reading Success.* New York: Guilford.

McCormick, R. L., and J. R. Paratore, eds. 2005. *After Early Intervention, Then What?: Teaching Struggling Readers in Grades 3 and Beyond.* Upper Saddle River, NJ: Pearson.

McCormick, S. 2007. *Instructing Students Who Have Literacy Problems.* 5th ed. Upper Saddle River, NJ: Pearson.

McGill-Franzen, A. 2005. *Kindergarten Literacy.* New York: Scholastic.

McKenna, M., and S. Stahl. 2003. *Assessment for Reading Instruction.* New York: Guilford.

McLaughlin, M. W., and D. Mitra. 2002. "Theory-Based Change and Change-Based Theory: Going Deeper, Going Broader." *Journal of Educational Change* 2: 301–23.

McMahon, S.I. 1997. "Book Clubs: Contexts for Students to Learn to Lead Their Own Discussions." In *The Book Club Connection*, ed. S.I. McMahon and T. E. Raphael, 89–106. New York: Teachers College Press.

McMahon, S. I., T. Raphael, V. Goatley, and L. Pardo. 1997. *The Book Club Connection: Literacy Learning and Classroom Talk.* New York: Teachers College Press.

McNaughton, S., S. MacDonald, M. Amituanai-Toloa, M. Lai, S. MacDonald, and S. Farry. 2006. *Enhanced Teaching and Learning of Comprehension in Year 4–9: Mangere Schools.* Auckland: Uniservices Ltd.

Morrow, L. M. 2003. *Organizing and Managing the Language Arts Block: A Professional Development Guide.* New York: Guilford.

Mosenthal, J., M. Lipson, S. Torncello, B. Russ, and J. Mekkelsen. 2004. "Contexts and Practices of Six Schools Successful in Obtaining Reading Achievement." *The Elementary School Journal* 41(5): 343–67.

Murphy, C., and D. Lick. 2004. *Whole-Faculty Study Groups: Creating Student-Based Professional Development.* 3rd ed. Thousand Oaks, CA: Corwin.

Nagy, W. E., and J. A. Scott. 2000. "Vocabulary Processes." In *Handbook of Reading Research, Volume III*, ed. M.L. Kamil, P. B. Mosenthal, P. D. Pearson, and R. Barr, 269–84. Mahwah, NJ: Lawrence Erlbaum.

National Reading Panel (NRP). 2000a. *Report of the National Reading Panel: Teaching Children to Read: Reports of the Subgroups* (NIH Publication No. 00-4754). Washington, DC: National Institute for Child Health and Human Development, National Institutes of Health.

Oczkus, L. D. 2003. *Reciprocal Teaching at Work: Strategies for Improving Reading Comprehension.* Newark, DE: International Reading Association.

Olness, R. 2007. *Using Literature to Enhance Content Area Instruction: A Guide for K–5 Teachers.* Newark, DE: International Reading Association.

Opitz, M. F., and J. L. Harding-DeKam. 2007. "Understanding and Teaching English-Language Learners." *The Reading Teacher* 60(6): 590–93.

Palincsar, A. S., and A. L. Brown. 1984. "Reciprocal Teaching of Comprehension-Fostering and Comprehension-Monitoring Activities." *Cognition and Instruction* (2) 117–175. Mahwah, NJ: Lawrence Erlbaum.

Palincsar, A., and A. Brown. 1986. "Interactive Teaching to Promote Independent Learning from Text." *The Reading Teacher* 39(8): 771–77.

Paratore, J. R., and R. L. McCormack, eds. 2007. *Classroom Literacy Assessment: Making Sense of What Students Know and Do.* New York: Guilford.

Peterson, D. S., B. M. Taylor, R. Burnham, and R. Schock. 2008. "Reflective Coaching Conversations: A Missing Piece." *The Reading Teacher* 62(6): 500–09.

Pressley, M. 2006. *Reading Instruction That Works: The Case for Balanced Teaching.* 3rd ed. New York: Guilford.

Pressley, M., S. E. Dolezal, L. M. Raphael, L. Mohan, A. D. Roehrig, and K. Bogner. 2003. *Motivating Primary-Grade Students.* New York: Guilford.

Pressley, M., L. Mohan, L. M. Raphael, and L. Fingeret. 2007. "How Does Bennett Woods Elementary School Produce Such High Reading and Writing Achievement?" *Journal of Educational Psychology* 99(2): 221–40.

Pressley, M., L. M. Raphael, J. D. Gallagher, and J. DiBella. 2004. "Providence-St. Mel School: How a School That Works for African American Students Works." *Journal of Educational Psychology* 96(2): 216–35.

Pressley, M., R. Wharton-McDonald, R. Allington, C. C. Block, L. Morrow, et al. 2001. "A Study of Effective First-Grade Literacy Instruction." *Scientific Studies of Reading* 5: 35–58.

Raphael, T. E., L. S. Pardo, and K. Highfield. 2002. *Book Club: A Literature-Based Curriculum.* 2nd ed. Lawrence, MA: Small Planet.

Raphael, T. E., and S. I. McMahon. 1994. "Book Club: An Alternative Framework for Reading Instruction." *The Reading Teacher* 48(2): 102–16.

Raphael, T. E., K. Highfield, and K. H. Au. 2006. *QAR Now.* New York: Scholastic.

Rasinski, T. V. 2000. "Speed Does Matter in Reading." *The Reading Teacher* 54(2): 146–51.

———. 2003. *The Fluent Reader: Oral Reading Strategies for Building Word Recognition, Fluency, and Comprehension.* New York: Scholastic.

Resnick, L. B., and S. Hampton. 2009. *Reading and Writing Grade by Grade.* Washington, DC: National Center on Education and the Economy.

Reyes, P., J. D. Scribner, and A.P. Scribner, eds. 1999. *Lessons from High-Performing Hispanic Schools.* New York: Teachers College Press.

Rog, L. J. 2001. *Early Literacy Instruction in Kindergarten.* Newark, DE: International Reading Association.

Rosenshine, B., and C. Meister. 1994. "Reciprocal Teaching: A Review of the Research." *Review of Educational Research* 64(4): 479–530.

Sailors, M., J. Lowe, and T. Sellers. 2009. Support for the Improvement of Practices Through Intensive Coaching (SIPIC): Literacy Coaching and Reading Achievement. Paper presented at the National Literacy Coaching Summit, Corpus, Christi, TX.

Samuels, S. J. 1997. "The Method of Repeated Reading." *The Reading Teacher* 32: 403–408. Also reprinted in the February, 1997, issue of *The Reading Teacher.*

Samuels, S. J., and A. Farstrup, eds. 2006. *What Research Has to Say About Fluency Instruction.* 3rd ed. Newark, DE: International Reading Association.

Santoro, L. E., S. K. Baker, D. J. Chard, and L. Howard. 2007. "The Comprehension Conversation: Using Purposeful Discussion During Read-Alouds to Promote Student Comprehension and Vocabulary." In *Effective Instruction for Struggling Readers K–6*, ed. B. M. Taylor and J. E. Ysseldyke, 109–37. New York: Teachers College Press.

Saunders, W. M., and C. Goldenberg. 1999. "Effects of Instructional Conversations and Literature Logs on Limited and Fluent English Proficient Students' Story Comprehension and Thematic Understanding." *The Elementary School Journal* 99: 279–301.

Schneider, W., E. Roth, and M. Ennemoser. 2000. "Training Phonological Skills and Letter Knowledge in Children at Risk for Dyslexia: A Comparison of Three Kindergarten Intervention Programs." *Journal of Educational Psychology* 92: 284–95.

Scribner, J. D., M. D. Young, and A. Pedroza. 1999. "Building Collaborative Relationships with Parents." In *Lessons from high-performing Hispanic schools,* ed. P. Reyes, J. D. Scribner, and A. P. Scribner, 33–60. New York: Teachers College Press.

Shany, M. T., and A. Biemiller. 1995. "Assisted Reading Practice: Effects on Performance for Poor Readers in Grades 3 and 4." *Reading Research Quarterly* 30: 382–95.

Slavin, R. E., C. Lake, S. David, and N. A. Maadden. 2009. *Effective Programs for Struggling Readers: A Best-Evidence Synthesis.* Baltimore, MD: Johns Hopkins.

Snow, C. E., M. S. Burns, and P. Griffin, eds. 1998. *Preventing Reading Difficulties in Young Children.* Washington, DC: National Academy.

Southall, M. 2009. *Differentiated Small-Group Reading Lessons.* New York: Scholastic.

Stahl, S. A. 2001. "Teaching Phonics and Phonological Awareness." In *Handbook of Early Literacy Research*, ed. S. B. Neuman and D. Dickenson, 333–47. New York: Guilford.

———. 2004. What Do We Know About Fluency? In *The Voice of Evidence in Reading Research,* ed. P. McCardle and V. Chhabra. Baltimore: Paul Brookes.

Stahl, S. A., and M. R. Kuhn. 2002. "Making It Sound Like Language: Developing Fluency." *The Reading Teacher* 55(6): 582–84.

Swan, E. 2003. *Concept-Oriented Reading Instruction: Engaging Classrooms, Lifelong Learners.* New York: Guilford.

Symons, S., H. MacLatchy-Gaudet, T. D. Stone, and P. L. Reynolds. 2001. "Strategy Instruction for Elementary Students Searching Informational Text." *Scientific Studies of Reading* 5: 1–33.

Taberski, S. 2000. *On Solid Ground: Strategies for Teaching Reading K–3.* Portsmouth, NH: Heinemann.

Taboada, A., and J. T. Guthrie. 2006. "Contributions of Student Questioning and Prior Knowledge to Construction of Knowledge from Reading Information Text." *Journal of Literacy Research* 38: 1–35.

Taylor, B. M. 2001. *The Early Intervention in Reading Program (EIR®): Research and Development Spanning Twelve Years.* Early Intervention in Reading Corporation, St. Paul, MN. www.earlyinterventioninreading.com.

———. 2002. *Characteristics of Schools That Are Effective in Teaching All Students to Read.* Washington, DC: National Education Association.

———. 2008. "Effective Classroom Reading Instruction in the Elementary Grades." In *Response to Intervention: An Overview for Educators*, ed. D. Fuchs, L. Fuchs, and S. Vaughn, 5–25. Newark, DE: International Reading Association.

———. (2010a). *Catching Readers: Grade 1.* Portsmouth, NH: Heinemann.

———. (2010b). *Catching Readers: Grade 2.* Portsmouth, NH: Heinemann.

———. (2010c). *Catching Readers: Grade 3.* Portsmouth, NH: Heinemann.

———. (in press a). *Catching Readers: Grade K.* Portsmouth, NH: Heinemann.

———. (in press b). *Catching Readers: Grades 4/5.* Portsmouth, NH: Heinemann.

Taylor, B. M., B. Hanson, K. J. Justice-Swanson, and S. Watts. 1997. "Helping Struggling Readers: Linking Small Group Intervention with Cross-Age Tutoring." *The Reading Teacher* 51: 196–209.

Taylor, B. M., L. Harris, P. D. Pearson, and G. E. Garcia. 1995. *Reading Difficulties: Instruction and Assessment.* 2nd ed. New York: McGraw-Hill.

Taylor, B. M., and P. D. Pearson, eds. 2002. *Teaching Reading: Effective Schools/Accomplished Teachers.* Mahwah, NJ: Lawrence Erlbaum.

Taylor, B. M., and P. D. Pearson. 2004. "CIERA Research on Learning to Read: At School, at Home, and in the Community." *The Elementary School Journal* 105(2): 167–81.

Taylor, B. M., P. D. Pearson, K. Clark, and S. Walpole. 2000. "Effective Schools and Accomplished Teachers: Lessons About Primary Grade Reading Instruction in Low-Income Schools." *Elementary School Journal* 101(2): 121–66.

Taylor, B. M., P. D. Pearson, D. S. Peterson, and M. C. Rodriguez. 2003. "Reading Growth in High-Poverty Classrooms: The Influence of Teacher Practices That Encourage Cognitive Engagement in Literacy Learning." *Elementary School Journal* 104: 3–28.

———. 2005. "The CIERA School Change Framework: An Evidence-Based Approach to Professional Development and School Reading Improvement." *Reading Research Quarterly* 40(1): 40–69.

Taylor, B. M., and D. S. Peterson. 2003. *Year 3 Report of the CIERA School Change Project.* Minneapolis: University of Minnesota, Center for Reading Research.

Taylor, B. M., and D. S. Peterson. 2003. *Year 1 Report of the REA School Change Project.* St. Paul, MN: University of Minnesota, Minnesota Center for Reading Research.

———. 2006a. *The Impact of the School Change Framework in Twenty-Three Minnesota REA Schools.* St. Paul, MN: University of Minnesota, Minnesota Center for Reading Research.

———. 2006b. *Year 1 Report of the Minnesota Reading First Cohort 2 School Change Project.* St. Paul, MN: University of Minnesota, Minnesota Center for Reading Research.

———. 2006c. *Year 3 Report of the Minnesota Reading First Cohort 1 School Change Project.* St. Paul, MN: University of Minnesota, Minnesota Center for Reading Research.

———. 2007a. *Year 2 Report of the Minnesota Reading First Cohort 2 School Change Project.* St. Paul, MN: University of Minnesota, Minnesota Center for Reading Research.

———. 2007b. "School-Wide Reading Improvement to Meet All Students' Needs." In *Effective Instruction for Struggling Readers, K–6,* ed. B. M. Taylor and J. E. Ysseldyke, 235–50. New York: Teachers College Press.

———. 2008 *Year 3 Report of the Minnesota Reading First Cohort 2 School Change Project.* St. Paul, MN: University of Minnesota, Minnesota Center for Reading Research.

Taylor, B. M., D. S. Peterson, M. Marx, and M. Chein. 2007. "Scaling Up a Reading Reform in High-Poverty Elementary Schools." In *Effective Instruction for Struggling Readers, K–6,* ed. B. M. Taylor and J. E. Ysseldyke, 216–34. New York: Teachers College Press.

Taylor, B. M., M. Pressley, and P.D. Pearson. 2002. "Research-Supported Characteristics of Teachers and Schools That Promote Reading Achievement." In *Teaching Reading: Effective Schools, Accomplished Teachers,* ed. B. M. Taylor and P. D. Pearson, 361–74. Mahwah, NJ: Lawrence Erlbaum.

Taylor, B. M., T. E. Raphael, and K.H. Au. 2010. "Reading and School Reform." In *Handbook of Reading Research, Volume IV,* ed. M. Kamil, P. D. Pearson, P. Afflerbach, and E. Moje, 594–628. New York: Routledge.

Taylor, B. M., R. Short, B. Frye, and B. Shearer. 1992. "Classroom Teachers Prevent Reading Failure Among Low-Achieving First-Grade Students." *The Reading Teacher* 45: 592–97.

Timperley, H. S., and J. M. Parr. 2007. "Closing the Achievement Gap Through Evidence-Based Inquiry at Multiple Levels of the Education System." *Journal of Advanced Academics* 19(1): 90–115.

Tyner, B. 2009. *Small-Group Reading Instruction: A Differentiated Teaching Model for Beginning and Struggling Readers.* Newark, DE: International Reading Association.

Tyner, B., and S. E. Green. 2005. *Small-Group Reading Instruction: A Differentiated Teaching Model for Intermediate Grade Reader, Grades 3–8.* Newark, DE: International Reading Association.

Valli, L., R. G. Croninger, and K. Walters. 2007. "Who (Else) Is the Teacher? Cautionary Notes on Teacher Accountability Systems." *American Journal of Education* 113: 635–62.

Van den Branden, K. 2000. "Does Negotiation of Meaning Promote Reading Comprehension? A Study of Multilingual Primary School Classes." *Reading Research Quarterly* 35: 426–43.

Vaughn, S., P. Mathes, S. Linan-Thompson, P. Cirino, C. Carlson, S. Pollard-Durdola, et al. 2006. "Effectiveness of an English Intervention for First-Grade English Language Learners at Risk for Reading Problems." *The Elementary School Journal* 107: 153–80.

Vaughn, S., J. Wanzek, and J. M. Fletcher. 2007. "Multiple Tiers of Intervention: A Framework for Prevention and Identification of Students with Reading/Learning Disabilities." In *Effective Instruction for Struggling Readers K–6*, ed. B. M. Taylor and J. E. Ysseldyke, 173–95. New York: Teachers College Press.

Walpole, S., and M. C. McKenna. 2004. *The Literacy Coach's Handbook: A Guide to Research-Based Practice.* New York: Guilford.

———. 2009. *How to Plan Differentiated Reading Instruction: Resources for Grades K–3.* New York: Guilford.

Wasik, B., and R. E. Slavin. 1993. "Preventing Early Reading Failure with One-to-One Tutoring: A Review of Five Programs." *Reading Research Quarterly* 28(2): 178–200.

Wharton-McDonald, R., M. Pressley, and J. M. Hampston. 1998. "Literacy Instruction in Nine First-Grade Classrooms: Teacher Characteristics and Student Achievement." *The Elementary School Journal* 99: 101–28.

What Works Clearinghouse. 2009. *Beginning Reading: What Works Clearinghouse Topic Report.* http://ies.ed.gov/ncee/wwc/ (Accessed March 24, 2009).

Wood, K. D., N. L. Roser, and M. Martinez. 2001. "Collaborative Literacy: Lesson Learned from Literature." *Reading Teacher* 55(2): 102–111.

York-Barr, J., W. A. Sommers, G. S. Ghere, and J. Montie. 2006. *Reflective Practice to Improve Schools: An Action Guide for Educators.* 2nd ed. Thousand Oaks, CA: Corwin.

Index